1970

This book may be kept

Victorian Poetry and the Romantic Religion

DEREK COLVILLE

Victorian Poetry

and the Romantic Religion

STATE UNIVERSITY OF NEW YORK PRESS

ALBANY

Published by State University of New York Press
Thurlow Terrace, Albany, New York 12201

Grateful acknowledgment is made
for permission to quote the poem
"The Most of It" by Robert Frost
from *Complete Poems of Robert Frost,*
Copyright © 1942 by Robert Frost
Reprinted by permission of Holt, Rinehart and Winston, Inc.

International Standard Book Number 0-87395-058-5
Library of Congress Catalog Card Number 76-97213
Printed in the United States of America
Designed by Rhoda C. Curley

To my parents, my friends

To my parents, my brothers

CONTENTS

ix

PREFACE

I should first like to say a word about the sort of book I attempt. Basically, it is a critical reading of Victorian poetry concerned with questions of outlook and belief. The approach is through a simple reformulation of the preceding Romantic work, based on well-known ground. I hope the book might provide a useful introductory approach to nineteenth century poetry. And while I hope that at a few points it may not be irrelevant to him, it is not a book for the specialist, as must be obvious both from the range of material it deals with, and from the elementary ground it covers at certain steps in its argument. The book is aimed at the reader who likes poetry, cares about the most ultimate human problems, and who may be interested in important poetry (and poetic prose) of the last century. This literature is very different, of course, from that of our own time, but it is the only other "modern" work we have—modern, that is, in its concern with problems of existence in an industrial, technological, and sceptical age.

The book springs from three convictions of mine, which have grown deeper during my teaching and discussion of the literature in question. The first is obvious enough, that English Romantic poetry has *at its core* the experience of vision, and the values enforced by that. Second, that most other characteristics cited in the ambiguities of Romantic definition are peripheral consequences of such central vision and values. My third conviction depends upon the first: if this central/peripheral pattern is held in mind in reading the great Victorians, certain conclusions emerge which reveal important mental stances behind the poetry of Arnold, Browning and Tennyson, at least as far as world-outlook is concerned.

I hoped also to write a demonstrative book about poetic effects and causes, and this has meant a large amount of quotation. There is no satisfactory substitute, in a book of this kind, for consulting the text as a point is being made. While the work, therefore, in a sense carries an intrinsic anthology, readers should realize the limitations of quotation and have ready access to the larger contexts where necessary.

My approach, of course, leads to—and stems from—value-judgements. My prejudices, which it will do no harm frankly to state, are an admiration for the tonal impact of Arnold's poetry, and a respect for Tennyson as a mind emblematic of what is most courageous in the Victorian struggle to retain faith. I also admit to a sense of embarrassed inadequacy at what seems to me a lack of consequence in some of Browning's generally admired "objective" work, and of wonder at the unconvincingness of his attempts elsewhere to deal subjectively and directly with matters of faith. These latter prejudices regarding Browning, I must own, disturb me, but they persist. Perhaps I need only add that a concern—really a rather Victorian concern—with problems of ultimate belief underlying poetry leads one naturally enough to the best of Arnold and Tennyson, but it leads to the weaker side of Browning. In his case particularly, the subject of this book leads often to minor poems, and away from much of his major achievement; this obviously does his artistry less than justice.

The book's general scope, in fact, makes it necessary sometimes to omit major works, and sometimes to treat only parts of others; this is especially true of the brief Romantic overview which begins the volume. One other word is necessary concerning this overview: the Romantic use of religious terminology is of course not Christian in implication. It is, as I hope is clear from my readings of such work as Coleridge's Conversation poems and Wordsworth's vision on Snowdon, a metaphor by which the poets exploit the associations of conventional Christianity to the advantage of their new worship of imaginative relationships.

I have tried to keep documentation to a minimum, and cite only what is necessary, given the nature of the book. Similarly, dates are cited only where they have relevance to the comment or argument being made. My use of secondary work, of course, reflects my preferences, and my assessments of its usefulness to my task. My direct debts to critics are not numerous, but once incurred they tend to be heavy. That is to say, I have avoided compiling references to critics who may agree or disagree with a single point or carry it further, but I have made pronounced use of a selected few whose general positions have offered what I feel to be illuminating support, or, sometimes, opposition, in a sustained way. This kind of value in secondary work is independent of date, and I have made no attempt to stress recent work merely because it is recent.

Academic life, once or twice in a lifetime if one is fortunate, provides colleagues who teach one by what they are as well as what they know. To find three such colleagues within twenty years of academic life in America has been my incredible good luck. If this book should be useful to some readers, credit for that would properly belong to the late Professor Vladimir Jelinek of Washington University, Professor Bernard F. Huppé of the State University of New York at Binghamton, and Professor Richard Sewall of Yale University.

I have incurred other, more direct debts in making the book, and the easiest to define must represent many others. Certainly I owe thanks to Professor Marshall Van Deusen of the University of California, Riverside, and to Professors Sheldon Grebstein, John Hagan, Bernard F. Huppé and Seymour M. Pitcher of the State University of New York at Binghamton for reading the manuscript and making many useful suggestions. The Macmillan Company kindly gave me permission to quote from Tennyson's *Armageddon,* as it appeared in *Unpublished Early Poems,* edited by Charles Tennyson (New York, 1932), and copyrighted in 1932 by the Macmillan Company. I am grateful to The Research Foundation of State University of New York for supporting the work, and I thank the students whose interest in this literature spurred whatever thought made the book happen.

DEREK COLVILLE

Maine, New York
July 1969

I
APPROACH TO VICTORIAN POETRY:
A ROMANTIC REFORMULATION

1. FOREWORD: VICTORIAN AND ROMANTIC ❧ Victorian poetry, as many of its teachers will concede, does not enjoy a reputation attractive to students. There are exceptions among readers, and among individual poems, but in general the poetry is thought to be outworn. Reaction tends more towards a spiritless disdain than an energetic dislike. The Romantics are better regarded, with Blake usually leading the way, but this relative enthusiasm is often granted for isolated reasons rather than comprehensive understanding. Considered generally, the poetry of almost no other epoch evokes so disappointing a reaction as that of the century nearest our own; and this despite shared interests in visionary experience and a host of common problems in the background.

A major reason, quite obviously, is that the nineteenth century poets shared a belief in the possibility of reaching absolute truth. The Romantics, indeed, believed they had reached it; the Victorians knew that they had not. For the existential modern, absolute truth is impossible. Often, the twentieth century mind, willing enough to recognize if not sympathize with the beliefs of periods remoter in time, cannot envisage the belief of yesterday, particularly when yesterday was beset by problems it knows only too well. Characteristically, the modern mind does not see, in nineteenth century poetry, what has no possibility of existence for itself.

Viewed in that way, Victorian poetry of moral struggle loses much of its impact. It becomes irrelevant and vacuous. It is highly metaphorical poetry, and it loses half (the tenor) of its metaphor. Tennyson's Bedivere, in the *Morte d'Arthur,* does not appear to us as a modern spirit caught between allegiance to a faith and the claims of rational scepticism. He appears only as the vehicle of metaphor, a character in a hackneyed tale trying to cast a sword into a lake. The poetry appears mere narrative, superficial, traditional, over-stylized and old-fashioned.

The Romantic poem, at least in its essential religious and philo-sophic aspects, fares as badly; and if it is more successful as "art" this is, ironically, only through the force of an underlying commitment which modern readers often cannot even see. A sense of puzzlement is a central reaction—conscious or otherwise—of most modern read-ers of Romantic poetry. Scholars are constantly having to explain that the wholeness of belief the poems express, however naïve it may now appear, was not only possible when they were composed, but did actually exist.[1] This suggests not only how far our own age has retro-gressed from Romantic certitude, but also that Romantic certitude has had a remarkably swift decay. The difficulty is not that the mod-ern reader does not understand the reasons for this decay; he shares fully in that part of nineteenth century experience. But he does not see the rest of the Victorian equation of conflict. It is the possibility of belief he cannot envisage. The resulting vacuum is a comment on his own time; it is not properly a comment on the last century's po-etry.

To be more positive: if it is possible to experience vicariously something of the quality of commitment or the search for it in the nineteenth century, its poetry might appear substantially different. To sense the power of Romantic belief is to bring back to poetry the grail the Victorians so frustratingly sought. It is to see what was mod-ern poetry for Arnold, Browning and Tennyson, and to see it as it was available to them, even if they themselves could not always un-derstand it fully. For these reasons I should like to attempt a simple reformulation of Romantic poetry as a pattern of core and periphery. The core is the experience of vision. The periphery emerging from it is a world-outlook which is, by modern standards, of staggering sureness and faith. Such a pattern reveals that the other myriad forces in Romantic poetry, which so often appear to make definition hopeless, are not an inchoate mass, but orderly and logical consequences.

My attempt at such a reformulation has one primary purpose. It will provide a critical norm against which to examine major Victorian poetry which deals with problems of world-outlook. Later I shall point to characteristics and techniques in Victorian work which provide significant comparisons and contrasts with those of the Romantics. I have no illusions that I have made new discoveries in Romanticism. I provide no definitions, but merely suggest patterns of stress. My attempt at reformulation may also provide one way of approaching the English Romantic poets, useful to those who read them for the first time, but that is only incidental to my purpose in turning to their poetry.

2. THE CENTER OF VISION: COLERIDGE AND WORDSWORTH The Romantics repeatedly wrote of experiences from which they drew intense conviction that they understood the meaning and design behind the phenomenon of being alive on the earth. Their interpretation forms a clear complex of ideas which, like any other, invites evaluation. What is really distinctive in their work, however, is not the ideas themselves—I doubt if any sympathetic reader of Romantic poetry values it foremost as philosophy—but the extraordinary sense of commitment and conviction it carries.

Other manifestations of what is generally called Romanticism—rebellion against classical rules, social and political revolt, escapism, stress on the imagination, exoticism and abnormality, emotionalism rather than reason, preoccupation with nature [2]—all these, except the last, probably represent the literature of our own century as much as that of the previous one. But the passionate certainty with which the Romantics invested the meaning of their experiences has not persisted in a comparable group of creative minds since Keats died in 1821, and it has not been asserted with grandeur since Carlyle wrote *Sartor Resartus* soon after that. The compendium of clear ideas and attitudes shared by the Romantics was held, despite natural variations in personality, with remarkable unanimity. While the word "vision" is often used to refer to Romantic presentations of experience, and while it suggests accurately that their experience was erratic and ephemeral, it was not vague. If we seek beyond the obvious leanings of their poetry—towards nature, the individual, the imagination, political radicalism, and so on, we shall find that these are not premises but concomitants of a unified way of connecting individual experience to the universe surrounding it. The clarity of what the poets saw and felt, and the homogeneousness of what they deduced from it, reveal a clear and definite order.

This order, and the steps by which it was revealed, are shown most simply by Coleridge and Wordsworth. (Blake, of course, is chronologically the first great Romantic poet, and a Romantic epitome in the passion of his belief in his experience and its meaning. But his vision and expression are more erratic and complex than those of Coleridge and Wordsworth, and I postpone him for later mention.) The Romantic order in Coleridge, however, is so plainly illustrated that it scarcely matters which of a number of poems are taken first to demonstrate it, and which are kept for purposes of corroboration.

The Eolian Harp is both the earliest (1795) of the poems I have in mind, and the simplest in its recording of the steps of the experience. It opens quietly, with a simple expression of personal affection as Coleridge sits with his wife Sara outside their cottage at Clevedon in Somerset. The poet then attempts to convey the quiet evanescence of the evening; it is a leisurely, almost idle recording of a mood of nature, treated in the manner of Collins or Gray. These elements— human affection and the quiet consciousness of nature—are gathered up (l. 13 ff.) into a feeling of mounting joy and excitement. It is different from and yet contains the elements which formed it; it is a sense of liberation from the particularized perception of surrounding objects, a sense which many people experience on hearing music in sympathetic mood and surroundings. The catalyst for this imaginative enlargement is the music of the eolian harp placed in a window. The fascination which the Romantic poets felt for this instrument, simply a kind of box with tuned strings, was inevitable, since it represented music played by nature. But here the more vital symbol is the wind, which Coleridge takes elsewhere (e.g., *Fears in Solitude,* ll. 20–21) as God's "breath" reaching and animating earth. Here the music it produces is itself the immediate stimulation in changing the essential *kind* of Coleridge's idling imagination into a higher one; imagination reaches beyond the confines of the everyday physical universe, beyond all that has preceded, beyond the evening, Sara, and the silence. This change is reflected in immediate "magic" imagery ("Such a soft floating witchery of sound/ As twilight elfins make, when they at eve/ Voyage on gentle gales from Fairy Land"). The images for the lute and its sound, in fact (coy maid, twilight Elfins, Melodies round honey-dropping flowers) progressively liberate the instrument from earth-bound associations. This level of imagination is itself a preliminary to the sudden, metrically-quickened, and exclamatory apprehension of the prime force, the Unity, behind both worlds:

> O! the one Life within us and abroad,
> Which meets all motion and becomes its soul,
> A light in sound, a sound-like power in light
> Rhythm in all thought, and joyance everywhere—

Coleridge is here expressing his experience by means of images of sound and light; these are familiar enough individually and in weaker form in the world of sense. But by mixing and uniting them, he suggests a whole process taking place in a subjective mental dimension which becomes itself unified and then overwhelmed by religious contact. This conviction of a glimpse beyond the curtains of the finite world is always the height of the Romantic experience. The descent from it may be, as it is in this poem, swift, and in Coleridge it is usually made by retracing the steps taken in the ascent. These steps are, however, now *not the same,* for the poet's view of them has been transfigured by the experience to which they had led. Here, as Coleridge returns to the elements of love and nature by way of the music of "the mute still air," the fading Collins-like recording of evening evanescence is transformed to a scene in the poet's imagination, bathed in a far stronger light:

> as on the midway slope
> Of yonder hill I stretch my limbs at noon,
> Whilst through my half-clos'd eye-lids I behold
> The sunbeams dance, like diamonds, on the main,

and the initial simple affection for Sara is now broadened:

> Methinks, it should have been impossible
> Not to love all things in a world so fill'd.

The rest of the poem consists chiefly of rather embarrassed withdrawal, almost as if Coleridge were perturbed by the intensity of an experience which Sara, who unwittingly had a hand in creating it, has not shared, being content (according to the poem) to meet her prime mover in a much more orthodox way.[3] But this simple descent, under her "mild reproof," does not occur before Coleridge has put forward the principal speculation of the poem; namely that the whole of nature is simply an instrument, a collective harp, for bringing together the human mind, the soul, and the absolute force which created and orders both, into a united harmony:

> And what if all of animated nature
> Be but organic Harps diversely fram'd
> That tremble into thought, as o'er them sweeps
> Plastic and vast, one intellectual breeze,
> At once the Soul of each, and God of all?

This Lime-Tree Bower My Prison was written two years later,[4] but the change in time, and in the circumstances of the poem's composition appear insignificant beside the striking similarity of the experience it describes to that of *The Eolian Harp,* both in its kind and in the steps of its occurrence. The opening situation is that Coleridge, accidentally prevented from joining Charles Lamb and a group of other friends on a walk, is left in solitude in the lime-tree bower, creating in imaginative reverie the sights and sounds his absent friends are enjoying. The picture he creates for himself exists at first solely within a "realistic" or documentary range, consisting simply of imagined impressions of physical phenomena well-known to Coleridge from memory. Their details, early in the poem, have a flat, dull aspect fitting the poet's mood of desolate confinement. Coleridge's first mental picture (ll. 9–19), in fact, is largely composed of a series of images of *partial fulfillment*—the slightness of actuality beside its unrealized potential: the dell which is "only speckled" by the mid-day sun, and the "dark green file of long lank weeds" near the waterfall. Most important is the "branchless ash," whose arched trunk grows away from the sky and light and towards the earth; its "few poor yellow leaves" are moved not by the breeze, but only "tremble still" through the movement of the waterfall. From this somber daydream of their probable surroundings, the poet's mind wanders next to an imagined picture of his friends in a far more open, brightly-lit panorama of land and sea, and then back to his friends themselves and particularly to Lamb—"My gentle-hearted Charles!"—in spontaneous affection. As in *The Eolian Harp,* the combination of human affection with nature (here only envisioned) has an electric effect. The mind-pictures and the sluggish imagination are both transfigured; the imagination moves beyond physical confines; it is suffused with excitement. It catches fire in a sense almost literal; the meter quickens into brief ejaculatory rushes, bound together by the sustained "s" alliteration. The contrast with the earlier imaginative state is dramatized by a tremendous shift from the former lusterless imagery—and for that matter from the open brightness of the sea-land panorama. The cumulative effect of the various images is almost blindingly bright:

> Ah! slowly sink
> Behind the western ridge, thou glorious sun!
> Shine in the slant beams of the sinking orb,
> Ye purple heath-flowers! richlier burn, ye clouds!
> Live in the yellow light, ye distant groves!
> And kindle, thou blue Ocean!

This imaginative eruption brings to Coleridge's mind an experience which is ultimately mystical—the overwhelming sense of contact with a universal creator; although Coleridge is here wishing it for Lamb, he is writing of an experience he has often had himself. The point of view becomes personal and reminiscent, the direct brilliance passes, but the awed hush of the alliteration is retained:

> So my friend
> Struck with deep joy may stand, as I have stood,
> Silent with swimming sense; yea, gazing round
> On the wide landscape, gaze till all doth seem
> Less gross than bodily; and of such hues
> As veil the Almighty Spirit, when yet he makes
> Spirits perceive his presence.

The descent is again swift, and is again to a sense-perceived world which has changed. The lime-tree bower, the "prison" in the physical world, is now seen with mental "eyes" retaining some of the light of the blaze they have witnessed. The bower, while not blazing with light as did the height of the vision immediately prior to mystical contact, is now made radiant by the effect of that vision on the poet's mind—a radiance expressed again by light and shade:

> Pale beneath the blaze
> Hung the transparent foliage; and I watch'd
> Some broad and sunny leaf, and lov'd to see
> The shadow of the leaf and stem above
> Dappling its sunshine! And that walnut-tree
> Was richly ting'd, and a deep radiance lay
> Full on the ancient ivy, which usurps
> Those fronting elms, and now, with blackest mass
> Makes their dark branches gleam a lighter hue
> Through the late twilight.

Although they describe the same physical phenomenon, the differing emotional connotations of "only speckled by the mid-day sun" and "dappling its sunshine!" exactly reflect, in the context of the poem, the poet's spiritual journey—the contrast of Coleridge's mental state before the central imaginative experience with his condition after it.

The emergence, the return to the physical world, is signalled by a brief suggestion of evening evanescence again in the manner of Gray and Collins:

> the bat
> Wheels silent by, and not a swallow twitters,
> Yet still the solitary humble-bee
> Sings in the bean-flower!

and by the naïve moralizing, "Nature ne'er deserts the wise and pure," and "sometimes/ 'Tis well to be bereft of promis'd good, / That we may lift the soul, and contemplate,/ With lively joy the joys we cannot share."

The poet, however, does not choose to leave us back in the physical world of fading evening and sensed "reality" without once more fashioning a memorable vignette to act as summation of the larger entity of which the immediate evening is a part. He does this by creating a symbolic reconstruction of this unity in the superficial form of a "chance" detail:

> My gentle-hearted Charles! when the last rook
> Beat its straight path along the dusky air
> Homewards, I blest it! deeming its black wing
> Had cross'd the mighty Orb's dilated glory,
> While thou stood'st gazing . . . .

Coleridge and Lamb, physically separated but as individual perceptions connected by love, and here brought together by the sight of the bird (nature) against the sun (God), the source of all.

The elements of the total experience are somewhat differently arranged in *Frost at Midnight* (1798), yet the vision, while rather less dramatic, is essentially the same as that just described. The poem begins, again, in that silence and solitude which liberate "the idling spirit," here mirrored by the "flaps and freaks" of the flame of the low-burning fire in the frosty night. The imaginative flaps and freaks of reverie move, not this time in place, but back in time to the past (boyhood); and with a rush of love—"echoed" by metrical acceleration—to the baby Hartley sleeping by the poet's side, and hence to the future. Thus human love is again combined with imagined and idealized scenes of nature which Coleridge foresees his son enjoying:

> *thou,* my babe! shalt wander like a breeze
> By lakes and sandy shores, beneath the crags
> Of ancient mountain, and beneath the clouds,
> Which image in their bulk both lakes and shores
> And mountain crags,

and this leads once again to the apprehension of God:

> so shalt thou see and hear
> The lovely shapes and sounds intelligible
> Of that eternal language, which thy God
> Utters, who from eternity doth teach
> Himself in all, and all things in himself.
> Great universal Teacher! he shall mould
> Thy spirit, and by giving make it ask.

The final lines form a gradual fading from this—a number of natural vignettes of contrasting seasons suggesting the world's temporal cycle. They terminate in the same silence with which the poem began, and they are emotionally enriched in impact by their contrast of a general background with sharply particular images, and the whole dramatized in vivid colors:

> Therefore all seasons shall be sweet to thee,
> Whether the summer clothe the general earth
> With greenness, or the redbreast sit and sing
> Betwixt the tufts of snow on the bare branch
> Of mossy apple-tree, while the nigh thatch
> Smokes in the sun-thaw . . . .

The images are chosen to represent the natural world outside the cottage, in contrast with the specific details within it which, like the narrow dell in *This Lime-Tree Bower*, were given to suggest the limits of the poet's consciousness at the beginning of the poem.

It is clear, then, that these poems, differing as they do in form and detail, are all finally concerned with a central imaginative and spiritual experience which is consistent in kind, takes place with some frequency, and proceeds to its climax through a number of steps susceptible to sharp definition. I have, moreover, selected the poems simply on the basis of the clarity with which they recreate this process. The same experience or, more precisely, its corollary of a "world" of deeper meaning than the normal physical confines of this one, is implicit in most of Coleridge's poetry, for example in the su-pra-rational world of the Ancient Mariner's voyage—a world with an order as positive as that of the Greek gods, as the Polar Spirits make clear:

> The other was a softer voice,
> As soft as honey-dew:
> Quoth he, 'The man hath penance done,
> And penance more will do.'

The entire morality of the poem implies this superior order:

> The self-same moment I could pray;
> And from my neck so free
> The Albatross fell off, and sank
> Like lead into the sea.

Beside this morality the slightness of the moral tag at the end of the poem ("He prayeth best, who loveth best/ All things both great and small"), once the Mariner has re-entered the rational world, fittingly reflects the slightness of that world compared with the imaginative one where the bulk of the poem's action has taken place. I think it is also essentially true to see the argument, and the glosses to the poem which appeared in its 1817 version, as emphasis of this dualism. While they do not confine their narration to events within the physical world, the point of view they seem to express is a mundane one beside the infinitely wider, emotionally provocative "superworld" created by the poem itself.[5]

It is important that the central experience of the poem, resulting in the Mariner's release from the bonds symbolized by the Albatross (Part IV), follows the visionary pattern familiar in the poems already considered. First, the water-snakes, which have been so horrifyingly vague in the becalming, are suddenly seen as beautiful. Next, though their beauty is declared inexpressible, its effect on the Mariner is a surge of love and blessing. He becomes one with the order of being, a connection finally expressed by his religious contact in the prayer which releases him.

Christabel likewise stresses this relationship, though its method differs. There is only one supernatural event in the whole of the fragment (and even this is explicable as hypnotism); but the entire effect depends on hints and understatements putting the burden on the reader's imagination and inviting his attention and awe into the realm of the order, beyond the rational, on which the poem operates. Thus the casual suggestion that "some say" the mastiff bitch "sees my lady's shroud" is followed by a "rational" view so precise, limited and final that its very confinement provokes the reader to reject it and turn to another: "Is the night chilly and dark? / The night is chilly, but not dark." Similarly,

> It moaned as near, as near can be,
> But what it is she cannot tell . . . .
> Is it the wind that moaneth bleak?

is followed by the chilling presentation of "normal," sense-observed "fact":

> There is not enough wind in the air
> To move away the ringlet curl
> From the lovely lady's cheek.

Dejection is much more specifically related to the experience treated in the first three poems I considered, though its approach is negative. The poem is the obverse of the various steps of the imaginative experience, and its theme is Coleridge's complaint at his failure, on this occasion, to ascend them. Again, the contrast between solitary confinement in the physical world and the imaginative exultation of reaching beyond it is made by means of light. That "real" —sense-apprehended—light at the start of the poem, which forecasts the storm, is given an illusory quality:

> For lo! the New-moon winter-bright!
> And overspread with phantom light,

> (With swimming phantom light o'erspread
> But rimmed and circled by a silver thread),

while even the abstract statement of what would be necessary to transcend this physical world by imaginative apprehension is suffused with light of an entirely different kind:

> Ah! from the soul itself must issue forth
> A light, a glory, a fair luminous cloud
> Enveloping the Earth.

 The clearest and most powerful presentation of Romantic experience in Wordsworth is the vision on Snowdon (*Prelude,* XIV, 1–62). Despite wide differences in form and style, it parallels Coleridge's visionary presentation in the distinctness by which it charts the steps of the ascent to vision. It is a famous passage, but I should like to reconsider it here as a paradigm of Romantic experience.

 The facts are concrete, even prosaic enough for the poet to mention the meal he and his companions took before beginning their climb up Snowdon. Three men—Wordsworth himself, a friend, and a shepherd—and the shepherd's dog climb the mountain in the predawn hours. There is a certain atmosphere of confinement in the "close, warm, breezeless summer night" with its "dripping fog," as though all the conditions which surround a man are pressing down on him to contain him within himself. They begin to climb, as if to break out of this confinement. But it persists, symbolized by the mist they continue to encounter, which again presses down upon each man, isolating him—from his fellows, from the world: "pensively we sank/ Each into commerce with his private thoughts."

 This state is reinforced by the profound silence, and the effect of the barking of the shepherd's dog, who has found a hedgehog, is not so much to break the silence as to dramatize its depth. (This is close to Coleridge's use of the "stilly murmur of the distant Sea" at the start of *The Eolian Harp,* the owlet's cry which sets off the silence in *Frost at Midnight,* and the sound of the "solitary humble-bee" after the vision in the lime-tree bower.) The silence resumes again. Wordsworth now tells us that he feels the sense of confinement, isolation and the deadness of silence is something to be fought against; it is identified with earth; its direction is downward, and it is an enemy (ll. 28–31).

The climb continues, and as Wordsworth takes his first step above the mist, an event occurs suddenly:

> . . . at my feet the ground appeared to brighten,
> And with a step or two seemed brighter still;
> Nor was time given to ask or learn the cause,
> For instantly a light upon the turf
> Fell like a flash, and lo! as I looked up
> The Moon hung naked in a firmament
> Of azure without cloud . . . .

The point of view is vital in this presentation. We are to apprehend this experience exactly as the beholder at the moment it occurred. We are not to seek its rational explanation and dismiss the event: "nor was time given to ask or learn the cause." We are to see it as what it is—miracle, and the language is that reserved for miracle (divine creativity) in the Bible: "and lo! as I looked up/ The Moon hung naked in a firmament." The poetry is used here to shock the reader out of the metaphorical mist in which he is apt to live, and which is inimical to the Romantic faith. By using the terms of miracle, Wordsworth forces us to question our normal, sense-bound, rational and blasé view of existence. Is it really so ordinary, he seems to ask, that we live in a universe of infinite space, where there is a moon, where we have eyes and consciousness to see it and be aware of something we call beauty? Or is there wonder, and something miraculous in these things to which we have become blind? There are two sharply distinct ways of reacting to experience here, and the dual view is crucial in the understanding of Romanticism: one involves sensed observation and rational acceptance, the other cosmic awareness and a capacity for wonder.

The confinement is now broken, and Wordsworth stands above the fog, beneath the open sky and with the moonlit sea of mist at his feet. But he makes it clear that there is movement, and towards an area far larger than, and essentially different from, the norm of earthly sensory experience. Here, at this transitional point, physical laws are dismissed, transcended, and in fact reversed. Here the hills move: "A hundred hills their dusky backs upheaved." Here the ocean, in the physical world so active, flowing, and tidal, is "silent" and "still." Here the vapors are "solid." Of course, we can say, it is all an illusion, a poetic metaphor for the mist, created from the conditions by the poet's imagination. But to dismiss it so is again to confine ourselves to the "rational" area. Is not what actually exists in the relationship between the conditions and the poet's imagination as real as—Wordsworth would say more real than—that rational view? The visionary climax comes with a rush of sound:

> . . . save that through a rift—
> Not distant from the shore whereon we stood,
> A fixed, abysmal, gloomy breathing-place—
> Mounted the roar of waters, torrents, streams
> Innumerable, roaring with one voice!
> Heard over earth and sea, and, in that hour,
> For so it seemed, felt by the starry heavens.

Wordsworth is here not merely describing, but trying to echo, to make the reader feel, at second-hand, something of the impact of the height of vision. It is an emotional and imaginative contact with what he feels to be the ultimate order, the essential reality, of the universe—of life itself. This contact and the exultant blinding sense of truth it brings carry limitless implications, and the poet has to suggest the impact he feels in terms we understand. Shifting from the visual suggestions he has mainly used to this point, he turns to symbolic sound. It comes to him from many sources, but is united in effect: to him it is specifically a cosmic sound and it comes, fittingly, through the rift which divides the earth from the greater infinitude beyond it. It unites the world we live in with the greater one: "heard over earth and sea" but "felt by the starry heavens."

Wordsworth follows this presentation of experience by a versified explanation of its significance. As a poetic statement—almost an abstract lecture—on philosophic meaning it is unique in Romantic work, but in its clarity, its considered perspective and above all its confidence it is entirely representative. The poet has had, he tells us, "a vision," which on reflection appears to have been the "type" or sign of "a majestic intellect." He has seen "the emblem of a mind/ That feeds upon infinity, that broods/ Over the dark abyss" (ll. 71–73). He is suggesting the religious meaning of his experience by echoing Milton's Creative Spirit at the start of *Paradise Lost,* that spirit which is to create the world in Milton's poem, and which

> . . . with mighty wings outspread
> Dove-like satst brooding on the vast Abyss
> And madst it pregnant.

There follow a number of most specific statements by Words-worth defining the meaning of his experience—creating, in fact, a whole order from it. Imagination in man is the lesser mirror of crea-tivity in God. Through imagination, the experience of the senses be-comes that of the spirit; it "conducts to ideal form." Nature, the "face of outward things," is the language of God, moving men imagi-natively until even the least sensitive "see, hear, perceive,/ And can-not choose but feel." It is the most creative imaginations, the "higher minds" of the poets, which therefore see most truly into the nature of existence. Making use of the old myth that the inspired poet hears the music of cosmic harmony, Wordsworth sees such minds as "angels stopped upon the wing by sound/ Of harmony from heaven's remo-test spheres."

This ordered larger harmony reached through the imagination embraces all we know: nothing is small in this conception of reality. God is quite literally in the palm of the hand, and eternity in a flower. Thus those who see life in this way see the enormous implica-tions of the humblest object, and humblest people. They "build up greatest things/ From least suggestions." To hold this outlook is to escape from the prison of judging all experience by the senses and by reasoning based on their observation. It is to escape into a larger world of spirit, to feel that eternity, and not time, is where we live. The relevant lines imply these things quite inescapably. Higher, po-etic minds are

> By sensible impressions not enthralled,
> But by their quickening impulse made more prompt
> To hold fit converse with the spiritual world,
> And with the generations of mankind
> Spread over time, past, present, and to come,
> Age after age, till Time shall be no more.

The movement here is repeatedly from the finite to the infinite side of Romantic dualism, though the terms themselves may vary. On the finite side are the earth, nature, man, the senses, rationality, and time. On the infinite side are the universe, God, imaginative or tran-scendent knowledge, and eternity. Between the two levels, and the means of connecting them, are imagination, love, and vision. Like Coleridge, Wordsworth saw love as catalyst to visionary experience, as well as its consequence. If all is to be accepted into Romantic order, and nothing excluded, the moral equivalent of such accept-ance is love:

> By love subsists
> All lasting grandeur, by pervading love;
> That gone, we are as dust.

He means love both earthly and human, and love in its "still higher" form, spiritual or religious love. Wordsworth ends his interpretation of the meaning of his experience by retracing its elements in descending order, using the figure of a river flowing down from God (ll. 188 ff.). But in Wordsworth's presentation of the entire outlook, perhaps the most characteristic lines are those which attack what is always anathema to the Romantic:

> The tendency, too potent in itself,
> Of use and custom to bow down the soul
> Under a growing weight of vulgar sense,
> And substitute a universe of death
> For that which moves with light and life informed,
> Actual, divine, and true.

"Actual, divine, and true": it is hard to imagine a more assertive and uncompromising statement of faith in a world-outlook.

Despite differences in expression, it is evident that Coleridge and Wordsworth were writing of experience common to both, of immense importance to both, and almost certainly discussed by both together. There is, however, one characteristic in Wordsworth's work, a steady inclination towards abstraction, which distinguishes him sharply from Coleridge as a poet. There are indeed times—and the long passage, just discussed, explaining the meaning of the Snowdon vision is the most obvious example—when Wordsworth becomes essentially a philosopher writing in verse. It is largely from this tendency that his special difficulties arise. "The light that never was," "sensations sweet/ Felt in the blood and felt along the heart," and "Thoughts that do often lie too deep for tears" do not carry literal meaning self-sufficiently. They can only express it when apprehended with some familiarity with the poet's experience, a certain trust in it and a sympathy for his view of its meaning.

Read casually, Wordsworth seems to be a simple poet who describes rather than recreates, and appears only to stray into metaphysical matters. This superficial view has some foundation, but his expressive resources are more extensive as well as more subtle than they at first appear. To take a simple example, he will often dramatize the contrast between the finite world and the one beyond it by sudden shifts in the scale of his images. The beauty in Lucy's humble obscurity is stated in the simplest metaphor:

> A violet by a mossy stone
> Half hidden from the eye.
> —Fair as a star, when only one
> Is shining in the sky.

But the primary simplicity serves to screen the essentially different suggestion, of cosmic scale and importance, made in the last two lines.

Wordsworth, again not appearing a symbolic poet on first reading, actually relies heavily on the device. He uses symbols in a way so elementary it is almost, but not quite, labored: his use, for instance, of the blind beggar in Book VII of *The Prelude* (637–649) to suggest the limitations of finite life:

> I was smitten
> Abruptly, with a view (a sight not rare)
> Of a blind Beggar, who, with upright face,
> Stood, propped against a wall, upon his chest
> Wearing a written paper, to explain
> His story, whence he came, and who he was.
> Caught by the spectacle my mind turned round
> As with the might of waters; and apt type
> This label seemed of the utmost we can know
> Both of ourselves and of the universe;
> And, on the shape of that unmoving man,
> His steadfast face and sightless eyes, I gazed,
> As if admonished from another world.

In *The Prelude* especially, Wordsworth's very consistency in using visual shapes (or Forms, to use his term) and architecture to express his vision makes it easy for readers to miss his point in seeking particularities. His "Forms" are among his most functional techniques. His consoling thought after crossing the Alps without having been aware of a summit (*Prelude* VI, 562–591), "For still we had hopes that pointed to the clouds," indicates what the idea of height meant to him. "The distant Alps," "mighty Forms," and "France standing on the top of golden hours" are all phrases packed together in his brief statement introducing his visit to France in 1790 (*Prelude*

VI, 322–341). From the meaning of mountains, which provide the closest points to the Maker of the Whole, the meaning of streams (God's love flowing down to man through nature) and lakes (aggregations of that love in nature) are consequent. Equally and logically inevitable is the height on Snowdon as setting for the events and reflections of Book XIV of *The Prelude*. Conversely, in Book III, the early references to flatness appear as background detail, but the constant stress on it becomes a visual representation of Wordsworth's spiritual state at Cambridge. And I think it encourages understanding of the nature of *The Prelude* to imagine its general architecture as transmitting the spiritual development of its author through the "form" of a mountainous topography—the "foothills" of the early visions, the flats of Cambridge, the sweeping descents into the valleys and shadows of Wordsworth's ultimate reactions to the Terror in France, and the gradual ascent to the Snowdon summit. Even the characteristic "Form" of Wordsworth's explanation of the Romantic order in Book XIV of *The Prelude* suggests a mountain. The description of the function of nature-stimulated imagination in men (ll. 86–129) moves upward to the summit of the mystical experience with which the book opened: the descent, as has been pointed out (page 18), is the restatement of the process, starting from its first cause, the Deity.

Resources other than architecture and symbolic use of forms attest to Wordsworth's view of the significance of his experience. I have mentioned his use of Miltonic echoes: he will also use chains of related imagery to suggest the ultimate meaning of what he describes overtly. In the first Book of *The Prelude* (31–58) occurs a passage describing at some length the emotional stirrings arising from Wordsworth's boyhood contacts with nature. Through the whole passage are scattered terms such as "consecrates" (l. 32), "punctual service" (l. 44), "Matins and vespers" (l. 45), "clothe in priestly robe" (l. 52), and "holy services" (l. 54)—terms which combine to suggest powerfully the Romantics' practice of transferring the language of orthodox religion to their own worship of the imagination.

The emphasis with which the imaginative world is differentiated from the physical one is as striking in Wordsworth as in Coleridge. I have already referred to Wordsworth's dramatizing of the distinction by shifts in the scale of his images. The relationship between the two is most important in those passages of *The Prelude* where the superior guiding world of imagination must speak through the inferior one of physical nature to erring humanity. The most revealing instance is probably the moral lesson the boy Wordsworth received after having stolen a boat (Book I, 357–400). The whole of the natural world becomes alive, threatening—not of itself, but working, almost speaking, through the boy's state of heightened imagination which is usually called conscience:

> . . . a huge peak, black and huge,
> As if with voluntary power instinct,
> Upreared its head. I struck and struck again,
> And growing still in stature the grim shape
> Towered up between me and the stars, and still,
> For so it seemed, with purpose of its own
> And measured motion like a living thing
> Strode after me. With trembling oars I turned,
> And through the silent water stole my way
> Back to the covert of the willow tree.

The presentation is hedged by "As if," "For so it seemed." We are still technically—and what a small area of meaning the term has here!—in the dimension of physical laws. But the most functional part of the whole affair is the method of Wordsworth's transition from this merely physical world to that from which emanates moral authority. It is done subtly through a detail perfectly explicable in physical terms, but appearing to take on a kind of life redolent of the supernatural—the boy's view of the peak. As he rows, its bulk, increasingly revealed with each stroke, appears to him to move, to tower over him threateningly. It suggests, therefore, both to the young Wordsworth and to the reader, a reproving nature coming to life. The impression is deepened by the minor symbolic (weeping) associations of the willow tree and the major ones of the peak's towering "between me and the stars." Still, the boundaries dividing the natural from the supernatural world have not actually been crossed, as they had also not been actually crossed in Coleridge's *Christabel*.

Such incidents stress the connection, yet sharp difference in moral authority, between the physical world's "reality," and the spiritual entity beyond it, which speaks through it by means of our imaginative perception. They imply the infinitely greater importance of the transformed world over the untransformed. In other words, what most of us call "illusion" is more true for Wordsworth than what we usually call "reality." The poet takes every opportunity, and uses a variety of methods, to impress this on his reader, often through symbols like the echo [6]—literally a speaking to human ears through natural laws, more eloquent, because more universal, than the eolian harp. Sometimes he is much more detailed. In the skating passage of Book I of *The Prelude*, the view is intensely subjective: it is the cliffs which appear to move after the skater has stopped:

> . . . yet still the solitary cliffs
> Wheeled by me—even as if the earth had rolled
> With visible motion her diurnal round!

The continuing movement can be given a physical explanation, dizziness, but Wordsworth omits any such suggestion, concentrating instead on the larger view beyond reason. He employs a kind of irony: *"as if* the earth had rolled/ With visible motion her diurnal round!" This is the limited, reasonable (and false) statement of what a larger cosmic view would show as simple fact, and which has been glimpsed here through an experience we normally discount as "illusion"!

To move from technique to outlook is to find in Wordsworth both correspondences with Coleridge, as well as extensions in ideas important to the understanding of Victorian poets who were to follow. Like Coleridge, Wordsworth insists on several occasions that initial loss or disappointment ultimately proves constructive in the universal moral scheme. There are many examples: Wordsworth, by Book VI of *The Prelude*, has established the symbolic meaning of mountains for himself. Then the "soulless image" (l. 526) of Mont Blanc is one anti-climax; the crossing of the Alps, with no sense of summit or crescendo (ll. 586–591) is another. But the lines following stress the later conviction that the disappointments were of sense only, and, taking the whole event as metaphoric, he becomes convinced that it is constructive in showing dramatically that its sensory vehicle is irrelevant, its spiritual tenor everything:

> I was lost;
> Halted without an effort to break through;
> But to my conscious soul I now can say—
> "I recognize thy glory:" in such strength
> Of usurpation, when the light of sense
> Goes out, but with a flash that has revealed
> The invisible world, doth greatness make abode,
> There harbours; whether we be young or old,
> Our destiny, our being's heart and home,
> Is with infinitude, and only there.

The same general affirmation, that suffering builds spiritual wisdom, applies to the experience described in Book XI of *The Prelude*. Here Wordsworth's long series of shocks and sufferings—the crumbling of youthful social aspiration after the French Terror, the searching of society to its heart, the yielding of moral questions in despair, the bitter philosophic accusations of divine unconcern, the turning to "abstract science"—all these later appear to have existed only to draw forth the loving, inspiriting care of Dorothy in his hour of need.

The young Wordsworth appears, at least as far as poetry is concerned, somewhat more explicit than Coleridge in assigning wide philosophic meaning to his experience. He makes certain extensions which cohere into a larger Romantic theory. The most concrete example of such an extension is probably the *Intimations of Immortality* ode. In brief, the ode takes the ultimate reality, which Wordsworth and Coleridge had apprehended by imaginative glimpses, to be the same unclouded whole which exists for men before birth—the beginning of life, which is itself the beclouding illusion. In changing the former for the latter, that is, in being born, a consciousness (or perhaps we should say an unconscious awareness) of the greater reality is retained by the child, and persists until sufficient time of earthly life—the "prison-house"—has elapsed to erode it. The longer a man lives confined by what he is apt to call (with unknowing irony in Wordsworth's view), the "real" world, the more completely is the vision of the divine remnant of former glory effaced (Section V). In this process nature works in two ways: it can help stimulate the ever-shrinking vision into flashes of reactivity, but in the other direction a concentration upon nature *for itself alone* will ultimately destroy and replace the capacity for vision:

> The homely Nurse doth all she can
> To make her Foster-child, her Inmate Man,
> Forget the glories he hath known,
> And that imperial palace whence he came.

As we shall see, Wordsworth himself later apologized for—and simultaneously defended—the literal view of the pre-existence of the soul which his poem expresses. But Wordsworth by that time, like most of his modern readers, was incapable both of vision and of unqualified belief in the poetic imagination. I am making the presumption that the Romantics, like most people with the capacity for enthusiasm, meant, in their work, what they said. Even granting this, it is easy in the twentieth century, abetted by the casual finality of the word *vision*, to shrug off the climax of all these experiences as a fairly familiar phenomenon, but one so intensely personal that it is hardly worth discussing, for it seems to defy translation into terms of meaning to the reader. The poets themselves were not content with this position, and their writings are frequently records of struggle to define what they had met at the height of their experiences, as in the *Tintern Abbey* lines: "And I have felt/ A presence that disturbs me with the joy/ Of elevated thoughts. . . ." In effect, what Wordsworth speaks of in the famous lines which follow is not unlike a Platonic ideal world, a perfect prototype of the physical universe, completed by an accompanying morality. His references to it are generally, as in *Tintern Abbey,* somewhat abstract, but he regards the poet's major task as the transmission of trust in it:

> the animating faith
> That Poets, even as Prophets, each with each
> Connected in a mighty scheme of truth,
> Have each his own peculiar faculty,
> Heaven's gift, a sense that fits him to perceive
> Objects unseen before . . . .

The "mighty scheme of truth" certainly exists for Wordsworth, but it is seen only after nature enlarges the mind's eye:

> oh, at that time
> While on the perilous ridge I hung alone,
> With what strange utterance did the loud dry wind
> Blow through my ear! the sky seemed not a sky
> Of earth—and with what motion moved the clouds!
>   *(Prelude,* I, 335–339)

It is not coincidental (for it itself illustrates that apparent separation often covers larger connections) that the passage immediately following this, though ostensibly beginning another section of Book I, is in fact connected by the image-coincidence of the central "hung" in the first passage with the equally emphatic "cling" in the second: ". . . there is a dark/ Inscrutable workmanship that reconciles/ Discordant elements, makes them cling together/ In one society." The "alone" and "together" respectively attached to these verbs likewise suggest progress towards the larger unity seen through such moments.

Wordsworth's treatment of the "mighty scheme of truth" is al-

ways somewhat dampened by his sense of the impossibility of revealing the infinite to finite men. There can at best be affinity "between
religion—whose element is infinitude, and whose ultimate trust is
the supreme of things . . . and poetry, ethereal and transcendent,
yet incapable to sustain her existence without sensuous incarnation." [7]

Coleridge is not so reserved in prose discussion of what he called
the Whole, and a return to him in this connection shows how his entire outlook was shaped by the overriding presence of its idea. He recalls that at eight years of age, when the night sky was explained to
him, he showed not "the least mixture of wonder or incredulity. For
from my early reading of fairy tales and genii, etc., etc., my mind had
been habituated *to the Vast,* and I never regarded *my senses* in any
way as the criteria of my belief. I regulated all my creeds by my conceptions, not by my *sight,* even at that age." [8] He goes on to argue
the case for children being permitted to read stories of magic: "I
know no other way of giving the mind a love of the Great and the
Whole." Are not the experimentalists, he goes on to ask, "credulous
even to madness in believing any absurdity, rather than believe the
grandest truths, if they have not the testimony of their own senses in
their favour?" There is in fact a natural need to apprehend the unity
of all things. In a letter to John Thelwall, Coleridge confessed, "I
can contemplate nothing but *parts,* and parts are all *little!* My mind
feels as if it ached to behold and know something *great,* something
one and *indivisible.*" [9]

In his essay *On Method,* Coleridge argued that each species and
each individual in nature is both a system in itself, "a world of its
own," and is also united by universal laws with the whole. He went
on to use this interconnection as analogy for an equally pervasive
moral order: "shall we not hold it probable that by some analogous
intervention a similar temperament will have been effected for the
rational and moral?" In such a system, the finite form is the mere
symbol of its infinite implications. The Romantic experience, then, is
simply a deeper than normal apprehension of this all-pervading system of God.

As M. H. Abrams has indicated, Coleridge's literary criticism is
the logical product of this world-outlook.[10] His celebrated conceptions
of Fancy, "the aggregating faculty of the mind" (that which suggests
equivalents and correspondences), and Imagination, "the modifying
and coadunating faculty" (that which unifies), are simply two
marked stages in his Romantic quest for final unity—the former

finite, the latter leading to perception of the infinite Whole. Coleridge, in fact, builds round his idea of the Whole, as Carlyle was later to do also, an entire set of dual terms describing experience in its unfulfilled and fulfilled forms: Understanding (logic relative to initial sensual observation—in short, the scientific method) and Reason (in Coleridge's special sense of near-intuition); "littlenesses" and the Vast or Whole; Fancy and Imagination; nature seen with the eyes, and nature irradiated by heightened imagination.

3. BLAKE ℰ Blake's early simple poetry, which antedates the work of Wordsworth and Coleridge I have used as prototype, shows him steeped in Romantic values from the start. His consciousness of the dual view of life shows itself most obviously in the title of the *Songs of Innocence and Experience*—Romantic potential put against the actuality of the world—and in the arrangement of the lyrics. These poems, essentially, are repeated demonstrative statements of Romantic values, made with a moving pathos and simplicity; and only secondarily do they express the vision that has led to them. Where vision occurs, it is flatly presented with the most naked and casual directness.

> On a cloud I saw a child,
> And he laughing said to me . . .

The Romantic dual awareness occurs in every poem. The *Songs of Innocence* (1789) open with an introductory lyric on what poetry should be: direct, spontaneous, steeped in nature, joyful and joymaking, and speaking to children. It is a Romantic manifesto.[11] Then follow poems overflowing with joy and love ("The Shepherd"), freedom and play ("The Ecchoing Green"), and tenderness ("The Lamb"). But the Songs are never earth-bound for long: there is a continual awareness of the force behind the joy of life:

> 'And we are put on earth a little space,
> That we may learn to bear the beams of love;
> And these black bodies and this sunburnt face
> Is but a cloud, and like a shady grove.

> 'For when our souls have learn'd the heat to bear,
> The cloud will vanish. . . .'

This poem, "The Little Black Boy," more specifically even than most of those around it, sets transcendent values against earthly ones: the black body against the white soul, the cloud of earthly life against the light of eternity, earthly love as the due reflection of eternal love.

So the *Songs of Innocence* proceed, varying the terms and focus, but not the outlook, in each poem. Duality is implied throughout: the actual and the potential in "The Chimney Sweeper," the theme of earthly *lost* and transcendent *found* in "The Little Boy" poems. In this the Songs are entirely representative of Blake. While his complex later work is beyond the scope of this brief overview, it is a simple matter to show that the poet held to the dual view of existence at all stages of his career. Some twenty years after composing the *Songs of Innocence,* for instance, Blake was to write one of the clearest statements of the dual view ever made by a Romantic poet; it occurs in the 1810 notebook passage known as *A Vision of the Last Judgment.* "This world of Imagination," he wrote, "is the world of Eternity; it is the divine bosom into which we shall all go after the death of the Vegetated body. This World of Imagination is Infinite & Eternal, whereas the world of Generation, or Vegetation, is Finite & Temporal. There exist in that Eternal World the Permanent Realities of Every Thing which we see reflected in this Vegetable Glass of Nature."

Also behind each of the Songs, implied where not expressed, is the doctrine of moral unity:

> . . . all must love the human form
> In heathen, turk or jew;
> Where Mercy, Love and Pity dwell
> There God is dwelling too.
> ("The Divine Image")

Equally omnipresent is the order which itself implies love, the order demonstrated in the rescue of the ant in "A Dream," an order which implies the oneness of all:

> Can I see another's woe
> And not be in sorrow too?
> Can I see another's grief,
> And not seek for kind relief?
> ("On Another's Sorrow")

The *Songs of Experience* (1794) are in general ratification of the values of the *Songs of Innocence;* Experience presupposes the same dual conscience, but teaches by negative example; that is, it usually sees the duality through the eyes of earthly reality grown-too-large. Hence from the admonitory "Why wilt thou turn away?" of the introductory poem, the group proceeds to the themes of love-grown-selfish ("The Clod and the Pebble"), social repression ("Holy Thursday" and "London"), the lesson so-called "savage" nature can teach ("The Little Girl Lost" and "The Little Girl Found"), jealousy ("Nurse's Song"), earthly longing and the eternity it seeks ("Ah! Sun-Flower"), and so on.

But Blake, if he can enforce a true value, is prepared to treat his scheme of arrangement itself as a restrictive blinker, and "The Tyger," a poem the ostensible converse to "The Lamb" in the *Songs of Innocence,* is not one of destruction or terror, but of wonder and awe at the power which could "frame" it. By simply placing "The Tyger" in the *Songs of Experience,* Blake enforces a dramatic demonstration of the lesson Wordsworth was to teach more prosaically in *The Prelude* (Book XI), that what seems terrifying or destructive is no less the product of God and a work of love, if apprehended with eyes and mind not blinded by viewing the senses and the present as sole realities.

This sense of something larger than neat opposition of dual values is pervasive in Blake's work, and it also accords with the centrally Romantic characteristics I have stressed. The *Songs of Innocence and Experience* are basically dualistic in the values they put forward, as I have suggested, but so simple a view does, it is true, appear disconcertingly inadequate after reading the poems. For they have an undercurrent of self-contradiction. To cite the simplest of examples, the introductory poem on the nature of art in the *Songs of Innocence,* "Piping down the valleys wild," has, for all its childlike joy, on one level of reading a disturbing counter-current in certain diction: the hollow reed, the *staining* of the clear water for the act of writing. Or one could cite the treatment of time in "The Ecchoing Green": must the joyous play be watched by the old folk, who comment on its remoteness as now seen in their lives? Is such a comment mere acceptance? With this as background, the poem's final image of the "darkening" green seems to carry a gloomier connotation than simply exhausted fulfillment. Or the seemingly mocking irony of the final line of "The Chimney Sweeper,"—"So if all do their Duty they need not fear harm," has a parallel effect. The fact is that both the *Songs of Innocence* and the *Songs of Experience* carry consistent undercurrents, counter-forces to their main implications, and the unbalanced, dynamic tension they create points to the direction Blake's vision was to take in the rest of his work. Romantic dualism, then, provides only an impetus, an initial direction, in Blake's poetry. To put it another way, it is easy to diagram the earthly, sensed forms of life in one column and the larger, eternal realities in another. But while this is central in the *Songs of Innocence and Experience* it is not exhaustive, and to represent the forces in the rest of Blake's work, and even in the *Songs* themselves, one would have to complete the diagram by drawing a "circle of Unity" around both columns or, better still, drawing nothing at all (since such a circle would imply limitation) but imagining both columns as highly limited parts of a limitless order. The bulk of Blake's poetry is given, not to dualistic division, but to a synthesis which he stresses even more than Coleridge and Wordsworth do in their work.

The Marriage of Heaven and Hell, in its title, its arrangement, and its pronouncements, makes this very clear, and it remains true on the various levels on which Blake's major work operates. The aphorisms of the *Auguries of Innocence,* as one example, are moral insights consequent to that synthesis. Nothing in Blake is clearer or more powerful than the magnificent passage accompanying the eighth plate of *America*—in its clarion call to its age, in its building of counter-currents into a triumphant and visual unity, through the agency of unfettered, or lawless, creative pleasure (Orc).[12] This synthesizing force, above all else, is always present in Blake. A poem such as *The Mental Traveller* may carry a wealth of tenable meanings; and whether one accepts a particular one, such as John H. Sutherland's, or not, one still has to accept his conclusion that "the poem is really about the dynamic relationships of eternal principles, and hardly about men at all."[13] Similarly the archetypes of the Prophetic Books, so fully the subject of speculative analysis elsewhere, do create a vision which is above all consistent, as Northrop Frye implies: ". . . what the artist has to reveal, as a guide for the work of civilization and prophecy, is the form of the world as it would be if we could live in it here and now."[14] Blake synthesizes because he stresses fundamental human unities and hopes for an age in which they can be realized.

There is, moreover, in a sustained reading of Blake a sort of chain-reaction, with each link having a completeness of its own, yet acting as catalyst to the next. If the *Songs of Innocence and Experience* are largely dual in their vision, they also carry, as we have seen, undercurrents suggesting synthesis. If much of Blake's work suggests synthesis, it is never complete, never in precise or final balance, never static. It is not the swing of one pendulum, or many: it is at once the pendulum which swings, the fountain which erupts, the explosion which destroys; all occurring within and beyond time and space, in a universe which itself metaphorizes infinity.

The very complexity of the private symbolism in the Prophetic Books, of course, indicates the difficulty of sustaining live poetic language for a vision uncompromising in its insistence and vitality over a long lifetime, as Yeats was to discover a century later. Indeed, while it is tempting to think of Blake as I have described him—the one English Romantic who kept the force of his vision over several decades—it is perhaps only the comparative background of Coleridge and Wordsworth, and the brief lives of the later Romantics, that make such a view seem so obvious and certain; and it might well be qualified by a view of Blake as undergoing some shrinking of vision in his own way. Geoffrey Keynes, for instance, sees him starting with early opposition to Christianity and going on later to reform of it: "Blake had been attacking original Christianity in the simpler poems of the Illuminated Books, but now his message was directed towards the cleansing of the Christian religion from its errors and establishing human consciousness of imaginative art as the supreme good." [15] If Blake is indeed seen as narrowing his range in that way as his work progressed, it would only move him closer to his fellow Romantics as well as to Victorians like Carlyle and Ruskin. And despite the apparent nakedness of his style and its later complexity, he meets with them at the center, his initial dual values growing into the assertion of an ever-active synthesis.

4. THE SECOND GENERATION: BYRON ❧ An admirably incisive historian reminds us—I think necessarily—of a fact obvious enough to be often overlooked. "The opinions of a man born in, say, 1780," remarks D. C. Somervell, "rest upon one set of data, while the opinions of a man born in 1800 or 1820 or 1850 rest upon quite another." [16] This observation (especially if we take "opinions" to include frame

of mind or attitude) is one on which this book is predicated. The second generation of Romantic poets, Byron, Shelley and Keats, spent their formative years against a background both more complex and more inviting to disillusionment than it had been even ten years before. I do not think that the new young poets entirely realized that it was a new and revolutionary *kind* of world—the one we call "modern"—that they lived in, and not simply a more tired, ugly, corrupt and evil version of the old one, which it was only in part.

In 1809, the birth-year of Darwin and Tennyson, Lincoln and Gladstone, Byron came of age, Shelley was nineteen and Keats fourteen, the same age as Carlyle, whose steady image as exclusively Victorian makes him seem quite apart from the Romantic group. The *Lyrical Ballads* had come out over a decade before, and the best of Wordsworth's creative work had been written. The previous twenty years had been dominated by the French Revolution, the Terror and the war with France. Sixteen years before, Godwin had produced his theoretical blueprint for a brave new world, *An Enquiry concerning Political Justice,* which had excited the young liberals (including Wordsworth and Coleridge). But England itself had remained relatively calm internally, and in 1809 it was entering its twenty-sixth year of a Tory administration which had shown, during its long tenure, remarkably little initiative in any but a repressive direction.

The following decade, in which lay the formative and productive years of the younger Romantics, was one of intense unrest, of overt struggle between repressive government and popular protest. In 1814, the future George IV was stoned and his carriage windows broken in the London streets. A year later the Corn Law was passed, forcing a considerable increase in the price of bread. It was a decade of widening gulf between landowners and workers; of slums and machinery-smashing riots in the cities; of hopeless poverty, poaching and man-traps, and rick-burning riots in the countryside. The decade closes characteristically with the charge of hussars on a crowd in St. Peter's Fields, Manchester; the crowd had been peacefully rallying for reform, and a few were killed and hundreds injured—the sardonically-named "Peterloo." One would think, in short, that the kind of disillusion felt by Wordsworth at the excesses of the French Revolution would have become far more immediate and powerful in the England where Byron, Shelley and Keats developed.

Yet they were poets whose whole tendency (with the exception of Byron) was to turn towards a metaphysical basis of life: they were closer to being prophets than politicians. Shelley's reaction to Peterloo admittedly was *The Masque of Anarchy* and its call to revolution, but Shelley is much more himself in giving mythical form to abstract aspiration in poems like *Prometheus Unbound*.

The main effect of their background on the younger Romantics comes down, I think, to this: they still felt a vision which had been given triumphant expression by Blake, Wordsworth and Coleridge, but they felt it in a less pure form, and they qualified it in individual ways. Indeed, judging by the kind of belief which I have regarded as the epitome of the English Romantic, Byron is scarcely to be considered. Shelley's devotion to the Romantic system is mingled with near-Blakean but abstract social values the system implies, expressed largely in myth. In Keats there is passionate belief tending to shade off into a preoccupation with aesthetics as such.

Byron's is the simplest case because he touches so lightly on the main matters of concern here. His early development, as a glance at his first lyrics shows, is entirely in the Augustan tradition, in strong contrast to that of Coleridge and Wordsworth. And until his disenchanted but poetically-redeeming maturity (certainly up to and including the composition of the first two cantos of *Childe Harold*) Byron's individual consciousness is egotistical, turned towards an ever-present vision, not of universal forces beyond the social world, but of himself, using the social world as backcloth. While his "romantic" earlier work is conventionally classified within the generous embrace of that promiscuous word, it becomes peripheral if one grants the centrality of the kind of experience, the idea of unity, the belief and indeed rhetoric I have concentrated upon in Coleridge and Wordsworth. Admittedly, Byron's egoism, apartness, and political liberalism are reasons why he may loosely be termed Romantic; and his disillusion, nostalgia, contempt of convention and cult of the excessive are strong veins in Continental Romanticism. But his references to experience and concerns comparable to those of Coleridge and Wordsworth are almost entirely confined to Cantos III and IV of *Childe Harold*. (*Manfred*, I think, is rather an appeal for such communion and a statement of its impossibility than any record of it.) And the *Childe Harold* references are so brief, are put so generally and turn up so casually, that they seem the result of a kind of osmosis from Coleridge and Wordsworth—actually mostly Wordsworth under the recommendation and direction of Shelley—than a direct genuine experience of Byron's. Nevertheless, there is this apparent record, and a few others like it, of the silent contemplation of nature leading to perception of unity and the deity:

> All Heaven and Earth are still: From the high host
> Of stars, to the lull'd lake and mountain coast,
> All is concentered in a life intense,
> Where not a beam, nor air, nor leaf is lost,
> But hath a part of Being, and a sense
> Of that which is of all Creator and defence.

Though he often bemoans the inexpressibility of his feelings at such moments (*Childe Harold*, III, 97; IV, 158), Byron never dwells on the meaning of the kind of contact described here. In short, there is brief record of the essentially English Romantic experience and order in Byron, and what there is strongly suggests absorption from secondary sources rather than Byron's own experience. He treats it as he treats other interesting poetic material, like the bullfight or a view of the Roman Coliseum, with a skillful and sometimes moving rhetoric but not much sense of spiritual conviction. The fragments which bear on the matter suggest rather a vaguely-desired view of life than a deeply-felt assertion of one. Much of the Romanticism there is in Byron is negative. It expresses itself in the longing for oblivion which characterizes *Manfred*, the melodramatic idealizing of the self in the Eastern tales, the steady egoism which is isolated rather than transcendent, and in the fear of serious reflection which marks much of his work. These things are indeed negative, but they clearly relate to the positive Romantic desire to transcend the earth.

It would be easy enough to cite sufficient isolated passages from *Childe Harold* III and IV to appear to place Byron also at that center of vision and assertion I have stressed as fundamental. But it would distort the proportions of the whole canon of his work. If his life, traditionally synonymous with the Romantic ideal, relates little to the centrality I emphasize, that is because the ideal is largely a Continental one, and because, again, Romanticism means so much to so many. Certainly Byron fits well enough those areas I have called concomitant—in his individualism, social rebellion, and that freedom for self-damnation which ran back to the Faust legend and was to run forward to Dostoevsky. These things had all been well-marked in *Werther*, created well before Byron was born, and even in Goethe's novella, I would argue, they are less integral than, and consequent to, the strong vein of religious nature-mysticism. In Byron, they mark much of his early work, like the Eastern tales, as they do his life as symbolic figure for his age, a figure with a special niche in the broad history of Romanticism. But much of his thought is of the eighteenth century, and his poetic expression, put beside that of any major English Romantic poet, is emotionally and imaginatively one-dimensional almost to the point of prose. As a man he remains a haunting figure, growing in tolerance, sympathy and worldliness until he could create a masterpiece which, despite its moments of quiet introspection, has more in common with Sterne than it does with Wordsworth. The vicarious Wordsworthianism in Byron arrived *via* Shelley, and, in its isolation and slightness, seems largely another Byronic posture.

". . . His *oeuvre*," remarks one historian of ideas, "lies in the tradition of Continental far more than of English Romanticism. Rousseau—Chateaubriand—Byron, the three great egocentrics, form a logical sequence, whereas Byron, viewed against the background of English Romanticism, must seem a freak, for English Romanticism, as Louis Cazamian has rightly remarked, does not consist in the triumph of the self." [17] Or, to put it as Paul West does, "If he [Byron] is great, he is so for reasons not primarily poetic. But we do not always want to be reading "great" poets; and our main pleasure in reading Byron is the contact with a singular personality." [18] And the recent view of John Wain beautifully dramatizes how far Byron, his status in the history of Continental Romanticism notwithstanding, stands outside the English transcendental tradition I have been considering. It was, writes Wain, "not possible for Byron to have a fully successful relationship with his poetic imagination." [19] A verdict like that would be the creative epitaph of a Blake, of a Coleridge or a Wordsworth, a Shelley or a Keats.

5. SHELLEY ॐ In turning to Shelley for his treatment of Romantic idea and attitude, we apparently confront some varied obstacles. The first is his natural preoccupation, as a prophetic poet, with myth, complex and sometimes self-made. Next, and seemingly clinching, is his "atheism." The third is his abiding concern with politics, his view of poetry as "words which were weapons" (*The Revolt of*

Islam, II, st. 20); poetry, as he says in the Preface to that work, is to kindle enthusiasm for "doctrines of liberty and justice." One might expect this to inhibit his concentration on the kind of experience and conviction I see as centrally Romantic. The difficulties, however, are more apparent than real. His use of myth merely limits the area of his vision and encourages the use of symbols. His "atheism" is illusory. He attacks "the erroneous and degrading idea which men have conceived of a Supreme Being . . . but not the Supreme Being itself" (Preface to *The Revolt of Islam*). Atheism in its literal sense is obviously antithetical to Romantic conviction, grounded in belief in a primal force; and Shelley shared with Coleridge and Wordsworth a reverence for such a force, which his vision had revealed to him. And despite his preoccupation with politics, his development moves generally from the practical to the philosophical, in sharp contrast to that of Carlyle and Ruskin in later decades. Certainly, under the influence of his reading of Wordsworth and others and his translation of Plato, he freed himself from his early domination by Godwinian ideas of institutional reform, and became increasingly involved with religious vision.

The poetic results of this development in Shelley are therefore most expressive for my purpose, and the *Hymn to Intellectual Beauty* (1816) chiefly so. "Intellectual Beauty," in fact, is simply Shelley's term for imaginative experience he assumes to be eternal, as opposed to the physical forms of the world. The *Hymn,* which is in a sense a climax in Shelley's spiritual autobiography, begins with a near-Coleridgean reference to certain moments of communion with supra-worldly force:

> The awful shadow of some unseen Power
> Floats though unseen among us,—visiting
> This various world with as inconstant wing
> As summer winds that creep from flower to flower.

The poem goes on, somewhat in the negative manner of *Dejection,* to express the inconsistency of the experience of Intellectual Beauty, by means of images of similar inconsistencies in nature. Vision is ephemeral, often inaccessible, but still of marvellous authority in the rare moments when it irradiates the imagination. Shelley stresses the puzzle of inconstancy, "Why aught should fail and fade that once is shown," and suggests that the human attraction towards Christian myth is a fruitless attempt to resolve this puzzle ("the names of

Demon, Ghost, and Heaven,/ Remain the records of . . . vain endeavour"). The poet then presents Intellectual Beauty as communion with supernatural unity reaching down through nature. He does so, much like Coleridge, using the images of light and music:

> Thy light alone—like mist o'er mountains driven,
> Or music by the night-wind sent
> Through strings of some still instrument,
> Or moonlight on a midnight stream,
> Gives grace and truth to life's unquiet dream.

This last line is only one of many which show how Shelley moves beyond Coleridge in his ability to suggest, through quiet reversals, the force of his highly Platonic belief in the meaning of his experience. Life has become the dream here, and the force which sometimes penetrates it is the reality. Reinforcing this reversal is:

> Thou [Intellectual Beauty]—that to human thought
> art nourishment
> Like darkness to a dying flame!

The symbolic technique seems so artless here it is easy to miss Shelley's insistence that even the highest kind of human, finite effort, thought (the dying flame), is almost nothing to the universal whole (the darkness) that surrounds it in all directions and gives it existence. We have, in other words, a brilliantly visual contrast, a passing dramatization of the theory of opposites worked into Shelley's presentation of his experience, and confirming it. The rest of the poem connects the experience of Intellectual Beauty with the political aspiration of the earlier Shelley and with universal love, but not before he has made a cutting comparison between the empty passivity of formal religion in his youth and the first impact of visionary experience: "Sudden, thy shadow fell on me;/ I shrieked, and clasped my hands in ecstasy!" He pays tribute to the inexpressibility of its meaning, recording his hope "That thou—O awful LOVELINESS/ Would'st give whate'er these words cannot express."

Essentially identical experience is recorded in *Mont Blanc*, written the same year,—the specific contact with a universal as opposed to a finite reality through which it is felt:

> Dizzy Ravine! and when I gaze on thee
> I seem as in a trance sublime and strange

> To muse on my own separate fantasy,
> My own, my human mind, which passively
> Now renders and receives fast influencings,
> Holding an unremitting interchange
> With the clear universe of things around.

The dichotomy of the two levels of being is dramatized in the poem; there is the finite world and the power behind it, which ". . . dwells apart in its tranquillity,/ Remote, serene, and inaccessible." It is the mountain which symbolically joins the two—the mountain, with its unseen snows and their meaningful evaporation in the sun, is the language of God:

> The secret Strength of things
> Which governs thought, and to the infinite dome
> Of Heaven is as a law, inhabits thee!
> And what were thou, and earth, and stars, and sea,
> If to the human mind's imaginings
> Silence and solitude were vacancy?

Shelley's use of the dome of heaven here, with its religious implications, recalls that other use he makes of it in *Adonais* (1821), and his power, beyond that of any other poet, to evoke the essentials of the Romantic system in a few simple symbols. In the famous lines I have in mind, they are so lucidly clear one does not have to mar them by prose explication:

> Life, like a dome of many-coloured glass,
> Stains the white radiance of Eternity,
> Until Death tramples it to fragments.

This brings us to a certain extension which Shelley made to the assumptions treated thus far: in bald terms it is concerned with the relationship of death to the Romantic order. As Wordsworth, in the *Intimations*, had connected the ultimate authority to a state before birth and in fading form to childhood, Shelley stresses the return to it in death. It is primarily because of this idea that *Adonais* ceases to be a competent but conventional elegy for Keats, and suddenly explodes, from the thirty-eighth stanza on, into the most assertive, magically comforting verse. The entire poem becomes radiant with conviction, poured out in tremendous rhetoric:

Dust to the dust! but the pure spirit shall flow
Back to the burning fountain whence it came,
A portion of the Eternal, which must glow
Through time and change, unquenchably the same . . .

He is made one with Nature: there is heard
His voice in all her music, from the moan
Of thunder, to the song of night's sweet bird;
He is a presence to be felt and known
In darkness and in light, from herb and stone . . .

He is a portion of the loveliness
Which once he made more lovely: he doth bear
His part, while the one Spirit's plastic stress
Sweeps through the dull dense world, compelling there,
All new successions to the forms they wear . . . .

The emotional eloquence of this nearly conceals the fact that at the same time the poem is among other things a serious statement of idea: the conception of the absolute Whole is related to the confines of time:

Who mourns for Adonais? Oh, come forth,
Fond wretch! and know thyself and him aright.
Clasp with thy panting soul the pendulous Earth;
As from a center, dart thy spirit's light
Beyond all worlds, until its spacious might
Satiate the void circumference: then shrink
Even to a point within our day and night.

And again inversion of the finite view is made to emphasize its boundaries, compared to the limitless authority of the Unity beyond it. "'Tis Death is dead, not he," and

Peace, peace! he is not dead, he doth not sleep—
He hath awakened from the dream of life—
'Tis we, who lost in stormy visions, keep
With phantoms an unprofitable strife,
And in mad trance, strike with our spirit's knife
Invulnerable nothings.

Similarly, in the *Hymn to Intellectual Beauty*, only faith in the meaning of that experience can save humanity from the hopeless, finite view of death: "Depart not as thy shadow came,/ Depart not —lest the grave should be,/ Like life and fear, a dark reality."

To refer to Shelley's development towards this kind of verse helps to explain its sense of delighted discovery. His growth, I think, falls into two stages, with their transition occurring in 1816. I have cited him in the later stage, at his most eloquent, when his view of experience and authority in the universe is most fully that ideal "Romantic" one I seek to define and dramatize.

To put the matter most simply, I am suggesting that Shelley's early stage (summarized in mythical form in *Alastor*) was one of fragmentary insights deriving from his reading and observation of nature; and that this stage was transformed in 1816 by direct mystical experience which made possible the philosophical and rhetorical assertion of his writing thereafter.

The change was in the breadth and unity of his view, not in its kind. The "atheistic" pamphleteer of 1811, engaged in implementing political means to Godwinian perfection, was at the same time a Shelley convinced of a number of individual metaphysical insights. Of the existence and importance of the soul, for instance: he could "love" Elizabeth Hitchener without "risking the supposition that the lump of organized matter which enshrines thy soul excites the love which that should alone dare claim." [20] He would sign such letters, with a flourish but quite significantly—"Yours beyond this being." He thought of God as "another signification for the Universe." [21] He saw nature as divisible and changing, but indestructible, and inferred from it that the soul is imperishable, and will exist in the future in unconceived form.[22] He thought of love as "the bond and the sanction which connects not only man with man but with everything which exists." [23]

In these and many other similar references he makes at the time, there is steady conviction, but not passion. Shelley knew, from his reading of Plato and Coleridge and Wordsworth at least, that a system which could unite his insights into a religious view of imaginative experience was possible. To know that, however, is not to experience it: in 1815, Shelley was searching for something which could bridge this spiritual gulf. *Alastor* is his record of this search transmuted into the vivid myth of a journey. The preface to the poem tells us more plainly about it. Alastor is a youth of "uncorrupted feelings and adventurous genius," led by "an imagination inflamed and purified through familiarity with all that is excellent and majestic, to the contemplation of the universe." So long as he remains in this state of aspiration, stimulated by the beauty of the physical world, he is joyous. But the time comes when he seeks a Being, a vision which "unites all of wonderful, or wise or beautiful, which the poet, the philosopher, or the lover could depicture." Shelley here is giving mythic form to hopes of experience which might transcend the insights of the past and unite them. The generally Platonic scheme which theoretically does so is for Shelley up to this point merely philosophy, not experience. "Axioms in philosophy," Keats was to write to his friend Reynolds, "are not axioms until they are proved upon our pulses." [24]

Alastor records Shelley's period of search to make the shift from the one to the other, and the search ends in disappointment. But not long after the appearance of the poem we have something quite different—Shelley's account of the experience of Intellectual Beauty. From this point on, his work, including the poems I have stressed, testifies to his passionate embracing of visionary experience which sweeps his insights into a coherent whole. His work has an assertive rhetoric, a concentration of impact, which his earlier poetry, however radical, does not. The poems of this period, the last half-dozen years of Shelley's life, are imaginative rather than fanciful, in Coleridge's sense of those words.

His final poem, *The Triumph of Life,* deserves brief consideration here to see how far it confirms my argument about Shelley's development. The problem is large, since, as Mrs. Shelley remarked in her 1824 Preface to the poems, this one "was left in so unfinished a state that I arranged it in its present form with great difficulty." Broadly, the poem is part of a Romantic allegory seeming to echo the *Divine Comedy* in form, general situation, and by allusion. It has a negative side, epitomized by the "ghastly dance" in the last lines, and the remnant of Rousseau who, acting as guide like Dante's Vergil, expresses at one point an ignorant agnosticism: ". . . by what paths I have been brought/ To this dread pass . . . my mind can compass not." Nevertheless, the general impression the work gives is that its problems are put forward for later resolution in the poem Shelley had planned. But we need not rely on that speculation to see the incomplete poem as in some measure confirming his progress to Romantic assertion. It contains several most positive Romantic elements. It begins, for instance, with the coming of dawn, presented in the linked diction of worship ("smokeless altars," "the Ocean's orison," censers with "orient incense"), much as Wordsworth begins *The Prelude.* The poem is highly Platonic in places, and also embodies Blakean reversals (ll. 149–154). Love is put forward as the one thing not needing transfiguration. There are images for Romantic unity, "magic sounds woven into one/ Oblivious melody." Most important, perhaps, is that the whole poem is "vision," given an opening frame of religious creativity, love and unity in the dawn:

> When a strange trance over my fancy grew
> Which was not slumber, for the shade it spread
>
> Was so transparent, that the scene came through
> As clear as when a veil of light is drawn
> O'er evening hills they glimmer; and I knew
>
> That I had felt the freshness of that dawn
> Bathe in the same cold dew my brow and hair,
> And sate as thus upon that slope of lawn
>
> Under the self-same bough, and heard as there
> The birds, the fountain and the ocean hold
> Sweet talk in music through the enamoured air,
> And then a vision on my brain was rolled.

This particular transition to vision was to be seminal for *In Memoriam;* certainly Tennyson seems to have been influenced by it in Poem 95 and elsewhere.

Just as the tremendous assertion in Shelley's later verse recreates the impact of Intellectual Beauty, so does his later prose. In his *Defence of Poetry* (1821) he writes of Romantic experience and its part in poetry-making. At first he relies on descriptive definition: "We are aware of evanescent visitations of thought and feeling . . . elevating and delightful beyond all expression. . . . It is as it were the interpenetration of a diviner nature through our own." Poets, he adds in using an argument of Wordsworth and Coleridge, "can colour all that they combine with the evanescent hues of this ethereal world. . . . Poetry redeems from decay the visitations of the divinity in man." Shelley, next returning to consider the nature of poetry, seems to respond even to his attempted prose description of Romantic experience, and his rhetoric becomes intense:

> Poetry turns all things to loveliness . . . it subdues to union, under its light yoke, all irreconcilable things. It transmutes all that it touches, and every form moving within the radiance of its presence is changed by wondrous sympathy to an incarnation of the spirit which it breathes . . . it strips the veil of familiarity from the world

and lays bare the naked and sleeping beauty, which is the spirit of
its forms.

6. KEATS &ᴥ Wordsworth and Coleridge, as we have seen, worked
from an awareness that natural beauty could stimulate the imagination into contact with religious reality. They had been concerned
with the meaning of that reality, "the sustaining thought/ Of human
being, Eternity, and God." For much of his brief creative career,
Keats concentrated on the human foundation of the Romantic order,
the experience of beauty itself. He shows a preoccupation with
aesthetics, and his development is a probing of the experience of
beauty, gradually broadening into the seeking out of its causes and
meaning.

He died at twenty-five, and it is difficult to do much more than
stress certain directions he took towards Romantic idea and attitude.
His last ambitious poem, *The Fall of Hyperion* (written in 1819), is
a fragment with its prime theme still a problem: as W. J. Bate sees
it, "the self as it tries to come to terms with reality." [25] On another
level Bate also sees the poem as a kind of anticipation of existential-
ism.[26] I merely cite these matters as illustrating the unresolved nature of Keats' unfinished journey. Given the ground he did live to
travel, however, it is possible to indicate a progress moving close to
the ideas of the earlier Romantics; there are certain points of seeming resolution and a growing, though never unqualified, affirmation.

The *Ode on a Grecian Urn*, among Keats' later work, makes the
most obvious though still tentative affirmation, and it deals with
beauty and art, not with a deity; but all the relevant Odes, as well as
the general development of Keats' writings, show consciously or otherwise that beauty is most important as the vehicle by which imagination reaches certainty and truth beyond the finite veil. It is not
necessary to speculate whether his conception of that truth might
have become nominally more religious had he lived; the high level of
Biblical imagery in his last poem, unusual for Keats, might be held
to suggest the possibility. But during his brief career he read the earlier Romantic poets and was able to find his own way, independ-
ently, along the general road they had trod, seeing the meaning of
his experience rather as philosophical than religious.

His earliest work shows no serious ideas beyond enthusiasm for a sensuous kind of experience both in the physical world and recreated by disorderly daydream:

> I slowly sail, scarce knowing my intent;
> Still scooping up the water with my fingers,
> In which a trembling diamond never lingers.
> *(To Charles Cowden Clarke)*

Sleep and Poetry, written late in 1816, is probably Keats' first poem of intellectual—if not poetic—importance. It bears witness to his reading of Wordsworth.

> No one who once the glorious sun has seen,
> And all the clouds, and felt his bosom clean
> For his great Maker's presence, but must know
> What 'tis I mean, and feel his being glow.

But Keats resists the temptation to imitate those central Wordsworthian concerns which the young poet has not yet felt: "Should I rather kneel/ Upon some mountain-top until I feel/ A glowing splendour round about me hung,/ And echo back the voice of thine own tongue?" At the same time, in the middle of the poem Keats pays tribute to beauty both for its own sake (". . . choose each pleasure that my fancy sees") and more significantly as puzzling contrast to its background of human suffering:

> And can I ever bid these joys farewell?
> Yes, I must pass them for a nobler life,
> Where I may find the agonies, the strife
> Of human hearts.

Here is Keats' first full contrasting of the ideal, his vision of the wondrous chariot (ll. 125–154), with the untransformed finite world once that vision has gone. Still finding his authority in the world of sense, he calls the untransformed world "real," though he recognizes its inferiority:

> The visions are all fled—the car is fled
> Into the light of heaven, and in their stead
> A sense of real things comes doubly strong,
> And, like a muddy stream, would bear along

My soul to nothingness: but I will strive
Against all doubtings, and will keep alive
The thought of that same chariot, and the strange
Journey it went.

In a poem written at the age of twenty-one, then, Keats is already emphasizing the difference between an imaginative view which has supreme importance to him and a finite, sensuous one which of itself does not.

Before moving on in the poem to the attack (which so offended Byron) on Boileau and the Augustan poets—and it is easy to miss the point that Keats' main charge here is that they had ignored the direct impact of "wild" nature as Wordsworth had felt it—Keats turns to Greece in a significant way. At the heart of his confusion, when the limitations of the "real" world flood back to drown imaginative vision, conviction trembles: ". . . the high/ Imagination cannot freely fly/ As she was wont of old. . . ." Though Keats is here referring generally to the greater certainty of moral orientation in ages which invited imagination to work, his references to Jove, the Muses, Apollo and Pegasus in the lines which follow (169–187) show him putting his pen intuitively on the crux of the problem. Greek myth had been an ordered system, with nature and the human imagination as integral parts. It had assumed the kind of belief in a coherent universal whole which at this point the poet has not found. He was, of course, to be drawn to the Greek metaphysical system in a sustained way in working out his problems.

The poem ends with a return to sensuous daydream, after another near-Wordsworthian passage connecting nature and religious significance:

> yet there ever rolls
> A vast idea before me, and I glean
> Therefrom my liberty; thence too I've seen
> The end and aim of Poesy. 'Tis clear
> As anything most true; as that the year
> Is made of the four seasons—manifest
> As a large cross, some old cathedral's crest,
> Lifted to the white clouds

—an association in formally religious terms which Keats was not to depend on in the better-known poems to come.

Endymion (written 1817–1818), like an extended and resolved

Alastor, is Keats' mythological record of his search for authority, and (unlike *Alastor*) of finding its key and some idea of what the key promises, in the experience of beauty. Endymion's search for the Moon Goddess Cynthia (the ideal), and his ultimate discovery that she and the Indian Maid (the earthly) are one, records a further step in conviction for Keats—that the door to final authority is opened by the key of transitory experience of beauty in the everyday world.

Though his poem is mythological, Keats, differing from Shelley, will step aside from his myth to clarify directly whatever he considers of paramount importance. He begins by insisting, more or less instinctively and again in a rather Wordsworthian manner, on the centrality of nature's beauty to human life:

> yes, in spite of all,
> Some shape of beauty moves away the pall
> From our dark spirits.

We do not "merely feel these essences/ For one short hour," they

> Haunt us till they become a cheering light
> Unto our souls, and bound to us so fast,
> That, whether there be shine or gloom o'ercast,
> They always must be with us, or we die,

and such manifestations Keats calls, using a symbol reminiscent of Shelley,

> An endless fountain of immortal drink.

What emerges as the poem develops is Keats' immense belief in the importance of the experience of beauty and where it leads—a certainty reflected in his letters:

> The mighty abstract Idea I have of Beauty in all things stifles the more divided and minute domestic happiness—an amiable wife and sweet Children I contemplate as a part of that Beauty—but I must have a thousand of these beautiful particles to fill up my heart. I feel more and more every day, as my imagination strengthens, that I do not live in this world alone but in a thousand worlds.[27]

Most of *Endymion* is in fact a kind of negative testimony to the force of this certitude. Beauty is felt to be so certain a key to the system behind everyday consciousness that the greatest tragedy, and the most extensive subject of the poem, lies in its infrequency and transitoriness. The most dramatic parts of the poem (see, for example, Book II, 728–827) result from excesses stemming from Keats' sense of tragic loss at the return to the (untransformed) world, as do some of the most unfortunate images ever written by a first-rank poet ("Those lips, O slippery blisses . . ."). The falsetto histrionics of the entire passage mentioned above are "romantic" in the worst of the word's many senses. Keats on this occasion is frenetically lavishing all rhetorical force on a single isolated feeling, extensively dramatizing and bemoaning it; he does not, here, seek to move beyond it. This travesty of Romanticism ominously suggests what its outlook and assertion were to dwindle to after Victorian decades of stress.

The puzzle of the brevity and deprivation of the experience of beauty is not solved in *Endymion*,[28] but the lines later added to the poem (I, 777 ff.) show more fully the place of beauty in a scheme which makes clear the nature of its ultimate authority:

> Wherein lies happiness? In that which becks
> Our ready minds to fellowship divine,
> A fellowship with essence; till we shine
> Full alchemiz'd, and free of space. Behold
> The clear religion of heaven!

In a letter to his publisher, John Taylor, requesting the insertion of the passage, Keats points significantly to the difficulties it may cause "consequitive" minds, but its great importance for himself:

> The whole thing must I think have appeared to you, who are a consequitive Man, as a thing almost of mere words—but I assure you that when I wrote it, it was a regular stepping of the Imagination towards a Truth. My having written that Argument will perhaps be of the greatest Service to me of any thing I ever did. It set before me at once the gradations of Happiness even like a kind of Pleasure Thermometer. . . .[29]

In the "whole thing," the "Argument," Keats goes on to give examples of chance entrances into such moments of "fellowship with essence"—the touch and scent of a rose, music ("Eolian magic") on the wind, giving rise to the romantic evocation of the past in the imagination. He proceeds:

Feel we these things?—that moment have we stept
Into a sort of oneness, and our state
Is like a floating spirit's. But there are
Richer entanglements, enthralments far
More self-destroying, leading, by degrees,
To the chief intensity: the crown of these
Is made of love and friendship, and sits high
Upon the forehead of humanity.
All its more ponderous and bulky worth
Is friendship, whence there ever issues forth
A steady splendour; but at the tip-top,
There hangs by unseen film, an orbed drop
Of light, and that is love: its influence,
Thrown in our eyes, genders a novel sense,
At which we start and fret; till in the end,
Melting into its radiance, we blend,
Mingle, and so become a part of it,—
Nor with aught else can our souls interknit
So wingedly . . . .

To turn to Keats' great volume of 1820, there are many interpre-
tive possibilities in both *Isabella* and *The Eve of St. Agnes,* and little
is gained by arbitrariness. In general, both poems deal with conflict,
between beauty and fulfillment on the one hand, and pain, deprivation and actuality on the other. Certain stanzas towards the end of *Isabella* emphasize Keats' growing awareness of the indissolubility of
beauty and pain (st. 55, for example), a movement to culminate in
the *Ode on Melancholy.* In *The Eve of St. Agnes* the stress is more
on the emotional and imaginative exploration of the two kinds of
awareness, metaphorized by the color and warmth of the love-idyll
against the miraculous chill of the harsh medieval setting.

   Lamia (also from the 1820 volume) records in myth Keats' own
progress, dramatizing a further idea he accepts as he mounts his own
poetic ladder—that the most intense aesthetic experience made permanent would not be the ideal condition in human life; we have the
obligation, as Shelley had implied in the *Hymn to Intellectual
Beauty,* to accept the limitations of the finite world. That beauty
which is not subject to mortal limitation (that is, what was sought
constantly in *Endymion*) is realized in Lamia; Lycius drains the cup
of Lamia's beauty, "and still the cup was full." But it is tainted. The
difference is stressed by contrasting the parting passages in the earlier
poem with those in *Lamia.* Lycius' pitiful appeals to Lamia not to

fade or leave (Part I, 257–271) are much like those Endymion had made, but Lamia can stay only *because* she is unnatural and corrupted, and this only delays the inevitable reassertion of the laws of aesthetic experience in the finite world. *Lamia* expresses, in its treatment of the myth Keats took from Burton, a definite stage in the development of the poet's philosophy. He is certain now that a concern for beauty alone diverts the imagination from human suffering and is probably suspect. His inner confidence in the authority of the experience of beauty is not destroyed, but has to be seen against violence such as the poem's ending brings. *Lamia,* among other levels of meaning, is a mature realization of the limits of what finite life can properly demand.

The Odes, written slightly before *Lamia*,[30] besides restating Keats' progress to this point, spell out a reconciliation as far as he is able to take it. The vision of the *Ode to Psyche* is set in a narrative frame, and the whole poem becomes a myth, like the myth of *Endymion,* for the experience of creative imagination. The poem, with its closing images of temple, altar, virgin choir, with the poet as "thy priest," and with its winsome reference to ancient Greek assumptions,

> When holy were the haunted forest boughs
> Holy the air, the water, and the fire,

is Keats' celebration of his literal worship of beauty attained through the creative imagination. Though the scattered images of formal religion are reminiscent of Wordsworth's technique in parts of *The Prelude,* the body of the verse surrounding them insists in a sustained way that what is being worshipped here is profane—not the sense of a religious ultimate, as in Wordsworth, but simply natural beauty as the key to spiritual beauty, which itself is authoritative.

We can be brief and specific about the remaining Odes pertinent here. A marvellous work in its emotional power, the *Ode on Melancholy* is intellectually another statement of the idea which occurs both in *Lamia* and in the Chamber of Maiden-Thought letter—that beauty is necessarily accompanied by pain, transience and disillusion, and that these are essential parts of one experience. Closely connected with this is Keats' insistence on the value of the quest rather than its fulfillment—also in *Lamia,* which exemplifies and rejects the antithesis of this, and in the *Ode to Psyche* ("Their lips touch'd not, but had not bade adieu,"), and in the *Ode on a Grecian Urn* ("Bold Lover, never, never canst thou kiss,/ Though winning near the goal —"). This stress on the quest is not only Keats' mature reconsideration of the plaintive longing of the poet in the untransformed world (*Endymion*) who aches for the experience of the transformed one again. It is the justification both for the hard-won development of his own poetry and its ideas, and incidentally a prophetic justification of the value of much of the Victorian literature of spiritual struggle which was to follow.

In citing them for the ideas they reveal, one is bound to do some injustice to the *Odes*, where the impact is above all emotional. For receptive readers Keats, like all the Romantic poets, creates images and associations which themselves are an aesthetic stimulus. This acts on the imagination until it perceives, as in a clouded mirror, at least something of the impact of the spiritual chain-reaction which the original experience of beauty provoked in the poet. In this way the best work of the Romantics suggests rather than describes.

The methods by which Keats forces the reader to experience this "echo" of the movement to vision are multifarious, and in the Odes are completely integrated, but one simple example may be offered from the *Ode to a Nightingale*. The poem, at one level, consists of a series of "runs" at transcendence, each a little more deeply suggestive than the last, each progressively smoother metrically, each increasingly sensuous in sound. The first stanza, after the speaker's dreamlike opening consciousness, presents a simple mind-picture of the nightingale singing within the forest, quite the sort of elementary visualization which is imagination on its least complex level. Even here, however, there is the suggestion of classical myth in "Dryad," and the effortless joining of sight with sound in the association of mottled "shadows numberless" with "full-throated." Stanza two continues to expand the imaginative range by similarly blending sight and sound ("sunburnt mirth"), and expanding further into the opposition between the coolness of the imagined wine and the warmth of the life it suggests. It is here that the life of the South, existing wholly in imagination, becomes paradoxically most deeply sensual and "worldly" in its lush plosive sound:

> O for a beaker full of the warm South,
> Full of the true, the blushful Hippocrene,

With beaded bubbles winking at the brim,
And purple-stained mouth.

Stanza three, with a confidence by now seeming to defy any sustained confinement to the merely sensed world, swings back to define
that world as anti-climax, deprivation. It is a fleeting, chilling fare-
well to a limited reality expressed in monosyllabic diminutives, thin
sounds, and the imagery of unreality:

Here, where men sit and hear each other groan;
Where palsy shakes a few, sad, last gray hairs,
Where youth grows pale, and spectre-thin, and dies.

The next "step," in stanza four, is a passionate reaction to this, as the
speaker, on "the viewless wings of Poesy," reaches his transcendence
—Already with thee!" Here is the magic, the Queen-Moon, the
starry fays, and from this point on the poem broadens into a perspective which includes both the world of the speaker and that of the
nightingale, and which becomes suffused with images of death and
the deathless beauty of the song which conquers it.

The assertions in the poem are strong. Considered merely intellectually, the Ode to a Nightingale is an account of Keats' own imaginative and temporary apprehension of visionary beauty leading him,
through that dimension of time which inhibits and beclouds, to a
sense of a greater, immortal reality in the song (art) of the bird.
Similarly, in the Ode on a Grecian Urn he suggests that art is a
means of making permanent such glimpses, since art is exempt from
time and other mortalities. In the Ode to a Nightingale, also, is the
suggestion that death would eternalize the transitory experience he
echoes in the poem. Such ideas are familiar Romantic assertions. But
they are, in Keats, placed against weighty counter-forces in the Odes,
and judgments of the balance are subjective and difficult. It is true
that the Ode to a Nightingale, like all of Keats' work, is no solution
but a series of discoveries and affirmations still remaining to be
placed against a background of unknowing. Thus the poem ends in a
dazed sense of its vision gone, and the untransformed world be-
clouded. The poem's moments of Romantic affirmation are powerful,
and I do not think they are destroyed by its ending; but the ending
is one of bewildered near-despair at the loss of vision, and it seems
prescient of a Victorian future.

The conceptions and attitudes I have sketched are drawn from the flux of a development necessarily overlapping and unresolved. For most sympathetic readers, what Keats was centrally concerned with is clear enough. As C. D. Thorpe puts it, "What the observer gets is . . . a vision of truth flashed on the inner eye: not mathematical nor scientific truth, but the shadowy, inexpressible sense of truth best described as emotionalized realization, which only art can convey." [31] But Keats' power to do this can divert attention from a quality on which his art depends. His work is perfectly consistent throughout in one thing only: his certain, unqualified faith that his aesthetic and imaginative experience is the one key to that understanding of all experience towards which he struggles. The kind of insistence I indicated in the latter part of Shelley's *Adonais* is in Keats' letters, which bombard their reader with assertions like: "I am certain of nothing but of the holiness of the heart's affections and the truth of Imagination—What the imagination seizes as Beauty must be truth."

> The Imagination may be compared to Adam's dream—
> he awoke and found it truth.
> (*To Bailey, November 22, 1817*)

Keats may not have carried his Romantic concerns to the same kind of primal cause as did Wordsworth and Coleridge; nor was his vision unqualified. But his conviction of the supreme importance of aesthetic and imaginative experience matches theirs at its height. In the famous final lines of the *Ode on a Grecian Urn,*

> "Beauty is truth, truth beauty,"—that is all
> Ye know on earth, and all ye need to know,

the last half of the clause is just as important as the first.

7. CARLYLE ࣔ Carlyle illustrates the difficulty and arbitrariness of classifying Romanticism. Even more than Coleridge he was indebted to German thought, and in that sense is in the European tradition. He shares, however, the visionary experience, the most crucial ideas, and the assertiveness of the English Romantics, and he was vital in passing these on to the Victorians who are my primary concern. Certainly Carlyle apprehended the Romantic order with enough vigor to preach it as prophet. Though the kind of private spiritual therapy

which John Stuart Mill derived from Wordsworth's poetry [32] can now be assessed as more lastingly influential, Carlyle was the only Romantic writer looked to overtly and widely as practical moral leader and prophet, partly because of the sheer dynamism of his prose. The light in which his biographer Froude regarded him was a fairly common one for some thinking Victorians:

> Carlyle taught me a creed which I could then accept as really true; which I have held ever since, with increasing confidence, as the interpretation of my existence and the guide of my conduct, so far as I have been able to act up to it. Then and always I looked, and have looked, to him as my master.[33]

But it is perhaps better to avoid this suggestion of solved problems. The young Carlyle wrote *Sartor Resartus* in the decade which brought the deaths of Keats, Shelley and Byron; that is, he was closer to them in time than his "Victorian" classification encourages us to think. Through *Sartor,* he became a Romantic prophet for mid-Victorians like Ruskin, who were striving to retain or regain some moral bastion from which they might face the problems of their day. Without the prophetic voice of Carlyle to gather and restate the Romantic heritage, it is probable that whole areas of Victorian literature (especially the large one influenced by Ruskin) would have been markedly different.

The truth of this is emphasized, not contradicted, by those matters in which Carlyle appears to differ sharply from the Romantic poets. First, there are his attacks on them, notably on Byron and Wordsworth.[34] Or there are Carlyle's ironic comments on "view hunting," which certainly seem provoked, and fairly justifiably, by Byron's isolated accounts of Romantic experience in *Childe Harold.* There is the deft dig in *Sartor* at the unintentionally comic solemnity of Wordsworth's *We Are Seven:*

> 'On fine evenings I was wont to carry-forth my supper (bread-crumb boiled in milk), and eat it out of doors. On the coping of the Orchard-wall, which I could easily reach by climbing, or still more easily if Father Andreas would set up the pruning-ladder, my porringer was placed: there, many a sunset, have I, looking at the distant Western Mountains, consumed, not without relish, my evening meal.'

But these things are Carlyle's attack, not on what the Romantic poets stood for, but on what he regarded as their sentimentalizing and cheapening of it. He attacked not because he disagreed with their ideas, but because he cared so much for them and felt that (as was bound to happen occasionally) the ideas had been treated shoddily. It is also probable that Carlyle felt a certain natural impatience with the poets, because he saw the artist's function differently from them. The poets felt that their main function was expressive—to fashion all the resources of language towards recreating, or at least echoing, imaginative experience and to suggest its meaning as spiritual conviction. Where they move further into the practical world and deal directly in common terms with religion, morality and politics, they shrink. Their effort becomes fragmentary and almost irrelevant. Shelley is the most obvious example, but the generalization holds for all those who tried. Carlyle was different; he was secondarily a poet (fittingly a prose-poet) and first a prophet. His writings were felt as means to an end, and he draws the practical applications from Romantic experience and ideas much more directly than the poets could.

A more imposing obstacle than his attacks on the poets in the way of appreciating him as arch-prophet of the Romantic order is the sheer richness and complexity of his greatest work.[35] But a close look at *Sartor Resartus* shows that its basic ideas—not surprisingly in view of their common direct roots in German philosophy and indirect ones in Platonism—form an extended and detailed summary of those of the Romantic poets. This enormous restatement becomes simpler once its foundation—Carlyle's idea of the cosmic setting and man's place in it—has been established, and Carlyle establishes it very plainly indeed.

The natural universe, he says, is literally infinite, without limits, and therefore quite beyond man's capacity to apprehend, much less explain: ". . . all Experience thereof [of nature] limits itself to some few computed centuries and measured square-miles" (p.257).

Among his Romantic predecessors, Carlyle bears the most striking resemblance to Coleridge in several ways. There is, for instance, his special insistence that physical science, by Carlyle's day appearing superficially more and more alluring as the key to understanding existence and consciousness, must always be confined by its nature within its own sphere of purely sensed phenomena. "These scientific individuals have been nowhere but where we also are; have seen some handbreadths deeper than we see into the Deep that is infinite, without bottom as without shore" (p. 257). Carlyle stresses and extends this view by brilliant symbols illustrating the cosmic scale he is assuming. Man is "a minnow, . . . his Creek this Planet Earth; his Ocean the immeasurable All; his Monsoons and periodic Currents the mysterious Course of Providence through Aeons of Aeons" (p. 258). A purely scientific approach assumes that nature is a "huge, well-nigh inexhaustible Domestic-Cookery Book," whose secret will one day be revealed. But the road which brings one nearer to revelation of the universe, "whose Author and Writer is God," is that of philosophy, "an ever-renewed effort to *transcend* the sphere of blind Custom, and so become Transcendental." Custom persuades us "that the miraculous, by simple repetition, ceases to be Miraculous." But the deepest illusions "for hiding Wonder" are space and time. There follows a sentence which, properly considered, goes straight to the heart of the understanding of Romantic poetry: "In vain, while here on Earth, shall you endeavour to strip them [space and time] off; you can, at best, but rend them asunder for moments, and look through" (p. 260). The central human error is to apply assumptions, formed entirely on the bases of space and time, to those spiritual areas which lie entirely outside them:

> Were it not miraculous, could I stretch forth my hand and clutch the Sun? Yet thou seest me daily stretch forth my hand and therewith clutch many a thing, and swing it hither and thither. Art thou a grown baby, then, to fancy that the Miracle lies in miles of distance, or in pounds avoirdupois of weight; and not to see that the true inexplicable God-revealing Miracle lies in this, that I can stretch forth my hand at all; that I have free Force to clutch aught therewith? (p. 262)

In this matter of man's relationship to his setting, then, Carlyle's "philosophy"—his thought transcending the limits of space and time —is simply that the truth is found when conclusions based on the senses are rejected and sometimes reversed. We may recall how Wordsworth in *The Prelude* does much the same: in the "earthly" sphere, your senses tell you that you have ceased to move on your skates. But your dizzy "illusion" tells you the cosmic truth, a larger one. You *are* moving through space, though your senses, which relate only to the earth, tell you quite falsely that you are not. In Carlyle's scheme, what we call "actual" life, as apprehended through the senses, is the merest phantom: we live out our brief sense-bound lives in a flash, before disappearing into the actuality, the eternity from which we came. That is the reality, "life" the illusion:

> Are we not Spirits, that are shaped into a body, into an Appearance; and that fade away again into air and Invisibility? This is no metaphor, it is a simple scientific *fact*; we start out of Nothingness, take figure, and are Apparitions; round us, as round the veriest spectre, is Eternity; and to Eternity minutes are as years and aeons.   (p. 264)
> Ghosts! There are nigh a thousand-million walking the Earth openly at noon-tide; some half-hundred have vanished from it, some half hundred have arisen in it, ere thy watch ticks once.   (p. 265)

It is obvious from this foundation that Carlyle's thought is dualistic, demanding division into ideas based on the observation of the senses, and those, infinitely more valid, which are not. He makes use of a system, similar to Coleridge's but wider-ranging, of dual terms—"correspondences" denoting the levels of the finite (Earth) against the Infinite. The rest follow: body (or sense) against spirit: the Actual against the Potential: time against Eternity: Reality against Idea: man against God: society against Men: clothes [36] against the real man (the Me) beneath them.

Carlyle saw that in his own time the permanent human tendency to view only the first of each pair of these dual terms seemed irresistible, and his opposition to this forms the foundation of all his criticism of his epoch. He called it the Mechanical Age, and "Mechanism" was his term not only for the social realignments forced by a new industrial society, but for the view that sees only the finite as reality, and does not see the infinite at all. "Men are grown mechanical in head and in heart, as well as in hand." [37]

Carlyle's treatment of certain of these dual levels deserves some exploration as clarifying his moving ideas in *Sartor*. We have already seen that the earthly realm of sense, extended to the infinite level, becomes the superior realm of spirit. It is this realization by which Teufelsdröckh pierces "the mystery of the World," and so far as its consequent ideas are concerned it is the heart of the book. Teufelsdröckh,

> recognising in the highest sensible phenomena, so far as Sense went, only fresh or faded Raiment; yet ever, under this, a celestial Essence thereby rendered visible: and while on the one hand, he trod the old rags of Matter, with their tinsels, into the mire, he on the

other everywhere exalted Spirit above all earthly principalities and powers, and worshipped it, though under the meanest shapes, with a true Platonic mysticism.   (p. 207)

The point at which the operations of the two levels meet is apt to impress and confuse minds stimulated solely by the senses, whose sphere is the physical. Hence miracles, which appear to be a violation of natural law, are to Carlyle manifestations of "some far deeper Law, now first penetrated into, and by Spiritual Force" (p.256).

In making clear the relationship between sense and spirit Carlyle reveals a system following almost exactly the steps by which the Romantic poets attained their experiences and convictions. The universe is a vast system of symbols of God, "one vast Symbol of God." These symbols exist to guide human beings beyond the world of sense. The human faculty for recognizing them and following where they lead, says Carlyle in quoting Schlegel, is the imagination ("Fantasy being the organ of the Godlike"). And though our senses often make prisoners of us, creating the illusion that they are the authorities of consciousness, our instincts are not deceived. Man, while often finding it necessary to rationalize his actions, works quite naturally and instinctively through symbols.

Have I not myself known five-hundred living soldiers sabred into crows'-meat for a piece of glazed cotton, which they called their Flag; which, had you sold it at any market-cross, would not have brought above three groschen? . . . It is in and through *Symbols* that man, consciously or unconsciously, lives, works, and has his being: those ages, moreover, are accounted the noblest which can the best recognise symbolical worth, and prize it the highest. For is not a Symbol ever, to him who has eyes for it, some dimmer or clearer revelation of the God-like?   (p. 222)

When manifestations of the godhead become conscious experience, they are, as we have repeatedly seen, glimpsed or temporary. The means of making them independent of time is through art—precisely the moving idea of the *Ode on a Grecian Urn*. In "all true works of Art," says Carlyle, "wilt thou discern Eternity looking through Time; the Godlike rendered visible" (p. 223).

Exactly the same relationship, with its dual levels of significance, applies to Carlyle's treatment of the phenomenon of life itself ("Reality") and Idea. Whatever is experienced through the senses is simply (and thoroughly in accord with Plato) the sign of the superior idea for which it stands. "Matter exists only spiritually," says Carlyle in transposing Goethe, "and to represent some Idea and body it forth" (p. 72). In this way, the earthly body ("the earth-visiting Me") and its sensations, the consciousness of which we call life, are the clothing or emblem of the "divine Me," the spirit, just as time is the sensed emblem of its infinite idea, Eternity. Real existence lies in this sphere, and is with God. Hence death is viewed, as it is by Shelley, as the return from the finite prison of time to the infinite freedom of eternity:

> Yet a little while, and we shall all meet THERE, and our Mother's bosom will screen us all; and Oppression's harness, and Sorrow's fire-whip, and all the Gehenna Bailiffs that patrol and inhabit ever-vexed Time, cannot thenceforth harm us any more! (p. 107)

In view of all this, it is not surprising that the prose *Sartor Resartus* contains direct Romantic experience exactly paralleling that of the poets: Teufelsdröckh

> gazed over those stupendous masses [the mountains] with wonder, almost with longing desire; never till this hour had he known Nature, that she was One, that she was his Mother and divine. And as the ruddy glow was fading into clearness in the sky, and the Sun had now departed, a murmur of Eternity and Immensity, of Death and of Life, stole through his soul; and he felt as if Death and Life were one, as if the Earth were not dead, as if the Spirit of the Earth had its throne in that splendour, and his own spirit were therewith holding communion. (p. 151)

The qualifying "almost" and the conditional "as ifs" and "weres" here perhaps point to a realization on Carlyle's part that he is no further protected here by his "editorship" from his own charge of "view-hunting" than Byron was by the figure of Childe Harold. But what is important is that Carlyle feels it necessary to express, despite his own mistrust of where direct expression on such a subject might lead, his conviction of the importance of Romantic experience by means of a rhetoric nearly as forceful, though not as aesthetically and emotionally exciting, as that of the poets.

Carlyle's own spiritual progress to belief in his scheme is described through Teufelsdröckh's biography in Book II of *Sartor Resartus*. Its general lines are reflected in the chapter headings: The Sorrows of Teufelsdröckh (the *Werther* parody is Carlyle's ironic dis-

missal of "muling and puking"); The Everlasting No; The Centre of
Indifference; The Everlasting Yea. Carlyle's central experience in this
spiritual process is his "conversion," which he describes, with a symbolic—and Wordsworthian—sense of placement, at the end of his
chapter "The Everlasting No":

> There rose a Thought in me, and I asked myself: "What *art* thou
> afraid of? Wherefore, like a coward, dost thou forever pip and
> whimper, and go cowering and trembling? Despicable biped! what
> is the sum-total of the worst that lies before thee? Death? Well,
> Death; and say the pangs of Tophet too, and all that the Devil and
> Man may, will or can do against thee! Hast thou not a heart; canst
> thou not suffer whatsoever it be; and, as a Child of Freedom,
> though outcast, trample Tophet itself under thy feet, while it con-
> sumes thee? let it come, then; I will meet it and defy it!" And as I
> so thought, there rushed like a stream of fire over my whole soul;
> and I shook base Fear away from me forever. I was strong, of un-
> known strength; a spirit, almost a god. Ever from that time, the
> temper of my misery was changed: not Fear or whining Sorrow
> was it, but Indignation and grim fire-eyed Defiance.   (p. 167)

This, said Carlyle, "occurred quite literally to myself in Leith Walk
[Edinburgh]." [38]

Teufelsdröckh passes first from morbid self-pity (The Sorrows)
—there is more than a hint here of his rejection of Byron ("Your
Byron publishes his Sorrows of Lord George, in verse and prose, and
copiously otherwise"). He moves through the overwhelming conviction of God ("The Universe is not dead and demoniacal, a charnal-
house with spectres; but godlike, and my Father's!"), through renun-
ciation of the self to blessedness and the love of God. "This is the
EVERLASTING YEA, wherein all contradiction is solved: wherein whoso
walks and works, it is well with him."

Thus by both example and a sustained if gyrating argument
based on recurring reference to Romantic ideas, *Sartor Resartus* is at
once a statement of its author's faith in those ideas, and a plea for
conviction and action based on such faith. Duty and Work are creative and (to apply Carlyle's dualism once more) the symbol of the
Godlike in man.

8. SUMMARY: ASSERTION AND DECLINE & All the writers I have discussed, with the exception, as I see it, of Byron, testify to their belief

in an energetic, creative system by which an infinite universe exists. They do not differ from Plato in assuming that the system operates in the moral as well as the physical sphere. It implies a prime force whose infinite nature is often suggested by the word God, used in a sense beyond that of formal religion.

There is a complex process by which human beings experience contact with this force and its moral directives. In the attention Romantic writers give to this, they depart from the abstraction of Platonic theory. The process is best illustrated by the metaphor of climbing to an apex or summit of full communion. The raw materials for this visionary experience, which characteristically takes place in solitude, are usually natural sights and sounds, aesthetically stimulating, and often combined with feelings of human affection. By these the imagination is raised from a receptive stage of "mind-wandering" to one of intense concentration from which the normally-sensed world fades. The clarity and power of the experience suggests that it extends to all universal matter, and thus brings conviction of the unity of all things. There is a sense of being part of this unity, its divine authority becoming a strong conviction at the height of experience. The return from this state is similar only in that its direction is a retracing of the path leading to it, for the experience so transforms the protagonist that even the materials which helped begin it appear transfigured afterwards. Feelings of universal love accompany his return to a natural world closer to him, and more eloquent for him, than it was before the experience. And (certainly if we take Wordsworth as example) so impressive is the experience that something of its chastening and ennobling effect returns to him, even years after, at the mere memory of the physical scene which first stimulated it; such as, to cite an obvious example, the daffodils in "I wandered lonely as a cloud."

The summit of the experience reveals that the physical world is only reflection or symbol of the authority it unveils. Certain writers go so far as to see earthly consciousness as only the temporary interruption of permanent immersion in that reality before birth and after death. Such extensions, however, are not central; they stress the debt of the Romantic order to former ideas—particularly to German transcendentalism, generally to Plato.

It may well be wondered, if what I have called an order be set out as baldly as above, how it can claim any originality. How does it differ, for instance, from another, like the deistic "gentleman's religion" of the eighteenth century intelligentsia? There are massive differences in the kind and stages of its apprehension, the means through which belief is acquired. But, viewed simply and generally, both are systems by which the universe, and human consciousness, may quite defensibly be held to operate. In deciding what is characteristically Romantic, then, the stress cannot fall on ideas as such. The Romantic poets move beyond Plato not in essential ideas, but in the attention they give to imaginative and spiritual experience, in the extent it seems to have been common to them, in the fervent conviction it led to, and the imaginative force they bring to expressing it.

The general pattern of experience, and certainly its summit, have not been uncommon, judging by literature other than Romantic. In English alone, mystical writers from Richard Rolle to Vaughan and Traherne have written of experience leading to the conviction of communion with a first cause. In our own time even a writer so limited in range, hardheaded in outlook, and precise in his terms as W. Somerset Maugham has recorded similar experience:

> I was sitting in one of the deserted mosques near Cairo when suddenly I felt myself rapt as Ignatius of Loyola was rapt when he sat by the river at Manresa. I had an overwhelming sense of the power and import of the universe, and an intimate, a shattering sense of communion with it.[39]

"I could almost bring myself to say," he adds, "that I felt the presence of God." "Almost"—and the contrast with the Romantic reaction is eloquent. Romantic writing is marked by the intensity of its reaction to a religious climax which Maugham finally dismisses.

It is just this intensity of conviction that is now the main barrier to sympathy with Romantic art. Viewed objectively, the religious implications of the Romantic order are more cohesive, conform further to general human experience, and are certainly of greater antiquity than those of Christianity in the various forms with which modern Western civilization is associated. But the intensity of belief the Romantics express has not been possible for any group of creative men since their time, and they seem divided from us by a gulf rendering them perpetually strange. In short, we come face to face with religious assertion when we expect only "literature." Once the stamp of a formal creed is put upon a system, we are generally willing, with a mental shrug, to place it in that special limbo reserved for such embarrassing speculations. Carlyle indicted this attitude as early as 1829.

Man does not, he said "believe and know" truth, "but only thinks it, and that 'there is every probability' . . . ." [40]

John Stuart Mill, in a memorable passage of *On Liberty,* points out that "the world, to each individual, means the part of it with which he comes in contact; his party, his sect, his church . . . and it never troubles him that . . . the same causes which make him a Churchman in London would have made him a Bhuddist or a Confucian in Peking." Even a Bhuddist or Confucian, however, as a formally religious man of an alien culture, may be granted "there is every probability." But what can one say of a group of writers of one's own tongue who claim to have frequently seen God in the palm of the hand, and eternity in a flower? And writing individually but implying in unison that this is the most important experience a living man can have!

After the assertive certainty of Romantic conviction, its most remarkable feature is the swiftness of its decay. One does not need much imagination to suggest its causes in Victorian England: the obliteration of much of an agricultural economy, and its replacement by an industrial one, bringing the sudden growth of cities and the varied problems of mass production; the struggle for political influence by large sections of the population; colonial expansion and exploitation; the pace and lack of leisure in materialistic life; the inadequacy of the church, despite attempts to reform it; science, especially in the fear, which Darwin symbolized, that nature, far from being a link in a chain leading to God, was itself the final reality—and one due to the operations of chance in an indifferent universe. All that has since happened to many of these thorny Victorian problems is that they have developed a broader milieu and have become more pressing.

Romantic decline is illustrated by almost all the writers I have mentioned who lived into middle age. A generally sympathetic critic of Wordsworth remarks of his development, ". . . for the most part after 1805 there is a shocking debilitation in his work. The symptoms of it are plain too: a flat and moralistic and not often very passionate adaptation of Christian and classical vocabularies; a tendency to increased garrulity; a soberly cheery optimism about the relations of man and nature, man and God, combined with a sort of peevishness against railroads and a zeal for capital punishment." [41] Wordsworth himself had been aware of the dangers as early as 1800. In the Preface to the *Lyrical Ballads* he observes "a multitude of causes, unknown to former times, are now acting to blunt the discriminating powers of the mind . . . to reduce it to a state of almost savage torpor." He mentions "the great national events daily taking place," "the increasing accumulation of men in cities," and "the uniformity of their occupations."

One often reads lamentations on the elderly Wordsworth as a political reactionary, but the reasons that conservatism is so sad a falling-away from radical idealism are not made clear. They should be: the early Wordsworth gained, as we have seen, a moral authority from his visionary experience; radical idealism is simply one of several corollaries to that moral authority. His later political stance is significant far beyond the purely political sphere, for it shows the great diminution in the influence of his early vision on him.

In later life, commenting in a note to the poem on the ideas of the *Intimations of Immortality* ode, Wordsworth considered this change. In his youth, he says, he had been

> . . . often unable to think of earthly things as having external existence, and I communed with all that I saw as something not apart from, but inherent in, my own immaterial nature. Many times while going to school I have grasped at a wall or tree to recall myself from this abyss of idealism to the reality. At that time I was afraid of such processes. In later periods of life I have deplored, as we all have reason to do, a subjugation of an opposite character . . . .

He goes on to apologize, much as a Victorian professor might do, for the poem's having invited the inference by "good and pious persons" of his championing the idea of a prior state of existence. The idea, he concedes, is "not advanced in Revelation," but "the Fall of Man presents an analogy in its favour." It is "in the popular creeds of many nations" and "is known as an ingredient in Platonic philosophy."

A comparable loss of vision, if not of assertion, is true of Carlyle. He could not sustain the outlook of *Sartor Resartus,* and one does not have to thumb the social history books to find the forces which destroyed it. The first six chapters of the work itself (appearing serially in 1833–34) concentrate on attacking those forces. From the opening pages, with their affable irony at the expense of spiritless and over-specialized research, occur a series of attacks: on the selfishness of business and industry; on exploitation of workers and the political system which encourages it; on excessive pragmatism; on money-power; on misapplied technical "progress" ("The first ground handful of Nitre, Sulphur, and Charcoal drove Monk Schwartz's pestle through the ceiling: what will the last do?"); on advertising ("puffery and quackery"); on popular newspapers; on the inactivity of the Church. As one follows Carlyle through his growing stress on hero-worship (which had been in *Sartor* a mere corollary to his central faith), through his idealizing of the Middle Ages in *Past and Present,* he appears—differing from Wordsworth in this—to lose even the consciousness of his former vision. Carlyle sees democracy in *Past and Present* as the tired dragging down of everything to the level of the meanest common denominator: "Democracy, which means despair of finding any Heroes to govern you, and contented putting up with the want of them,—alas, thou too, mein Lieber, seest well how close it is of kin to *Atheism,* and other sad Isms." There is no reason to condemn a writer for preferring autocracy to democracy; it is still an arguable matter, and the preference in 1843, after decades of mob disturbances, probably appeared natural and sensible. What is sad here is not the position Carlyle takes, but the fact that the prophet alive with faith has shrunk into political propagandist. Carlyle might have seen himself that the *scope* of his concerns here, slightly more than a decade after the assertive faith of *Sartor,* was very close of kin to agnosticism and other sad isms. His attention is no longer on ideals, but on a social situation, the lack of "hero" material. Raymond Williams, who sees Carlyle's shift as moving from a real insight predicated on human needs to the substitution of what he (Carlyle) desired personally, comments, "The phenomenon is indeed general, and has perhaps been especially marked in the last six or seven generations." He goes on to describe the process:

> This indeed is the tragedy of the situation: that a genuine insight, a genuine vision, should be dragged down by the very situation, the very structure of relationships, to which it was opposed, until a civilizing insight became in its operation barbarous, and a heroic purpose, a 'high vocation', found its final expression in a conception of human relationships which is only an idealized version of industrial class-society.[42]

A sense of the withdrawal from Romantic attitudes is perhaps most succinctly suggested by various hints drawn from nineteenth century literature as a whole. Professor Walter Houghton suggests that love of woman, as expressed in Patmore's *The Angel in the House,* was one substitute for certainty of belief.[43] Or if we put the kind of duty we associate with Kipling beside the kind Carlyle speaks of in *Sartor,* it is hard to avoid the impression that Kipling's is an isolated vestigial survival. Or again, Wordsworth had used "forms" to express his vision, but later in the century their significance dwindles. As we shall see, for Arnold natural forms are the inscrutable symbols of a lonely, remote and inexorable existence, essentially fruitless clues in a dispiriting puzzle. For Ruskin they were initially what they had been for Wordsworth, the language of moral guidance spoken by God; but as Ruskin develops they are more often seen only as background to human diminution or repression of spirit, and their main level of meaning becomes social. The logical conclusion of this general loss of significance comes in the eighties and nineties, where the sensual experience of the form entirely dominates the artist's interest, and the contrast with Romanticism becomes complete.

"Disorder," Carlyle once wrote, "is dissolution, death. No chaos but it seeks a centre to revolve round." [44] He was at the time pleading the case for hero-worship, but this itself was only the political expression of his need for faith, and for the return, in political clothes, of the Everlasting Yea. We might recall, in moving to our own time, how far our most widely-read literary form, the novel, has been shaped round a parallel idea, though now "love" in various aspects is its main center. Judging by the number of twentieth century novels pleading for this, Matthew Arnold's brief and pathetic aside in *Dover Beach,* "Ah, love, let us be true to one another!" speaks for a whole legion of the lost.

NOTES

[1] For example, Harold Bloom in *Shelley's Mythmaking* (New Haven: Yale University Press, 1959), p. 41. Professor Bloom, dealing with the lines in the *Hymn to Intellectual Beauty,*

> Sudden, thy shadow fell on me
> I shrieked, and clasped my hands in ecstasy!

explains: "When the religion is as personal and undefined as it is here, readers are likely to feel a certain impatience with the emotion evoked by the enthusiast, emotion which is hardly transferable and therefore felt by them to be illicit in a poem."

2 I select, with some additions of my own, from S.C. Chew's consideration of the nature of Romanticism in *A Literary History of England* (New York, 1948), pp. 1122–1127. The list could be prolonged almost indefinitely.

3 In stressing the assertiveness of Coleridge's sense of unity in this early poem, I do not mean to minimize the apology with which he ends it. I see the apology as *poetically* important, as a crude and exploratory means of dealing with the "return to earth" from a height of vision. The problem of apparent apology does not recur in the other "Conversation" poems. Here it is complex, and several interpretations exist. See R. C. Wendling, "Coleridge and the Eolian Harp," *Studies in Romanticism*, VIII (Autumn, 1968), pp. 26–42. Mr. Wendling sees the apology as "Coleridge's deliberate refusal to rest complacently in a vaguely defined Romanticism"—a description of the poem's assertion I cannot accept.

4 I mention the dates of these Conversation poems to place them within Coleridge's early development. This is not to suggest, of course, that the experience and conviction they present was a new or sudden literary development introduced by Coleridge, Wordsworth or even Blake. Goethe, for instance, had expressed similar experience of vision and unity, with equal clarity and conviction, as early as 1774, when Coleridge was two years old and Wordsworth four. Thus *The Sorrows of Young Werther*, trans. by Victor Lange (New York, 1949), entry of August 18:

> . . . when I heard the groves about me melodious with the music of birds, and saw the million swarms of insects dancing in the last golden beams of the sun, whose setting rays awoke the humming beetles from their grassy beds . . . all this conveyed to me the holy fire which animates all Nature, and filled and glowed within my heart. I felt myself exalted by this overflowing fullness to the perception of the Godhead, and the glorious forms of an infinite universe stirred within my soul!

5 In using *The Ancient Mariner* as I do here, I am in accord with a great deal of "standard" criticism of the poem. It is fair to add, however, that the poem's richness of suggestion renders my use here very limited, though not (I think) incorrect. Mrs. Irene Chayes, for instance, sees the Mariner's story as a kind of allegorical journey through the errors of metaphysical speculation. See "A Coleridgean Reading of 'The Ancient Mariner'," *Studies in Romanticism*, IV (Winter, 1965), pp. 81–103. But even such an ingeniously worked out level of meaning does not of course deny the sort of simple dualism I stress.

6 See, for example, Wordsworth's treatment of the echo in *The Prelude*, I, 438–444.

7 Essay, Supplementary to the [1815] Preface to the *Lyrical Ballads*.

8 Letter to Thomas Poole, October 16, 1797.

9 [October 16,] 1797.

10 *The Mirror and the Lamp* (New York, 1953), p. 119.

11 Piping down the valleys wild,
Piping songs of pleasant glee,

On a cloud I saw a child,
And he laughing said to me:

"Pipe a song about a Lamb!"
So I piped with merry chear.
"Piper, pipe that song again;"
So I piped: he wept to hear.

"Drop thy pipe, thy happy pipe;
Sing thy songs of happy chear:"
So I sung the same again,
While he wept with joy to hear.

"Piper, sit thee down and write
In a book, that all may read."
So he vanish'd from my sight,
And I pluck'd a hollow reed,

And I made a rural pen,
And I stain'd the water clear,
And I wrote my happy songs
Every child may joy to hear.

[12] The Terror answer'd: "I am Orc, wreath'd round the accursed tree:
The times are ended; shadows pass, the morning 'gins to break;
The fiery joy, that Urizen perverted to ten commands,
What night he led the starry hosts thro' the wide wilderness,
That stony law I stamp to dust; and scatter religion abroad
To the four winds as a torn book, & none shall gather the leaves;
But they shall rot on desart sands, & consume on bottomless deeps,
To make the desarts blossom, & the deeps shrink to their fountains,
And to renew the fiery joy, and burst the stony roof;
That pale religious letchery, seeking Virginity,
May find it in a harlot, and in coarse-clad honesty
The undefil'd, tho' ravish'd in her cradle night and morn;
For everything that lives is holy, life delights in life;
Because the soul of sweet delight can never be defil'd.
Fires inwrap the earthly globe, yet man is not consum'd;
Amidst the lustful fires he walks; his feet become like brass,
  His knees and thighs like silver, & his breast and head like gold."

[13] "Blake's 'Mental Traveller'," *ELH*, XXII (1955), p. 147.
[14] "Blake's Treatment of the Archetype," *English Institute Essays* (New York, 1950), p. 177.
[15] *William Blake: Poet, Printer, Prophet* (New York, 1964), p. 24.
[16] *English Thought in the Nineteenth Century* (London, 1929), p. vii.
[17] H. G. Schenk, *The Mind of the European Romantics* (London, 1966), p. 141.
[18] *Byron: A Collection of Critical Essays* (New York, 1963), p. 1.
[19] "Byron: The Search for Identity," *The London Magazine*, V, No. 7 (July, 1958), p. 45.

20 Letter to Elizabeth Hitchener, dated October 16, 1811.
21 Letter to Elizabeth Hitchener, dated January 2, 1812.
22 Letter to Elizabeth Hitchener, dated June 20, 1811.
23 *Essay on Love*: of doubtful date, but probably composed in 1815. See *Shelley's Prose*, ed. David L. Clark (Albuquerque: University of New Mexico Press, 1954), p. 169.
24 May 3, 1818.
25 *John Keats* (Cambridge, Mass.: Harvard University Press, 1963), p. 587.
26 *Ibid.*, p. 591.
27 To George and Georgiana Keats [September 17, 1819].
28 The often-quoted "Chamber of Maiden Thought" letter, written soon after Keats had finished *Endymion*, records the poet's conviction that the resolution of the puzzle must lie in the examination of deprivation and pain themselves (to Reynolds, May 3, 1818).
29 January 30, 1818.
30 With the single exception of *To Autumn* (Sept., 1819), I am reversing the order of composition here by taking up *Lamia* (July-end of August, 1819) before the odes (April-May, 1819). My order is determined by the apparent development of Keats' ideas: normally, it accords with the order in which he composed his poems. The time between the odes and *Lamia* is roughly two months. What the apparent difficulty shows, I think, is that a man struggling to resolve a personal philosophy may advance a step or two and yet still write a poem (here *Lamia*) allegorizing his state of mind before these recent advances.
31 *John Keats: Complete Poems and Selected Letters* (New York, 1935), p. xli.
32 See Mill's very specific and important account of this in Chapter V of his *Autobiography*.
33 *Carlyle: Life in London*, I, p. 296. Professor Walter Houghton's *The Victorian Frame of Mind: 1830–1870* (New Haven: Yale University Press, 1957) cites this and other evidence that Carlyle was regarded, through his works, as a religious leader—not simply as a "writer."
34 See "The Sorrows of Teufelsdröckh" chapter of *Sartor*, or *Characteristics*, Essay III, or *Goethe*, Essay I.
35 The most succinct aid in coming to terms with the complexities of *Sartor Resartus* is the excellent introduction in C. F. Harrold's Odyssey Press edition (New York, 1937), and it is to this edition that I refer in quoting Carlyle.

Carlyle lived to be an elderly Victorian, and, for reasons soon to be briefly discussed, and implied by this book generally, was unable to retain so assertive a vision as *Sartor* is built on. The book is thus Carlyle's only full statement of his Romantic ideas, and is therefore central here. Around these ideas so much more is constructed, however relevant, that the general reader who turns or returns to the work with my selection of ideas in mind may find only confusion. Though they are not my concern here, it may help to separate some of the other important levels in *Sartor* from the philosophic conviction.

(a) The style: the creation of huge panoramas, the breathless presentation of the world's complexity through piled-up hyphenation, sub-clauses, sustained Miltonic metaphors, and the vivid animated-cartoon-like quality of descriptions.

(b) The humor: Parody (e.g. of Wordsworth, see p. 52); quaintness in scene-painting (the old-Germany background to Teufelsdröckh's life is very like Washington Irving); the Swiftian satiric techniques, the use of Carlyle's "editorship" as device for making fun of his own style, and, more importantly, as apology to disarm criticism, and for hinting how much more could be said.

(c) Structure: Book I: the editor, dealing with Teufelsdröckh's parchments, builds up and comments on their philosophic scheme. Book II: the moral biography of Teufelsdröckh (Carlyle's own spiritual progress). Book III: The Clothes Philosophy applied to religion, politics, nature, social regeneration, etc. Or, to put the emphasis more generally—Book I: what's wrong with the world, and the strange scheme of Teufelsdröckh which might correct it. Book II: the path to personal enlightment. Book III: the lessons of both applied to the world.

(d) Arising from this are sustained attacks on Victorian developments (see pp. 62–63).

[36] Clothes, in *Sartor*, carry a variety of meanings; one of the most important is that they stand for society as a structure, against the individuals who make it up.

[37] "Signs of the Times" (1829).

[38] According to Froude, *Carlyle's Early Life*, I, p. 101.

[39] *The Summing Up* (New York, 1938), pp. 270–271.

[40] "Signs of the Times."

[41] David Ferry, *The Limits of Mortality* (Middletown, Conn.: Wesleyan University Press, 1959), p. 172.

[42] *Culture and Society 1780–1950* (New York, 1960), pp. 83–84.

[43] *The Victorian Frame of Mind: 1830–1870*, p. 393.

[44] "The Hero as King," in *Heroes and Hero-Worship*.

II
ARNOLD

II

ARNOLD

1. THE BACKGROUND ℬ℘ In trying to clarify and stress the essential assertiveness of Romantic vision, I have in passing suggested the nature of its concomitant—the quick fading and ultimate failure of that vision in the minds of individuals. As the third decade of the nineteenth century moved into the fourth, however, the Romantic vision of poets like Wordsworth diminished, and younger versifiers imitated Romantic style while remaining apparently untouched by its visionary force. Since I do not wish to discuss at any length work at best insignificant and at worst fraudulent, I shall refer only briefly to the Spasmodics.[1] But it is relevant that a poem like Bailey's *Festus* (1839) should consist of torrents of Romantic rhetoric with no genuine vision behind it, and that it should be characteristic of a whole movement. Broadly speaking, the Spasmodics accepted the early Byron as patron saint, the arch-Romantic "poetic" personality. (The choice itself is ominous, granting the view that Byron had touched only the periphery of English Romantic experience.) Adopting also the more undisciplined sort of Shelleyan rhetoric as their style, they produced poetry as voluminous in mass as it was divorced from any rigorously observed human

experience. In their verse desires, passions, egoism and fantasies appear, but no sense of vision, individual or group. Their poetry never echoes immediate visionary experience in the Romantic manner. Between Romantic work and its Spasmodic imitators is all the difference between a man struggling to force words to convey the religious meaning his most intimate experience holds for him, and another who thoughtlessly strings together a certain sort of diction because it suits his voice—or his own idea of his voice. Although the two may superficially sound the same, the difference is crucial.

There are many other literary works with a place in the aftermath of full Romanticism, and some are of far more consequence than Spasmodic poetry. There is, for instance, George Darley's best poem, *Nepenthe* (1836), which departs sharply from Spasmodic work in having all the impact and artistic convincingness of direct vision. While a lengthier and less striking poem, it is to some extent comparable to *Kubla Khan*. But while Coleridge's poem had been an unfinished and fragmentary work of vision, in other complete poems Coleridge had not failed to imply throughout the meaning of such vision, the order it reveals, and the moral guidance to be inferred from it. Despite its fullness and power, the isolated vision of *Nepenthe* is not comparably significant; it has no comment to make on the ordinary world of poet and reader. It is quasi-Romantic vision in a moral vacuum.

There is, however, one major work of genius, the novel *Wuthering Heights*, which relates both to the fullness and ultimate decline of Romantic certitude. It is manifestly, within the terms I and others have set up, the most "Romantic" English novel ever written. No other so fully expresses that philosophic dualism which appeared as overt statement in Coleridge and Carlyle and is implicit in the work of the other Romantics. In *Wuthering Heights* the finite world, and especially that social part of it into which the young Heathcliff and Cathy peer through the windows of Thrushcross Grange, and that Christian aspect of it so sententiously urged by Nelly Dean and Joseph, do not matter at all. They are only springboards to the assertion of the immensely greater validity of a cosmic order motivating Heathcliff and Cathy and the moors of wind and storm, which in their oddly shrunken, "finite" periods of calm also appear irrelevant. Many characters and events in the novel, in fact, exist primarily *to provoke* rejection of the standards and ideals of the finite world, and consequently our imaginative acceptance of the cosmic one.[2]

In the sheer weight of its emotional assault on the reader's sense of *what is real*, in its overwhelming presentation of a universal and superior reality at the expense of a finite one, the novel is as impressive as the best Romantic poetry.[3] There is, however, one immense difference, apart from form, between the novel (published in 1847) and those works I have regarded as centrally "Romantic." Carlyle and the poets, true to Platonic tradition, infer a moral order from the cosmic one to which imagination has led. Emily Brontë does not: she may have chosen to live apart from the immediate stresses of her day, but she was sufficiently of her time to have disassociated her intensely-imagined cosmos from any moral function. What she asserts about the cosmos of *Wuthering Heights* is its reality, its relentlessness beside the human scale, its quiescent peace when its order is preserved, and its fury when it is violated by any finite considerations, including moral ones. Despite all its "Romantic" duality, *Wuthering Heights* carries no moral ordering of things; nothing, that is, beyond a fatalistic agnostic anarchy and the message that we go where we are driven. As it had for Darley, genuine vision, analogous to that which the Romantics had known, does exist for Emily Brontë, but it no longer relates to that everyday world of commerce and competition, invention and evolution, religious struggle and deepening scepticism which the intelligent Victorian reader saw around him.

All the work I have just mentioned, however varied in quality, provides interesting flotsam in the withdrawal of the tide of assertive Romantic faith, and at the same time varieties of escape from the bare philosophical beach on which the Victorians found themselves. There is evidence that the relationship between reader and writer had also changed towards that general Victorian reliance on the "great writer"—the poet or prose writer of poetic gifts (Carlyle), or of immense integrity (Newman or Mill) as guide, teacher, and even prophet. Clearly the poets seemed to offer special authority in this regard. The Romantics, at least before Carlyle, had never really been circulated on a broad enough scale to attain such a position (Wordsworth being some exception), nor had they been, as a whole, sufficiently appreciated or understood.

But the great activity of the Browning Societies and the welter of texts on the theme of Tennyson-as-teacher which poured from the presses before the end of the century testify that the Victorian reader expected of his "great poets" both philosophy and personal guidance. It was not, on the face of it, an unreasonable expectation. In a world of increasing confusion, where conventional religious belief seemed more shaken with every year that passed, what could be more natural than to turn to the most thoughtful, creative, "spiritual" and articulate minds which could be brought to bear on Victorian dilemmas? Such minds would of course be themselves reacting to the general problems of the environment, as Arnold saw it, of "two worlds, one dead, / The other powerless to be born"; they would be familiar with the problem John Stuart Mill had articulated in his autobiography—that to know that one could be happy with the faith that makes possible a view of life as integrated and purposeful is in itself no help in attaining such a faith. There is a tacit acceptance, throughout the work of the three great Victorian poets, of the relevance of their personal struggles with this situation to the lives of their readers, and of the need of their readers for guidance.

Tennyson, of course, was seen as the great moral teacher and guide. Browning, once the reputation of *The Ring and the Book* had stimulated his admirers into searching his work for moral and philosophic guidance, and with his earlier poems then appearing more relevant to the purpose, attained a considerable following also. Though his prose criticism had considerable impact, Arnold in his own century was never accorded a comparable position as poet. It is at first curious, and ultimately important to the understanding of the state of mind of the three poets, to realize that modern assessment tends towards the reverse position. Of the three, Tennyson in the early twentieth century suffered spetacular diminution in reputation, which only comparatively recently has begun to recover: Browning remains problematical: Arnold on the whole has worn best—and certainly has shown the most consistent advance—of all. I am speaking here of total poetic reputation as perspective has developed, not of value as philosopher and guide. But the two affect each other; twentieth-century reaction against the Victorian view of Tennyson as philosophic teacher has certainly been a major factor in diminishing the general poetic stature he has had since his own day.

Conversely—and I hope my analysis of Arnold's poetry which follows will suggest reasons for this—Arnold has come closer to the modern reader *in direct proportion to* his failure to provide constructive guidance (as poet) to his own generation. Obviously this involves changes in attitude and expectation of the reader, as well as conclusions about the nature of the poet. But for the moment it is sufficient to say that Arnold is inevitably the logical starting point (granting that it is useful to try to infer the poet's attitudes of mind, in the face of Victorian stresses and problems, from his work). He is, in the emotional and conceptual attitudes his work suggests (though not in its techniques), by far the most modern of the three poets. He is, often for the precise reasons for which his Victorian readers found him comparatively unfruitful, a point of familiar understanding for the modern reader—a recognizable, near-modern norm (again in content if not style) from which Browning and Tennyson may be seen as variations.

There is, for instance, something curiously modern—one might almost say insecure—in the very distinctness of the categories by which Arnold channels his life's effort. His daily work as school-inspector is practical, of demonstrable value: the prose criticism is so-cial, or, where it centers on literature, socially-oriented—here Arnold is consciously doing his duty as teacher and guide. His poetry appears purely personal, consisting of tortuous vignettes of mind and spirit. Versatility in itself, of course, is no logical ground for charging a lack of confidence or commitment. Still, the whole corpus of Arnold's writing encourages the perhaps quite unfair image of a man's rather ponderous attempt to achieve, like Mycinerus, "something . . . be-fore the shadows fall" by means of a varied permutation of effort quite opposite from the dedication of particular passion.

It is not my design to treat Arnold's prose here except in so far as it offers certain hints, general evidences of his cast of mind, serving as useful introduction to the poetry. Arnold's prose is pleasant to read in its apparent clarity and movement; and in the relevance of its subject matter to many problems and situations still with us, it is thought-provoking. But it is remarkably diffuse prose, and if one per-forms the kind of précis exercise the young John Stuart Mill was brought up on (Reduce the Passage to its *Essential Thought!*), one emerges with remarkably few headings from the large mass of, say, *Culture and Anarchy*. Against this diffuseness of idea, forming a striking dichotomy, is Arnold's conception of truth. Like that of most Victorian thinkers until quite late in the century, his thought rests on the assumption that absolute truth exists somewhere, and, like the Holy Grail, is ultimately to be held as attainable. It is not relative, shifting and personal, as the modern mind tends to regard philo-sophic truth. Arnold's absolute conception of truth, however, does not permit him as critic to advance far along the road to it: his ideas are broad and few, and the bulk of his prose is simply elaborative.

A similar sense of strain arises between, on the one hand, the consistency and absoluteness of his pursuit of standards, and on the other the memorable vagueness of his terminology in setting them out. Arnold's desire as critic for absolute criteria is manifest everywhere. The object of the 1853 *Preface,* for example, is to establish them for poetry (the young writer needs "a voice to prescribe to him the aim which he should keep in view"). There is the careful piece on *The Literary Influence of Academies;* there is the touchstone theory ("there can be no more useful help for discovering what poetry belongs to the class of the truly excellent, and can therefore do us most good, than to have always in one's mind lines and expressions of the great masters, and to apply them as a touchstone to other poetry"). There are also Arnold's constant urgings to have the reader place beside lines under discussion "this passage—or this." Against this yearning for the critical absolute, however, we find an astonishing looseness of terminology in Arnold's criticism, and the flow of the reader's thought is constantly being brought to a temporary standstill by expressions like "the conditions of excellence," "to see the object as in itself it really is," "the best ideas . . . current at the time," "the best that is known and thought in the world," "a high and perfect ideal," "perfection," and so on—even *sweetness* and *light.* They are roughly meaningful terms within the context, perhaps, that Arnold sets up, but they are hardly consistent with the rigid precision of the kind of "truth" he envisages.

In his criticism we are, so to speak, brought up repeatedly and flatly against a philosophical wall beyond which lies absolute truth, but which Arnold has no real hope of surmounting. His poetry in general is the metaphorical and sometimes myth-vehicled expression of his inward thought and attitudes as he reacts to the impasse—or attempts to. For this reason it is an extremely static body of work. It is not useful, in considering Arnold's poetry, to be guided by its chronology in an attempt to trace developments of thought and attitude, for Arnold shows very few indeed.

This stasis in his poetry has led to a correspondingly static general view of him as poet. In the process of quietly gaining rank comparable to that of Tennyson and Browning, Arnold has come to be seen as the poet of resignation, an elegiac nature poet, imbued with classical stoicism, and presenting Victorian dilemmas through a restrained and individual pathos which has become the basis of his appeal. There is nothing false in that assessment, except that it is partial. It does not suggest the complex elements of Arnold's personal and losing struggle to progress towards spiritual orientation in the Victorian world. It does not relate his work to the previous poetry—much of it Romantic—by which Arnold was, consciously or otherwise, moved and affected. And it gives no place to variations within his work, in particular to the special kind of animation—not in itself Romantic, though faintly echoing the Romantic—which Arnold was capable of whenever his creative imagination (though never his entire mind) could be drawn away from contemporary problems.

While his themes usually concern estrangement (*The Forsaken Merman*, the *Marguerite* poems, *Sohrab and Rustum*, *Thyrsis*, *The Scholar-Gipsy*, *Dover Beach*, etc.) they appear only as symbols for what Arnold feels to be his own position drawn against the human situation. Life is seen as an eternal puzzling process with which the poet—or his projection—cannot come to terms. Hence Mycerinus:

> Into the silence of the groves and woods
> I will go forth, though something I would say—
> Something—yet what, I know not; for the gods
> The doom they pass revoke not, nor delay;
> And prayers, and gifts, and tears, are fruitless all,
> And the night waxes, and the shadows fall.

This outlook is Arnold's basic one in poem after poem regardless of subject: *Mycerinus* is ostensibly about the injustice of condemnation by the gods, but Arnold uses the embellished dramatic monologue to present and dramatize, though not to answer, his basic puzzle which centers on the conditions of life itself. Arnold constantly surveys the human predicament from without—from the position of one cut off from that kind of belief and orientation which alone can bring real involvement and relief from concern. As explanation of the "curiously classic fatalism" in Arnold's earliest poetry, E.D.H. Johnson has remarked that while Arnold refused to grant that man is accidental, he could not share either the orthodox religion or romantic religion.[4]

2. CENTRAL POEMS OF ARNOLD ⁊ Before raising poetic questions which bear on Arnold's difficulties of belief, I think it useful to set out a rough indication of the kind and direction of such questions.

An analytical reading of a short, fairly early (1849) and quite characteristic Arnold poem, *The Forsaken Merman,* provides at this point the opportunity to set out, as parts of a unified context, tendencies which can later be examined as consistently functional in all Arnold's poetry.

The Forsaken Merman is fundamentally a lyrical dramatic monologue presenting, with muted emotions, a situation Arnold takes from what is, broadly speaking, fairy story—specifically Danish legend. The merman and his children have been forsaken by the mortal "mermaid"—inevitably named Margaret—who has heard the Easter church bells from the land, and has been drawn back to the world of mortals. The poem, obviously then, has loss and alienation as its general theme, though, as we shall see, the kind of alienation Arnold is presenting turns out to be a rich and complex matter. The emotional effect of a mother abandoning her children is obvious enough; that she abandons a kind of primal life in the sea for the sake of conventional religion is also clear. But we might also note that Arnold, in choosing his source, has played on traditional associations to effect an ironic reversal, which suggests that it is generally true of life at any level that lasting security can never be established. The mermaid "tradition" usually places man, as the center of his world, tempted from a set path by the blandishments of mermaids. Here, the merman, in the background of events both described and implied, had once found his center in love, faith, and home. Arnold's chosen story is one that reverses the "tradition" by having the "mermaid" herself tempted away from merman and family. The very difference in detail itself stresses the sameness of effect, an echoing and hopeless deprivation.

Arnold presents his situation, evoking throughout a tone of remote plaintiveness, by means of remarkable skills in structure and technique. The poem opens at the most dramatic moment of the Merman's speech, as he summons the children back to the sea, before telling them to call one last time to their mother. From this last fruitless call the poem presents, in a series of flashbacks ("was it yesterday?"), the fulfilled sea-world as it was in the days of family unity (ll. 30–53), the temptation of the "mermaid" and her desertion (ll. 54–62), the fruitless visit of the family to the land, their appeal to her to return with them and its rejection (ll. 65–82), and the merman's vision of her divided feelings in the land-world. Returning to the narrative present, the merman continues his envisioned account of his wife and his family in their different kinds of isolation, and ends with the resigned, hopeless expedition to the beach-borders dividing the two irreconcilable worlds of sea and land, which will take place in the future. The poem, therefore, generalizes its situation not only through the gnomic qualities of its legend, but also through its emphasis on the sheer endlessness of the solitude it presents in past, present, and future.

The opening of the poem uses techniques exploited throughout: the repeated use of long vowels, particularly at line endings, for a tone of echoing forlornness; sufficient variation in line length to permit suggestion of both the brisk choppiness of waves (l.7) and the violent burst of feeling in abrupt exclamation (l.11):

> Come, dear children, let us away;
> Down and away below!
> Now my brothers call from the bay,
> Now the great winds shoreward blow,
> Now the salt tides seaward flow;
> Now the wild white horses play,
> Champ and chafe and toss in the spray.
> Children dear, let us away!
> This way, this way!
>
> Call her once before you go—
> Call once yet!
> In a voice that she will know:
> "Margaret! Margaret!"

As almost always in Arnold's work, the very certainty of structure and technique makes an astringent contrast with the themes and divided mental attitudes which are orchestrated and augmented by the tone. These "divided mental attitudes" need examination; that sense of alienation I called rich and complex is, I think, at once the basis of the emotional force of the poem and a revealing expression of Arnold's own outlook. The impact of the poem as a whole is not merely that of a skillfully-expressed dramatic lament: it has, carefully woven within it, a series of tensions. If the poem's overt theme is alienation, it makes clear in its most central passage that it is alienation from belief—here Christian belief—which Arnold has in mind, and the passage is elaborately symbolic of his own position:

> From the church came a murmur of folk at their prayers,
> But we stood without in the cold blowing airs.

We climbed on the graves, on the stones worn with rains,
And we gazed up the aisle through the small leaded panes.
She sate by the pillar; we saw her clear:
"Margaret, hist! come quick, we are here!
Dear heart," I said, "we are long alone;
The sea grows stormy, the little ones moan."
But, ah, she gave me never a look,
For her eyes were sealed to the holy book!
Loud prays the priest; shut stands the door.

But if the door stands shut to the merman and his children, it has surely opened to Margaret? Hers is the only religious commitment in the poem: is Christian belief and dedication therefore a possibility for others? Not at all: Margaret sings joyfully back in the mortal world, but the very joy she feels is mortally limited and qualified; it is a worldly joy of living, not a spiritual one. Although she longs for "the blessed light of the sun," she mentions it only after a string of far more mundane desires, first for "the humming street, and the child with its toy," and next, in the same unspiritual way, for "the priest, and the bell, and the holy well." The suggestion is that modern religion itself is worldly, and for Margaret it is, therefore, short-lived, qualified, and ultimately destroyed by longing:

And so she sings her fill,
Singing most joyfully,
Till the spindle drops from her hand,
And the whizzing wheel stands still.
She steals to the window, and looks at the sand,
And over the sand at the sea;
And her eyes are set in a stare;
And anon there breaks a sigh,
And anon there drops a tear,
From a sorrow-clouded eye,
And a heart sorrow-laden,
A long, long sigh;
For the cold strange eyes of a little Mermaiden
And the gleam of her golden hair.

While there is in Margaret enough faith—or while she feels sufficiently the attraction of faith—to move her away from her adopted sea-world to another one, there is not enough faith in that one to sustain her thereafter, and she herself appears as divided and forlorn as the family she has abandoned.

Again, it is suggested that Margaret, back in the mortal world, will see her former home of sea and storm with mortal eyes, so that her vision is deceiving; to the merman and his children, however, their natural habitat of sea and storm will have the wholeness, integration and security of a sort of heaven:

> We shall see, while above us
> The waves roar and whirl,
> A ceiling of amber,
> A pavement of pearl.

Yet this apparent security and beauty for the merman and his family in their natural home are in their turn immediately destroyed by the next lines, which revert to the theme of perpetual solitude:

> Singing: "Here came a mortal,
> But faithless was she!
> And alone dwell forever
> The kings of the sea."

The kings of—the sea! The irony within the phrase sums up admirably the conflicting forces throughout *The Forsaken Merman.* The poem, indeed, poses two distinct but related problems: the first is Arnold's own, that of standing, like the merman, outside the door of orthodox faith and finding it impossible to enter; the other, which provides a reason for that impossibility, is the conviction that where faith appears within reach for others—like Margaret in the poem—it will inevitably fail to sustain them. To cite Mill's classification of non-believers, the poem concerns not only those who reject or fail in faith, but also those who "never really had it." And since the exploitation of the dramatic situation in the poem falls chiefly on the merman, perhaps Arnold's stress is on the last category. In case, however, the merman and his wife Margaret might be assumed to turn again to each other as relief from their individual solitudes, the poet bathes the borders of their two worlds—the beaches—in the moonlight of illusion. It becomes quite clear that those borders, pictured though they are with indefinite patches of light, are a barrier, not a bridge, and any apparent joining of the different worlds over them must be illusive.

> But, children, at midnight,
> When soft the winds blow,
> When clear falls the moonlight,

When spring-tides are low;
When sweet airs come seaward
From heaths starred with broom,
And high rocks throw mildly
On the blanched sands a gloom;
Up the still, glistening beaches,
Up the creeks we will hie,
Over banks of bright seaweed
The ebb-tide leaves dry.
We will gaze, from the sand-hills,
At the white, sleeping town;
At the church on the hillside—
And then come back down,
Singing: "There dwells a loved one,
But cruel is she!
She left lonely forever
The kings of the sea."

This ending is in some ways the part of the poem most characteristic of Arnold, and it is where his interest appears most clearly to lie. The half-realized, half-suppressed and pathetic beauty of the border-beach (here a kind of anticipation of what is exploited more fully and clearly in *Dover Beach*) represents the idea of connection-in-appearance and isolation-in-reality which eternally haunted Arnold. The beach in *The Forsaken Merman* leaves the dimension of the fairy-story and (again setting up a kind of tension) becomes a part of our world; and, like Keats' nightingale, returns the reader to it. It is as if Arnold were simultaneously indicating the limitations of the fairy-tale fragment and yet also pointing out its relevance to the world we do have to live in.

The view of that world expressed by the poem is important. The merman and his wife Margaret, the vague "children" and the sea-creatures suggest associations which belong to folk-literature: the whole poem gains, as has been suggested, a gnomic quality from this. It is not so much one poet speaking, as people of all ages and places through the voice of legend, and on the scale of all human fears and fantasies. Morever, the domain of the merman and his children in the "sand-strewn caverns, cool and deep" in the depths of the sea has great creative force: it compels the imagination; like the world of *Kubla Khan*, it becomes more real for the moment than the reader's immediate and concrete surroundings.

This brief glimpse of the merman's world is related to Romantic vision in imaginative force, but it does not carry Romantic implications. It is tinged with desolation, not at the withdrawal of vision as in Romantic poetry, but *throughout* at the want of that extensive, unqualified commitment which makes Romantic vision possible. For both these reasons—the gnomic theme and associations of the poem and the imaginative compulsion of the merman's world—the view of the conventional world, presented through the merman's visit to it, appears, comparatively, very small indeed, its religion hollow. And such a reversal of the conventional view, which sees the everyday world as central and authoritative, again relates to Coleridge's and Wordsworth's use of such reversal, though they had immensely different aims. Here, so far from shocking us into an awareness of the impact of vision, it merely functions as part of the poem's capacity to disturb the order of the reader's world and move it towards disruption and alienation in a highly negative way. The entire poem, working chiefly through its reversals and tensions, dramatizes the active but ultimately frustrated ways in which Arnold's whole sense of dilemma affects him. The poem can be read as simple fairy-story, as folk-myth about human alienation, and as personal allegory involving Arnold's own view of his time and its problems of belief. It should also be read as a sustained cry of pain made more affecting by the qualities of its sounds, meter and exclamation. This very ambivalence of level is itself functional in presenting the eloquent, balanced fragmentation of feeling which underlies Arnold's own personal incapacity for involvement in belief.

A series of subordinate questions and manifestations of doubt arising from the poet's central dilemma, often conflicting with each other, and forming a web of various tensions, similarly occurs in poem after poem. It is Arnold's method of securing animation and direction for the individual parts of a poem, but of so balancing them as a total that the entire poem becomes static, and thus mirrors its maker's own lack of commitment. The result is a complete lack of Romantic assertiveness, often with an affecting pathos. This technique of various individual tensions working to create a static whole is basic to Arnold; it occurs frequently; it is simple to illustrate. The two situations metaphorized in *The Forsaken Merman*—that of the individual who is cut off from faith and thus harmony, and that of one who feels faith intermittently or partially but never wholly—are similarly woven into *A Summer Night*, where they are treated as alternatives between withdrawal and involvement. But Arnold's conflict is not so much that dilemma in itself as the fear of risking total commitment *at all*—to either:

> And the calm moonlight seems to say:
> *Hast thou then still the old unquiet breast,*
> *Which neither deadens into rest,*
> *Nor ever feels the fiery glow*
> *That whirls the spirit from itself away,*
> *But fluctuates to and fro,*
> *Never by passion quite possessed*
> *And never quite benumbed by the world's sway?—*
> And I, I know not if to pray
> Still to be what I am, or yield and be
> Like all the other men I see.

Arnold develops the alternatives he senses, in the rest of the poem, to those logical conclusions he most fears. Total withdrawal from thought is a living death which he symbolizes, on this occasion, much as Carlyle and Ruskin would have done, in the spiritless mechanism of the industrial life he saw around him:

> With heads bent o'er their toil, they languidly
> Their lives to some unmeaning taskwork give,
> Dreaming of naught beyond their prison-wall.

But the alternative, the search for commitment, invites inevitable loss of belief, which Arnold develops, as Cowper had in *The Castaway*, as shipwreck. The central dilemma, and most of all the pain of attempted commitment to either of its alternatives, is developed throughout the poem:

> Is there no life, but these alone?
> Madman or slave, must man be one?

The same pattern of unresolved forces in tension is echoed by the cosmic background Arnold gives the poem. The heavens are unmoved, remote from human conflicts: "so calm . . . so great . . . untroubled and unpassionate," but at the same time they are "a world above man's head," to suggest to him, agonizingly and ultimately mockingly, his own fleeting and intermittent belief in the possibility, at least, of finding fulfillment:

> to let him see
> How boundless might his soul's horizons be,
> How vast, yet of what clear transparency.

A similar though more simple tension informs the poem *Self-Dependence*. On the one side the poem records what is clearly Arnold's Romantic longing:

'Ah, once more,' I cried, 'ye stars, ye waters,
On my heart your mighty charm renew;
Still, still let me, as I gaze upon you,
Feel my soul becoming vast like you!'

and on the other the stars, uncommitted, uninvolved, "self-poised . . . bounded by themselves" suggest another way to think and live —"in their own tasks all their powers pouring." It is true to say that almost all Arnold's major poetry rests considerably on the dichotomy he expresses in these poems, and in *Stanzas in Memory of the Author of "Obermann":*

Ah! two desires toss about
The poet's feverish blood.
One drives him to the world without,
And one to solitude.

In *Thyrsis* we find the same tensions expressed in different terms. In the bulk of the poem Arnold blends several themes: elegiac mourning for Clough; memories of their youth and of the past in general; hope for his own future belief; natural beauty. In somewhat the Romantic manner, he symbolizes the totality of these as brightness (light). As the sunset fades, and with it the prospect of belief in the complex meaning Arnold has given its bright beauty, the implication is that all—the hope for everything positive involved in the poem—is as transient and meaningless as the passing of Clough, and the only ultimate reality is the total darkness of night. But this would result in the poem's being given a kind of commitment to total pessimism, and Arnold does not let that fully develop; before the symbolic darkness drowns all, he has located the tree which once meant, for himself and Clough, the possibility of individual faith and achievement. But, again, it is, in its turn, not unqualified faith Arnold finds in the tree. That full, bright light which, in poem after poem, symbolizes faith fades even as he makes his rediscovery, and the light which replaces it is of a partial kind fitting the poet's special mixture of doubt shot through with half-defiant, faintly intuited hope:

Eve lets down her veil,
The white fog creeps from bush to bush about,
The west unflushes, the high stars grow bright,
And in the scattered farms the lights come out.

It is enough, for Arnold, to put Clough in a kind of classical-artistic heaven (ll. 172–190), but it also leaves Arnold himself unfulfilled, though with both a limitation and a hope:

I cannot reach the signal-tree tonight,
Yet, happy omen, hail!

A new tension has taken over: faith is possible (Clough is envisaged by Arnold as having found final acceptance), but the speaker himself is shut out from it. In short, the poet is using shifts in kind of light to represent his own abrupt shifts of feeling, and when he is finally left in the concrete world, outside the fulfillment he accords Clough, it is with little but an isolated determination not to despair. It is true that the imagined closing echo of Clough's voice whispers optimistic reassurance to the speaker, but as so often in Arnold's poetry, the optimism is disjointed and does not follow from what has gone on in the poem.

This characteristic progress of Arnold's mental attitudes as the poem proceeds rests upon a technique of retrogressive development; each forward step suggests at first that it is considerable and definite, but each is followed by a qualification or counter-check. The poem begins, for example, with a general lament on the changes time has wrought in the Oxford countryside: then, as the light of the sunset floods the city and brings out its beauty, the poet drops his lament and moves into lyric appraisal:

leafless, yet soft as spring,
The tender purple spray on copse and briars!
And that sweet city with her dreaming spires,
She needs not June for beauty's heightening,
Lovely all times she lies, lovely tonight!

Arnold's progress to this point seems to have moved towards that gentle mood in which consciousness drifts away from the actual world into imaginative animation—towards the sort of aesthetic experience reminiscent of the Romantic. But, just as the light of the sunset introduced it, it is sharply checked, in the lines which immediately follow, by images of darkness:

> Only, methinks, some loss of habit's power
> Befalls me wandering through this upland dim;
> Once passed I blindfold here, at any hour;
> Now seldom come I, since I came with him.

This pattern of assertion—or near-assertion, more often—and counter-check is frequently marked by considerable subtlety. The assertive lyrical lines on early summer (ll. 51 ff.) are checked by the sudden storm and the "cuckoo's parting cry":

> *The bloom is gone, and with the bloom go I!*

This in turn is counter-checked by the protest of the poet himself, with another assertively lyrical passage on the color, scent and beauty of full summer to come:

> Too quick despairer, wherefore wilt thou go?
> Soon will the high midsummer pomps come on,
> Soon will the musk carnations break and swell,
> Soon shall we have gold-dusted snapdragon,
> Sweet William with his homely cottage-smell,
> And stocks in fragrant blow;

but the very evocation of the summer's beauty is then given a fading, stilled quality which accords more with the cuckoo's cry than with the full richness of summer the poet envisages:

> Roses that down the alleys shine afar,
> And open, jasmine-muffled lattices,
> And groups under the dreaming garden trees,
> And the full moon, and the white evening star.

And Arnold goes on to say that although spring and cuckoos pass, they will return another year; yet, he goes on, Thyrsis will not—and by this elaborately circuitous route the poet is led back to his lament on time and change.

These methods of holding alternatives in tension, and of apparently moving the poem "forward" by means of a series of partially retrogressive checks followed in their turn by counter-checks, are basic to a great mass of Arnold's work, and I have tried here merely to suggest their nature. But even in what I have said so far, it appears that in a poem like *Thyrsis* matters other than developments of idea and attitude loom very large indeed. The simple but eloquent symbolism —the tree, the use of various kinds of light—I should like to put aside for the moment pending discussion of Arnold's general use of symbols as such. In his use of light, however, in the way in which his whole view of nature will often flush into an intensity, and in certain features I have mentioned in dealing with *The Forsaken Merman,* Arnold moves close to the Romantics, and I want now to put forward certain comparative considerations of that relationship.[5]

3. Arnold and the Romantics 🙌 In a number of places in his work, Arnold seems to display an urge towards transcendence which is sometimes (compared to his usual practice) oddly unqualified: *The Buried Life,* for example, presents "an unspeakable desire/ After the knowledge of our buried life;/ A thirst. . . . " It is

> A longing to inquire
> Into the mystery of this heart which beats
> So wild, so deep in us—to know
> Whence our lives come and where they go . . . .

Again, in *Self-Dependence,* the Romantic longing for unity similarly appears. In that poem, however, Arnold does place, as counter against the yearning for transcendence, the "self-poised," unfevered self-sufficiency of the stars. In general, he retains the Romantic sense of solitariness, but it is only felt in the force of his desires and the realization of his alienation, and not, as with the Romantics, as a condition ultimately leading to fulfillment. Thought and affection in isolation had often led, for the Romantic poets, to that kind of imaginative experience they valued above all else—that of Coleridge, for instance, in *This Lime-Tree Bower.* Thought and affection, or thought and desire, simply lead Arnold to realize and lament his own isolation, which has become a negative thing, and the only relief is for thought to cease.

A similar retreat from the Romantic attitude is seen in the use of poetic form. To the Romantics, poetry was, as I have said, a stuff, a part of, an echo of, the largest religious reality. It flows, it overflows, and sometimes it dries up. Hence the Romantics write fragments, exploit the freedom of the ode, and generally bend the forms of poetry to the free unpredictability of the experience behind it. But for the Victorian poets form becomes again very much the cistern which contains. They tend towards the carefully completed and symmetrical poem, and particularly towards forms based on previous authority. It is significant that in considering the two great long personal poems of the two eras, we should put beside the quiet places and surges of the flowing *Prelude* a poem like *In Memoriam,* itself symmetrically architected from complete lyrics. Arnold also is characteristic in his return to complete and traditional form and to previous authority, and the tradition he turns to, in *Empedocles on Etna* and other poems, is classical as well as English.

There is abundant evidence that Arnold was directly affected as a poet by his reading of Romantic writings, though as a critic he hardly understood the essential basis on which they rested. To take a simple example, the Carlylean tone and phrasing are steady elements of *Empedocles on Etna:*

> Mind is the spell which governs earth and heaven.
> Man has a mind with which to plan his safety;
> Know that, and help thyself!
> > *(Act I, Sc. ii, 27–29)*

> Be neither saint nor sophist-led, but be a man!
> > *(Act I, Sc. ii, 136)*

> Thou hast no *right* to bliss,
> No title from the gods to welfare and repose;
> > *(Act I, Sc. ii, 160–161)*

Arnold even uses Carlyle's exact phrase in *Sartor Resartus,*[6] putting it into the mouth of Empedocles,

> Man's measures cannot mete *the immeasurable All.*
> > *(Act I, Sc. ii, 341)*

However, what is remarkable about these phrases is not so much their direct similarity to Carlyle's, as the tremendous difference between their context and Carlyle's. The last sentence, "Man's measures cannot mete the immeasurable All," is a clear example. Carlyle had used the like aphorism in *Sartor Resartus* as positive religious affirmation. Arnold, in echoing it, is not concerned at all with religious affirmation, but with presenting the phrase negatively as merely antiscientific, as one of a number of negative contentions showing the inevitable frustration of belief, whether it turn to science or somewhere else. His stress is on the "cannot." A comparable difference, of course, exists between the cuckoo's song in *Thyrsis* and Keats' nightingale.

The first merely gathers up and symbolizes in its parting cry the inevitable fall of the combined elements the speaker prizes—Clough, youthful faith and hope, beauty and brightness. The nightingale's song provokes, and Keats' poem records, both a personal imaginative revelation and an assertion of its meaning, despite the return to the untransformed world. Arnold's bird merely records and symbolizes pain at the ephemeral order of life in the finite world which the poet never leaves. Keats' ode in part deals with this too, but beside it, and not necessarily overriding it, is his assertion of the authority of his vision. What optimism there is in Keats' poem is deeply involved with his faith in his own spiritual and aesthetic experience, and that is not destroyed by his pathetic dazed return to worldly reality. The final note of optimism in *Thyrsis*, however, has the impact only of disconnected afterthought.

Indeed, while Romantic poetry deals continually with communion and alienation, the first carries the emphasis, while alienation is dealt with only secondarily as its obverse. Arnold generally reverses that order, so that it is the possibility of human communion which becomes the afterthought (see *The Buried Life*, ll. 16–23).

While there is a constant dualism in Arnold's work, it is neither of the same scope nor kind as Romantic dualism. The latter connects what are seen as finite with infinite realities. The range of Arnold's dualism remains completely within the bounds of the temporal, and its utmost limit is shown by those places in his work where his imagination is momentarily caught by story or situation, for example, the merman's home in the sea, or the similes in *Sohrab and Rustum*. It is imagination compellingly transmitted through the verse, but it is of a worldly kind. Beside the climactic vision of *The Prelude* it appears as worldly escape; it exists for its own sake, and there is nothing beyond it. It is essentially a tasteful mature version of Keats' early daydreaming, though often made relevant to a story.

The difference does not turn merely on matters of technical ability or taste; in the first Arnold's ability is usually not significantly inferior to Keats', and he is never guilty of Keats' kind of banality. The difference lies in the kinds of emotional power produced by the widely contrasting scope of vision between Arnold and the Romantic poets.

The precise effects of this decline in vision upon Arnold's work may be illustrated. His poem *The Scholar-Gipsy*, for example, has, as frame to the evocation of the Gipsy himself, a quasi-Romantic, step-by-step ordering of the speaker's imaginings. The opening stanza of the poem sets up, first, an impression of the Oxfordshire countryside as active, deeply alive in its sounds and growth; this is followed, in Arnold's familiar manner of immediate contrast, by a portrait of the landscape in the quietness of night:

> But when the fields are still,
> And the tired men and dogs all gone to rest,
> And only the white sheep are sometimes seen
> Cross and recross the strips of moon-blanched green . . . .

This pattern of withdrawal from activity to quietness is followed by the poet's presenting himself musing in a still upland amid the sounds of a summer's day. In his solitude, the world of nature blooms and almost literally reaches out to the poet, moving his imagination:

> Through the thick corn the scarlet poppies peep,
> And round green roots and yellowing stalks I see
> Pale pink convolvolus in tendrils creep;
> And air-swept lindens yield
> Their scent, and rustle down their perfumed showers
> Of bloom on the bent grass where I am laid;
> And bower me from the August sun with shade;
> And the eye travels down to Oxford's towers.

> And near me on the grass lies Glanvil's book—
> Come, let me read the oft-read tale again!

What has happened thus far in the poem is not essentially different from what happens to Coleridge at the start of *The Eolian Harp* and *This Lime Tree Bower*. But what goes on to fill Arnold's imagination in his poem is not the Romantic experience with its consequent sense of certainty, but *an imaginative re-creation of someone else, living two hundred years before, who did have that kind of certainty*—the Gipsy, and the possibility of fulfillment shifts an entire dimension away from its place in Romantic imaginative experience. And when the figure of the Gipsy fades away, the poem turns into an extended lecture on the shortcomings of the Victorian world, the frustrations of which do not permit prolonged contact with the Gipsy's kind of assertion, not even vicariously.

If it is true that Arnold could sustain belief in neither the Christian nor (as I regard it) the Romantic religion, the vacillations in his critical views of the Romantic poets become understandable. He was drawn to them and moved by them, as his eloquent tributes to Wordsworth in particular show, but he was also disappointed in their lack of relevance to life as he saw it, and above all he shows no evidence of having understood the spiritual and imaginative motivations of their work—least of all in its religious aspect. He felt sympathy for them, but not empathy. He accuses the body of Romantic work of lacking "materials and a basis; *a thorough interpretation of the world,*" he goes on, "*was necessarily denied to it*" (my italics).[7] A thorough interpretation of the world! Arnold does not say a false interpretation, or the unacceptable one that modern readers seem to find; he goes out of his way to suggest that it was just that quality of dedication to an integrated world-view—of seeing life as whole—which the Romantics lack, but which, as I have tried to show, is one thing they unquestionably have. Here, what is finally wrong with Arnold's assessment of Romantic poetry is that it fails to see the Romantics as religious and philosophical poets, and it does so not because they do not have a thorough philosophical and religious interpretation of the world, but because they hold one which Arnold is so far from sharing that he does not see its existence.

As Lionel Trilling and others have sensibly pointed out, Arnold's famous tribute to Sophocles, "Who saw life steadily, and saw it whole," does not mean that Sophocles' vision of life included its every aspect, but that his vision of it was integrated, complete.[8] And this, despite the fallings off—the glory that passes from the earth, the sceptical unrest of Byron, the Coleridge of *Dejection,* and so much more—this kind of vision was the most constructive achievement of the Romantics. The achievement of youth it undoubtedly was, and while the later career of Wordsworth, the sad diminution of the ageing Coleridge, and the shrinking of Carlyle into political propagandist may remind us of its ephemeral nature, they change neither the reality of its existence nor the quality of its assertion. That the Romantic achievement was less than apparent to Arnold was not primarily due to imperfections, distractions and diminuendo in Romantic work itself. For Arnold, as for his contemporaries Browning and Tennyson, a thoroughly integrated view of life was no longer a real possibility. The time for that had gone, and it has not since returned for their successors.

Arnold himself never sees nature, in fact, as material and catalyst for vision in the Romantic sense, but often as an inexorable, enigmatic and painfully beautiful background against which human isolation looms as more deeply pathetic. If Wordsworth's central symbol had been the mountain, Arnold's is consistently the island—or rather the strait of separation—or the beach between two kinds of world (meaning world-view), and all suffused by a tragic and deceptive beauty. *Dover Beach* is in some ways Arnold's most characteristic poem. It is too well-known to need detailed treatment, except to note how it depends heavily on the poet's manipulation of his favorite symbol, light. The distinct kinds of light in the poem transmit the emotional content of the varied ways in which Arnold sees the world. The signal of the lighthouse across the Channel is a kind of light (a kind of faith) which gives orientation but is seen only ephemerally. It is akin to the bright girdle of faith which once (ll. 21–23) enwrapped the earth steadily. But between that and the realities of the darkling plain of Arnold's Victorian world is the moonlit beach— "Where the sea meets the moon-blanched land"—a metaphorical statement of Arnold's view of a kind of no-man's land of nature, given (in the light of a moon which has itself drawn back the tide of faith) a surface of deceptive and illusive beauty.

In Arnold's longer poems, most clearly in *Empedocles on Etna* and *Sohrab and Rustum,* his view of natural beauty shifts and turns like a shuttle weaving the fabric of the poem. In one place he will present it as a silent, eloquent rebuke to the realities of the human dilemma; in another it will become consolation; in yet another it will be invitation to escape. In brief moments it seems on the verge of suggesting entrance to a higher world of greater certainty, but Arnold's withdrawal at such times is immediate.

His entire view of natural scenery almost always has this ambivalence. To the Scholar-Gipsy, the Oxfordshire countryside has almost Romantic intensity: it is his instinctive language (the wordless handing of the flowers to the village maidens), and he is himself, by means of glimpses of him which follow the progress of the seasons, presented as part of the round of nature. He is seen as so integral to it that his distinction as human, apart from the world of wild things, is blurred over:

> The blackbird, picking food,
> Sees thee, nor stops his meal, nor fears at all;
> So often has he known thee past him stray,
> Rapt, twirling in thy hand a withered spray . . . .

But the poet shares none of this: to him nature is an escape, a peaceful refuge from the world, and a stimulus to the kind of reverie which seems to bring the Gipsy back to life. Similarly, throughout *Empedocles on Etna* the natural world is used as a background, a stage on which the life-drama is played, and through its beauty it intensifies both joy and pain, stressing the enigma of existence. Beyond this, Arnold is also able to use his nature-descriptions to imply comments through a careful parallelism. The scenery surrounding Etna is sung of by Callicles as rich, verdant and lush (Act I, Sc. ii, 36–51). Then, inevitably, he qualifies this:

> but glade,
> And stream, and sward, and chestnut trees,
> End here; Etna beyond, in the broad glare
> Of the hot noon, without a shade,
> Slope behind slope, up to the peak, lies bare;
> The peak, round which the white clouds play.

Callicles then sings of Chiron and Achilles, of the Greek world and cosmology (ll. 57–76). The juxtaposition of this passage against that which notes the change in the scenery implies that, in the years since faith in the Greek cosmology was held, succeeding faiths have also become empty and bare—the same change the scenery has undergone in the song.

In treating the natural world, Arnold often suggests that however beautiful it may be, it can only offer even its maximum—a consolatory sort of semi-fulfillment—to those able to approach it paradoxically through a withdrawal: for others it can only be a sad, ephemeral reminder of their own mortality. The Scholar-Gipsy, by means of his literal withdrawal from mundane ambition, finds immersion in the natural world, and thus purpose, singleness of aim, fulfillment and even a kind of immortality. In his turn, the poet, as has been indicated, gains only the secondary vision—of the Gipsy himself—through a withdrawal to remote nature, and he gains, if not that personal commitment which is out of the question for him, at least enough understanding to spark his indictment of his own era. At times the fulfilled view of the Gipsy seems to use that of the unfulfilled poet as a species of sub-plot, as the two come together:

> But, 'mid their drink and clatter, he would fly.
> And I myself seem half to know thy looks,
> And put the shepherds, wanderer! on thy trace.

The idea that somehow truth might be reached through a shy instinctive withdrawal from the sphere of fact and action occurs elsewhere in Arnold's work. It is the motif of the controversial simile of the Tyrian trader which closes *The Scholar-Gipsy*.

The theme of the simile is not simple escape as such. It carries the half-promise of fulfillment; and seen beside the fruits of the Gipsy's withdrawal and the lesser ones of the poet's, the simile appears less disjointed from the meaning of the entire poem than has sometimes been said. This kind of shy, half-realized withdrawal, with its half-promise of fulfillment, echoes Keatsian negative capability. The echo, however, falls within a paler context of Arnoldian non-commitment, and its character is reduced accordingly.

Arnold's treatment of time bears a corresponding relationship to that of the Romantics. To them, time had appeared uniformly as the shell, at the limit of the sensed world, which transcendence could break. To Arnold, it is insurmountable, implacable: it means simply transitoriness, and therefore inevitable pain. The small changes the years bring, however gradual, constantly threaten the ultimate and total loss of all. (Arnold's verse is full of sad revisitings like those in *Thyrsis* and *A Summer Night*.) It so happens that in Rustum's sad remembrance of his lost youth Arnold comes close to a phrase of Wordsworth's describing his own, "its aching joys . . . And all its dizzy raptures." [9] Arnold has:

> tears gathered in his eyes,
> For he remembered his own early youth,
> And all its bounding rapture.

The slight similarity of phrase is incidental, the difference in connotation vital. Wordsworth was stressing what had replaced the animal joys of youth, and he was doing so in describing the various stages of a system of apprehending reality. Arnold merely creates (with more complex technical resources) a remote, pervasive lyric sadness at the passing of time (*Sohrab and Rustum*, ll. 620–631).

Aesthetic experience is likewise treated by Arnold within comparably narrow scope. The relationship between beauty and the imagination is quite different from that which the Romantics saw. The very order and calm of beauty is to Arnold neither entrance to nor exit from deeper experience, but an ironic goad to the poet's lack of internal calm:

> That night was far more fair—
> But the same restless pacings to and fro,

And the same vainly throbbing heart was there,
And the same bright, calm moon.
                                    (*A Summer Night*)

And when at certain moments the quiet lyric surge in Arnold seems
on the point of discovering a level of greater certainty, a deep sense
of its unattainability sweeps forlornly over him: of the islands in *To
Marguerite,* he writes:

> But when the moon their hollows lights,
> And they are swept by balms of spring,
> And in their glens, on starry nights,
> The nightingales divinely sing;
> And lovely notes, from shore to shore,
> Across the sounds and channels pour—
>
> Oh! then a longing like despair
> Is to their farthest caverns sent;
> For surely once, they feel, we were
> Parts of a single continent!

These strained, careful, multi-directional qualifications and
counterpoints in Arnold's work reflect a mind permanently withheld
from dedication, either positive or negative, and while in Tennyson
and in *The City of Dreadful Night* there is passion, in Arnold there
is nothing beyond the bounds of pathos. Arnold seemed to realize the
effects of his philosophical suspension of belief on his work, for there
are signs that he attempts compensation—to give his poetry certain
kinds of positive force, without putting into it a spiritual commitment
he did not feel. Usually his ways of doing this are elementary and
highly practical—his critical insistence on the supreme importance of
"an excellent action," for instance. There is his care with topography
in *Thyrsis* and *The Scholar-Gipsy;* the visual sharpness of his observation:

> when hay time's here
> In June, and many a scythe in sunshine flames,

the care and detail of flowers and colors, and the three-dimensional
effect of showing exactly what the eye sees, in depth, from places like
the heights above Oxford at the beginning of *The Scholar-Gipsy.*
Sometimes this compensatory solidity is given by traditional forms or
suggestions of them—dramatic in *Empedocles on Etna,* elegiac in

Thyrsis, Greek epic in *Sohrab and Rustum.* And sometimes the structure of a poem will be positively mathematical in its symmetry, like that of *The Scholar-Gipsy.* The first two verses form a frame, in which, as has been observed already, contrasting scenes and moods of nature are used to initiate the poet's withdrawal to a mood of daydream. Then follows, for precisely one hundred lines (31–130), the story from Glanvil's book and the poet's imaginative evocation of the Scholar haunting the countryside. The next line ("But what, I dream! Two hundred years are flown") returns the poet to reality and begins a further hundred lines—again, precisely that (131–230) —presenting the envied lesson the Scholar's single-mindedness can teach Victorian doubt and fragmentation of effort. Finally, there are the two closing verses, corresponding to the frame at the start, which form the simile of the Tyrian trader. "The necessity of accurate construction," so "vitally important" for the writer and the "one point," Arnold tells us in the 1853 *Preface,* "on which the Greeks were rigidly exacting," is well illustrated by *The Scholar-Gipsy.*

4. THE SOLID FOOTING: A QUALIFICATION ☙ There are two individual and sharply contrasting poems, *Empedocles on Etna* and *Sohrab and Rustum,* which make special contributions towards revealing Arnold's cast of mind and his relationship to the poets preceding him. The first, *Empedocles on Etna,* would appear, of all Arnold's work, to be most obviously relevant to these questions, since it is fundamentally a dramatizing of the philosophical speculations of one who has lived into an age which confuses and alienates him. There has been a good deal of discussion of the exact relationship of Arnold himself to the figure of Empedocles.[10] To what extent are the speeches of Empedocles the direct thoughts of his creator? Certainly it would be misleading to attribute each statement of Empedocles in the poem as literally a part of Arnold's own creed. It would, moreover, be remarkably confusing, for the long lyric reverie of Empedocles is itself the logical and overt conclusion of all those conflicting philosophical tensions which have been observed elsewhere in Arnold's poetry. But the totality, the gloomy philosophical still-point at the heart of the poem, is Arnold's emblem of the thinking Victorian mind, fashioned through his own, and he says as much in the 1853 *Preface.* He points out that his intention had been "to delineate the

feelings of one of the last of the Greek religious philosophers . . . having survived his fellows, living on into a time when the habits of Greek thought and feeling had begun fast to change, character to dwindle, the influence of the Sophists to prevail," and says that in his opinion he had been successful in doing this. He goes on to discuss the question of the poem's relationship to his own day:

> Into the feelings of a man so situated there entered much that we are accustomed to consider as exclusively modern; how much the fragments of Empedocles himself which remain to us are sufficient at least to indicate. What those who are familiar only with the great monuments of early Greek genius suppose to be its exclusive characteristics, have disappeared; the calm, the cheerfulness, the disinterested objectivity have disappeared; the dialogue of the mind with itself has commenced; modern problems have presented themselves; we hear already the doubts, we witness the discouragement, of Hamlet and of Faust.

Why, then, was the poem withdrawn from the 1853 edition? Because, in a word, it was not sufficiently positive; it was too passive; it was not inspiriting; and Arnold's reasons for these conclusions, when extended, form a revealing self-judgment of his poetry as a whole. *Empedocles*, he implies, is *not interesting*; it is the sort of poetry which does not add to our knowledge, "a representation which is general, indeterminate, and faint, instead of being particular, precise, and firm." [11] He goes on:

> What then are the situations, from the representation of which, though accurate, no poetical enjoyment can be derived? They are those in which the suffering finds no vent in action; in which a continuous state of mental distress is prolonged, unrelieved by incident, hope, or resistance; in which there is everything to be endured, nothing to be done. In such situations there is inevitably something morbid, in the description of them something monotonous. When they occur in actual life, they are painful, not tragic; the representation of them in poetry is painful also.
>
> To this class of situations, poetically faulty as it appears to me, that of Empedocles, as I have endeavoured to represent him, belongs.

It may be argued that Empedocles' suicide is presented in the poem as a positive, assertive action—a point I shall return to later—and that the final note of the poem is thus one of calm fulfillment.

But like all Arnold's conclusions which appear to border on peace and optimism, it is essentially separate from what has preceded it in the poem. It shares the curious disjointment of the conclusions to *A Summer Night* and *Thyrsis* and *Rugby Chapel*. And Arnold's critical case against the whole poem does in fact hold good. The poem *is* monotonous and unbalanced; the "state of mental distress" *is not* countered by "action," or by "incident, hope, or resistance." The criticism is important for Arnold's view of how far his work should go in offering the Victorian reader the guidance he sought. A poem can be, should be, animated, enlivened by hope and resistance to its universal background of the human condition, but—and Arnold's omission here is eloquent in its implications—it cannot be expected to assert with vision, or real force, or passion, more than a view of that condition as essentially finite.

In the classical theme of the poem Arnold finds less the "solid footing" he speaks of in the *Preface* than a stage-setting providing a mood for the poem. The remoteness of ancient associations combines with Arnold's familiar use of natural scenery: this is presented as a way of sensuous escape, alternated with moods of pain at the incongruity of its beauty as background to the human situation.

The initial impetus of the poem is to consider the situation stated at the start of Empedocles' long lyric monologue in Act I, Scene ii; it appears at first a memorable definition of Romantic deprivation:

> Hither and thither spins
> The wind-borne, mirroring soul,
> A thousand glimpses wins,
> And never sees a whole;
> Looks once, and drives elsewhere, and leaves its last employ.

Empedocles' long speech which follows is an introspective survey of available philosophical positions, seen negatively. The shadow of *King Lear* seems to be behind parts of the diatribe: "The gods laugh in their sleeve/ To watch man doubt and fear." And the human predicament is best borne by an equivalent of Edgar's "Ripeness is all":

> What were the wise man's plan?—
> Through this sharp, toil-set life,
> To work as best he can,
> And win what's won by strife.

THE SOLID FOOTING: A QUALIFICATION 99

Edmund's sneering at human inclination to see destiny, not humanity itself, as responsible is reflected in:

> We, peopling the void air,
> Make gods to whom to impute
> The ills we ought to bear;
> With God and Fate to rail at, suffering easily.

The poem is a welter of conflicting positions; the unremitting cyni-
cism in the last quotation is itself countered earlier in the speech by
the assertion of a faith in human potentiality, leading to the middle
road, and expressed in Carlylean rhetoric:

> The sophist sneers: Fool, take
> Thy pleasure, right or wrong!
> The pious wail: Forsake
> A world these sophists throng!—
> Be neither saint nor sophist-led, but be a man!

and, as we have seen, the hand of Carlyle is scattered throughout,
with the differences in meaning already noted.

Individually each position is familiar, but it is given the brittle
starkness of suppressed eloquence largely through the verse form Arnold chooses, which is quite similar to what Fitzgerald was to exploit
with such success in the *Rubaiyat* seven years later. Thus Arnold:

> These hundred doctors try
> To preach thee to their school.
> We have the truth! they cry;
> And yet their oracle,
> Trumpet it as they will, is but the same as thine.

The similarity underlines a sensitivity on Arnold's part to the mood
and interests of his time. Again, a shadowy but definite awareness of
the implications of evolution, at a time when the subject was much
in the intellectual air but some seven years before the publication of
The Origin of Species, underlies parts of the poem:

> Other existences there are, that clash with ours.

> Like us, the lightning-fires
> Love to have scope and play;

> The stream, like us desires
> An unimpeded way;
> Like us, the Libyan wind delights to roam at large.

But the total effect of these fragmentary positions and counter-positions is static—even more so than usual for Arnold—a spiritless marshalling of philosophical possibilities, concluding with an anti-climactic stoicism itself halting and doubtful:

> Fools! That so often here
> Happiness mocked our prayer,
> I think, might make us fear
> A like event elsewhere;
> Make us, not fly to dreams, but moderate desire.

> And yet, for those who know
> Themselves, who wisely take
> Their way through life, and bow
> To what they cannot break,
> Why should I say that life need yield but *moderate* bliss?

And the final note of Empedocles' speech (before escape is sought in the lyrical description of scenery by Callicles the harpist, a kind of personified remnant of Romantic outlook) is an exactly-balanced still-point:

> I say: Fear not! Life still
> Leaves human effort scope.
> But, since life teems with ill,
> Nurse no extravagant hope;
> Because thou must not dream, thou need'st not then despair!

In short, where we might expect relatively animated self-revelation from Arnold, considering the directness of the poem's bearing on the Victorian situation, there is only a kind of detachment, as if the mind were working out an intellectual exercise entirely without personal involvement. The trouble lies in the theme of the poem. Empedocles is too close to Arnold's own spiritual state to act as a vehicle through which the poet's internal struggles can be given artistic form. He is neither a focus nor a catalyst for Arnold's creativity. He is not a character revealing an inner self—and simultaneously that of Arnold—in response to any developing situation. He is merely—

whatever his relationship to the poet—a disembodied and passive voice, with no artistic force to catch the imagination and make it real, which vents a complex series of intellectual doubts, and which is given the name Empedocles and placed in an ultra-formal and chilly convention of drama. For example, when Empedocles is drawn into consideration of what may lie beyond this life, he can only suggest a more troubled reincarnation of the same thing, "the sad probation all again" (Act II, 367–8). "Sad probation," or trial—but for what? For a kind of dimly-envisaged and vaguely-put image of true fulfillment, coming from no stated or even hinted experience of the poet's, but, like some tired Romantic ghost, emerging from time to time in the surrounding context,

> [. . . Mind and thought will]
> . . . keep us prisoners of our consciousness,
> And never let us clasp and feel the All
> But through their forms, and modes, and stifling veils.
> *(Act II, 352–354)*

> To see if we will poise our life at last,
> To see if we will now at last be true
> To our own only true, deep-buried selves,
> Being one with which we are at one with the whole world.
> *(Act II, 369–372)*

But the failure of such passing hopes and fancies is complete, unremitting:

> And we shall feel our powers of effort flag,
> And rally them for one last fight, and fail;
> And we shall sink in the impossible strife,
> And be astray for ever.
> *(Act II, 387–390)*

Yet even so gloomy a view is not presented as Arnold's emotional conviction, but as abstract argument. The thousand glimpses of that whole which Empedocles is never to see is not a case of Romantic deprivation; of a vision, once glimpsed, falling away. Romantic glimpses of fulfillment, brief as they were, had been the culmination of a complex series of imaginative steps. Such glimpses had been painful when they withdrew, as is plain in poems like *Dejection* or *Endymion,* precisely because of the force of the affirmation they had led to. But the glimpses Arnold speaks of are quite different; they are brief, isolated fancies of a whole that might have been; he has no reason to assert belief in the possibility. Arnold's "whole" is an abstract counter in the cause of argument, and Empedocles' great speech before his leap of suicide is predicated specifically (as the last quotation shows) on the impossibility of Romantic commitment.

The suicide itself, it is true, is surrounded by an atmosphere of affirmation, but this relates not at all to any wish to eternalize aesthetic experience as in the *Ode to a Nightingale,* but exactly the reverse. Life is to be ended at the point of bewildered pessimism because that is all, ultimately, that it offers, and in life the thoughts of vision and nobility can only mock. *Empedocles on Etna* is the intellectual statement, given the outer forms of poetry, of a man who never lost faith because he never really had it.

While possessing intermittent flashes of awareness of Romantic possibilities (apparently through a kind of intuitive fancy both isolated and inexplicable), but without Romantic experience and hence commitment, Arnold's poetry functions, in much the same way that science does, by mounting a range of speculative and introspective thought upon a basis of sense-observation. Within this range, *Empedocles on Etna* forms the most arid extreme: at the other extreme is a poem also worth considering in detail. *Sohrab and Rustum* is a poem different in kind from any other Arnold ever wrote, and presents a unique and important, though undeveloped, side of his work. In the 1853 *Preface* he had, we may recall, criticized *Empedocles on Etna* as painful but not tragic. I doubt if Arnold's poetry ever has the impact of tragedy: it lacks that human assertion of the defeated individual self against fate at the height of suffering—"I am Antony yet!" "I am Duchess of Malfi still!"—but *Sohrab and Rustum* is Arnold's closest approach to tragedy as opposed to pathos. It is animated throughout, and at times assertive. Arnold himself considered it the best poem he ever wrote—an opinion widely at variance with many critical estimates. I must say I agree with Arnold's minority opinion: if the business of poetry is to create an integrated emotional whole which emanates authority, the poem is his best.

It stands by itself because, for one thing, Arnold is drawn out of his introspective and passive self-retreat by the theme. It is the "great action" he advocated in his criticism. The story of the mighty father and the young valiant son, estranged by human affairs and ignorant of each other's identity, meeting in fated opposition, is a fitting symbol of the ironic cruelty of life as Arnold often saw it. The plot sustains interest throughout its series of chronological episodes; and since it has such force, the representation it offers of Arnold's own spiritual outlook becomes secondary—that is, subordinate to the narrative—and not, as in almost all his other poems, primary. Here is Arnold, certainly, writing of his own restlessness, but first he is writing of Sohrab within the frame of the story:

> Sohrab alone, he slept not; all night long
> He had lain wakeful, tossing on his bed.

And Arnold's own search is reflected in that of Sohrab for his father, which similarly remains a convincing condition of the train of events. The entire poem, also, is "an episode," that is, it is given an understood context, and is to be thought of as a fragment of a Homeric whole (the first two lines, in fact, begin with "And"). It is dual—an energetic story and, not too obviously (to transpose Arnold's phrase), an allegory of a state of mind, whereas the bulk of his work is primarily the latter. The protagonists of his poems usually, with the thinnest disguise, represent his own urges, reactions, and positions. In a deeper sense than the literal, Arnold is the poet surveying the past in *Thyrsis*; he is the estranged merman and the alienated Empedocles. The faint vision of fulfilled escape which the Scholar-Gipsy metaphorizes is Arnold's own. But in *Sohrab and Rustum* it is only the armies (and the reader) who are onlookers of the human drama of universal tragedy. The protagonists themselves are immersed in action.

The Greekness of the poem, the "solid footing" which Arnold said he found only among the ancients, is equally integrated. The view of fate is both deterministic, "The doom which at my birth was written down," and uncertain:

> For we are all, like swimmers in the sea,
> Poised on the top of a huge wave of fate,
> Which hangs uncertain to which side to fall.

There is sustained irony, as in Rustum's responding to Sohrab's fame with "would that I myself had such a son," and "come to Iran/ And be as my son to me." It is an irony sustained by Sohrab as he dies, saying,

> Surely the news will one day reach his ear,
> Reach Rustum, where he sits, and tarries long,
> Somewhere, I know not where, but far from here.

There are echoes of Greek myth: Rustum as Achilles:

> aloof he sits
> And sullen, and has pitched his tents apart

or Rustum despoiling himself (ll. 698–705).

The poem is shot through with Arnoldian tensions, but they are externalized dramatically and worked into the fiber of the narrative. The scene of the action, the world of meandering river, of storm and wind, sun and clouds, varied and inexorable, is the human setting. Glimpsed beyond this is the world of Zal and Sohrab's mother—an ideal world of peace for which Rustum longs, but which is only hazily felt through boyhood memories. Indeed, the range of Arnold's views of life is mirrored in the two extremes of the anxious questing Sohrab and the jaded, gloomy Rustum who seeks only escape and peace. The young Sohrab is torn by inner struggle; his father is more preoccupied with the memory of an alluring, half-forgotten other world—and bears the one he lives in only with a mild stoicism. Both attitudes represent moods of Arnold, but they are also dramatically compelling.

In smaller compass, but quite in Arnold's familiar manner, the black of the Tartar camp is put against the steel and scarlet of the Persians; the uneasy silence of night against the battle-ring of day; the strange immobility of the watching hosts against the vital action of the fighters; the remote inexorability of the natural background against human violence. The constant elements in the poem are the ones Arnold treats elsewhere—time, age, grief, separation, nature— and his view of them is not changed, but they are, this time, integrated with drama and action. Rustum's grief, for instance, is presented as part of the eternal living order of things:

> And his soul set to grief, as the vast tide
> Of the bright rocking ocean sets to shore
> At the full moon.

Arnold's old familiar sense of the slightness of life is totally assimilated and expressed in his handling of the ordeal as Sohrab lies dying —lines later repeated in agreement by Rustum:

> And thou must lay me in that lovely earth,
> And heap a stately mound above my bones,
> And plant a far-seen pillar over all,
> That so the passing horseman on the waste
> May see my tomb a great way off, and cry,
> 'Sohrab, the mighty Rustum's son, lies there,
> Whom his great father did in ignorance kill!'

Time itself is not the isolated sad orchestration to a personal predicament that it is in so many of Arnold's poems, but expresses itself through plot and characters—the contrast of age between Sohrab and Rustum, and between the aged Peran Wisa and his deputy who is "still in his lusty prime." Similarly, the varied ways in which Arnold sees nature are no longer used as opposed tensions to stultify a poetic statement of remote indecision: within the development of *Sohrab and Rustum* each separate view falls into its place as naturally consequent to events. Arnold's recurrent view of nature as uninvolved, the unheeding, near-Darwinian cosmic order (the direct opposite of Shelley's in *Adonais*) exerts itself strongly in the poem, but chiefly as Rustum's threats:

> "thy bones shall strew this sand, till winds
> Bleach them, or Oxus with his summer-floods,
> Oxus in summer wash them all away."

Arnold's plaintive, escapist love of natural beauty becomes Rustum's memory of his far-off youth in the passage I quoted earlier. But the poet is not only able to give his familiar views dramatic expression and integration in the poem: he is able, even, to broaden them in an unfamiliar way under the stimulus of event. So nature also appears as reproach to human folly:

> And he saw that youth,
> Of age and looks to be his own dear son,
> Piteous and lovely, lying on the sand,
> Like some rich hyacinth which by the scythe
> Of an unskilful gardener has been cut,
> Mowing the garden grass-plots near its bed,
> And lies, a fragment tower of purple bloom,
> On the mown, dying grass—so Sohrab lay,
> Lovely in death, upon the common sand.

Nature also suggests, in the last lines as the night falls on the river, a kind of ultimate completion, a sense of exhaustion at the fulfillment of tragic events; but it is fitting to put this aside until last in discussing the poem.

In much the same way, the poem offers a definite creative vehicle through which Arnold can express what he normally leaves implied in the rest of his work. I mean the area beyond which his discussion of philosophical possibilities ceases, the area beyond the point of enveloping doubt at which he figuratively throws up his hands in agnostic despair. This area, in *Sohrab and Rustum*, becomes simply the supernatural: it exists, its manifestations are recorded as details in the story, but they cannot be understood; the action carries them, and there seems no need for comment. There is no rational cause for the "something" which so affected Sohrab:

> something, I confess, in thee,
> Which troubles all my heart, and made my shield
> Fall; and thy spear transfixed an unarmed foe,

or for

> Thou say'st thou art not Rustum; be it so!
> Who art thou then, that canst so touch my soul?

or for the cry of Ruksh, the horse, at the height of the duel:

> a dreadful cry—
> No horse's cry was that . . . .

Allied to this are the cosmic reactions to the struggle:

> And you would say that sun and stars took part
> In that unnatural conflict; for a cloud
> Grew suddenly in heaven, and darked the sun
> Over the fighters' heads; and a wind rose
> Under their feet, and moaning swept the plain,
> And in a sandy whirlpool wrapped the pair.
> In gloom they twain were wrapped, and they alone;
> For both the on-looking hosts on either hand
> Stood in broad daylight . . . .

A device to suggest (as it certainly does) epic hugeness of scale? Certainly, but something more than that: it resembles, within its small compass, the near-Romantic dualism of *Wuthering Heights,* and again it is brilliantly integrated with the action.

It is, of course, the epic tradition which allows Arnold so fully to immerse himself and create, from his inmost philosophic and religious doubts, a unified and animated voice which is also a poem. The traditions of epic nudge the poem into purposeful movement: it shifts easily from ironic understatement—"his not unworthy, not inglorious son"—to epic enumeration of the Persian tribes in the Miltonic manner (ll. 110–140); and as it moves from simile to simile, it is not hard to imagine the sense of creative excitement Arnold must have had as the poem provided expressive vehicle after vehicle for his usually introverted feelings.

The similes, of course, play the greatest part in giving the poem its remarkable animation, as well as its universality. Every significant action in the poem can be tied to life as lived generally by others, and brought close to the reader.[12] They have a luminous detail which is not generally characteristic of Arnold, and seem to draw him out of himself. Whereas, in most of his work, Arnold seems to be standing outside it, and sometimes at a distance, here the poet appears for once to be almost like Browning, entirely immersed in the drama, his whole personality subsumed in the intensity of what he creates. Thus a mere plot detail, the identifying sign on Sohrab's arm, grows into:

> As a cunning workman, in Pekin,
> Pricks with vermilion some clear porcelain vase,
> An emperor's gift; at early morn he paints,
> And all day long, and, when night comes, the lamp
> Lights up his studious forehead and thin hands—
> So delicately pricked the sign appeared
> On Sohrab's arm . . . .

The similes are multi-functional: they contain much of the scenery and atmosphere of the poem; they sometimes create a whole additional dimension of feeling—suspense, for instance:

> But as a troop of peddlers, from Cabool,
> Cross underneath the Indian Caucasus,
> That vast sky-neighbouring mountain of milk snow,
> Crossing so high, that, as they mount, they pass
> Long flocks of travelling birds dead on the snow,
> Choked by the air, and scarce can they themselves
> Slake their parched throats with sugared mulberries—
> In single file they move, and stop their breath,
> For fear they should dislodge the o'erhanging snows—
> So the pale Persians held their breath with fear.

The frailty of things—the trembling uncertainty of an ephemeral world ("milk snow")—are often worked into the metaphor itself: thus the boyish slenderness of Sohrab appears to Rustum as a shadow of a presence rather than as actuality:

> Like some young cypress, tall, and dark, and straight,
> Which in a queen's secluded garden throws
> Its slight dark shadow on the moonlit turf,
> By midnight, to a bubbling fountain's sound.

The tree becomes only a shadow; the fountain only a sound; the garden a queen's, not a king's. Moreover, the similes are frequently linked together throughout the poem to construct a dimension of life seen as always ephemeral, always slight, always trembling on the instant: the breathless crossing of the high snows, the image of a pearl of dew on the corn, of the pearl diver's pale wife and the pale Persians. Against this, in the old counterbalance, is a natural background always hungry, always seeking its prize. Almost all the many birds in the poem (with the exception of the cranes) are birds of prey or concerned in acts of prey.

Finally, the similes are made so functional, are so fully integrated into events, that they occasionally form what is essentially a sub-plot; a perfect example is the simile immediately after the fatal wounding of Sohrab—the female eagle killed by the hunter:

>   anon her mate comes winging back
> From hunting, and a great way off descries
> His huddling young left sole; at that, he checks
> His pinion, and with short uneasy sweeps
> Circles above his eyry, with loud screams
> Chiding his mate back to her nest; but she
> Lies dying, with the arrow in her side,
> In some far stony gorge out of his ken,
> A heap of fluttering feathers—never more
> Shall the lake glass her, flying over it;
> Never the black and dripping precipices
> Echo her stormy scream as she sails by—
> As that poor bird flies home, nor knows his loss,
> So Rustum knew not his own loss, but stood
> Over his dying son, and knew him not.

It is probably an indication of how fully Arnold was able to project himself into the poem that it contains the only place in his poetic output where he can fairly be accused of bathos. When a poet is so fully drawn into his subject, or feels so passionately its importance, he is apt to inject that feeling into situations which, dispassionately seen by the reader, will not bear it, and the result is mawkish. Bathos, not surprisingly, abounds in poetry of Romantic dedication, Wordsworth, Shelley and Keats being frequently guilty. In all the poems where Arnold, a poet of steady good taste, appears to stand beside his utterance rather than immerse himself in it, bathos does not arise. In *Sohrab and Rustum* it does, as Ruksh, the horse, in "mute woe,"

> First to the one then to the other moved
> His head, as if inquiring what their grief
> Might mean; and from his dark, compassionate eyes,
> The big warm tears rolled down, and caked the sand.

Arnold clearly mars his poem here, but, in considering the man behind the work, and the remote good-breeding of the rest of it, I find the bathos something of a human relief.

The poem is given a quiet, integrated fulfillment distantly related to the sense of exhaustion that authentic tragedy provides. I shall quote the passage in a moment. This ending of quiet fulfillment, and its implied, unspecified optimism, is not in itself uncharacteristic of Arnold, but his use here is quite atypical. For once it arises naturally from the poem and is not the usual distinct afterthought of tremulous, causeless hope. The integration here depends on the symbol of the river which begins the poem, is referred to throughout, and ends it. The River Oxus is the flowing of life itself, distant, remote from human events, and mysterious. But, apart from bonding the events of the poem by the full circle it forms around them, the river itself seeks an end, and finally becomes something more than what it is in the body of the poem; after the inexplicable meanderings which mirror the human drama it emerges as a diffident but consequential suggestion of ultimate, half-agnostic fulfillment. It does so by means which are themselves derived from Romantic ones. After the tragic events of the poem have been stilled, the river moves on through degrees of gradually intensified light: from the "mist and hum of that low land," out into the "frosty starlight," under the "solitary moon," flowing "Right for the polar star . . . / Brimming, and bright," until:

Oxus, forgetting the bright speed he had
In his high mountain-cradle in Pamere,
A foiled circuitous wanderer—till at last
The longed-for dash of waves is heard, and wide
His luminous home of waters opens, bright
And tranquil, from whose floor the new-bathed stars
Emerge, and shine upon the Aral Sea.

The final seven lines in particular suggest a conclusion—even a subdued affirmation—of the sort of vision of life Wordsworth had set down in *Intimations of Immortality*. The birth which is a sleep and a forgetting comes in Arnold also from "afar"—and also from an eminence, the "high mountain-cradle in Pamere." In Wordsworth, the difficulties, the failures, the shades of the prison house soon follow, like the Oxus' "foiled circuitous wanderings." Then, the high mountain-cradle, like the joyful youth of Rustum and the loving sheltered childhood of Sohrab, and like the vital splendor of youth in Wordsworth's poem, become remote and dim. And finally Arnold brings the river to the fulfillment Wordsworth had predicated—by guiding steps of steady brightness to the calm home of the sea. It is, for a moment, only a slightly weaker echo of Romantic vision. The technique *is* Romantic, but this is not the blinding, all-revealing brightness of the lime-tree bower or the vision on Snowdon; nor does the Oxus, like a Wordsworthian river, flow from the infinite to the finite world. At its strongest, it is a fainter light it flows under, and this quietly suppressed demi-Romantic echo exactly evokes Arnold's spiritual attitude at its most optimistic.

5. ARNOLD: A SUMMARY ஜ» This closing scene of *Sohrab and Rustum*—in its most visual sense—works for Arnold as a kind of language objectifying three distinct matters: the dispassionateness of the natural background against which the human drama has been played; Arnold's distant and rootless hope, which is in mild contrast to it; and a near-tragic exhaustion, part of the eternal problematic stasis to which humans and events must return. These ideas all, at various times, co-exist and conflict in Arnold's mind. He constantly uses symbols, with greater clarity and sensitivity than almost all previous English poets except Shelley, to express the various shades of

his outlook on the world and the human condition.[13] In this, no less than a painter, he is stating *how* he sees, not merely what he sees: the inferences drawn from Arnold's symbols in nature are essentially revelations of facets of himself. The moonlit shore in *Dover Beach* is the best-known scene in all Arnold's poetry because it seems to represent that poetry and its creator's mind. It is the border between the land on which we and the poet stand, and the sea of faith which has withdrawn from our time; from it can occasionally be glimpsed flashes of genuine guidance, and around it is the unending darkness of confused unbelief, but the beach itself belongs to neither. Its dim moonlight gives it beauty through which comes hope of truth, but it is of neither light nor darkness; the beauty is illusive and a bitter comment on the quest for truth. While the complexities in Arnold's outlook force him to use intricate methods in handling light imagery, his techniques, in *Dover Beach* and elsewhere, are not different in kind from those of Coleridge in *Dejection: An Ode*.

Arnold works as naturally in symbols as the Romantics did; but while they, Coleridge in particular, had used them—light and sound for instance—to objectify the steps and heights of Romantic experience and the various stages of its deprivation, Arnold gives the same symbols meanings shaped by the limitations of his vision. The sea, for instance, constantly shifts in meaning. In *Sohrab and Rustum* it is, exceptionally, fulfillment if not infinitude; but it is also the withdrawn faith of *Dover Beach,* and most often life seen as the uncharted and menacing waste of *A Summer Night.* The island is not, as it is for Wordsworth (*Prelude,* Book II, 164–174), the isolated human experience which reveals the glory of which it is the gift, but human isolation itself. For Arnold, the mountain is not the Wordsworthian high point of spiritual aspiration, but an apex from which, with weary bitterness (*Stanzas in Memory of the Author of Obermann*), with determined optimism (*Obermann Once More*) or fatalism (*Empedocles on Etna*), he looks down only on the human situation. The river is not Wordsworth's flowing down of divine love, but —with the qualification already noted in *Sohrab and Rustum*—an enigmatic and uninvolved nature seen as background to human trials. Arnold reinforces these by other symbols of his own—the strait of separation, the Marguerite of unfulfilled longing for human communion. He will also often use light in the reverse way from the Romantics—to deny rather than affirm. He depends heavily upon it as symbol; in *Thyrsis,* as we have seen, light carries the affirmation of the entire poem; it is Clough, brightness, beauty, belief—but the final impression is negative; the day draws to a close, and despite the optimism of the poem's ending, the imaginative stress is on the symbolic meaning of Arnold's dying of the light.

This handling of a traditional poetic device, here the symbol, in a highly individual way to transmit the exact tone and accent of his outlook is typical of Arnold in other poetic matters. He is, technically, a poet deriving a great deal from tradition. It would be easy, if ultimately rather misleading, to point to exact resemblances to the Romantics: for instance, Arnold, like Wordsworth, is adept at suggesting the quality of overlying silence by means of underlying sound:

> to my ear from uplands far away
> The bleating of the folded flocks is borne,
> With distant cries of reapers in the corn—
> All the live murmur of a summer's day.
> (*The Scholar-Gipsy, ll. 17–20*)

But it is not a matter of direct Wordsworthian or Romantic influence. Arnold is here drawing on the traditional effects of English poetry, and assimilating them into an individual whole. It is the same in matters of construction: Arnold's critical insistence on the importance of precise structure is verified by his own poetry—sometimes, as I have suggested in treating *The Scholar-Gipsy*, exaggeratedly so. Usually, however, he manipulates within traditional forms differing developments and viewpoints (*The Scholar-Gipsy* and *Thyrsis* are clear examples); and he does it in such a way that each stage of the poem transmits—through symbol or simile or the action itself or tone or allusion—its own thread or counter-thread in the shifting web of Arnold's outlook. Usually, the derivative quality in Arnold's poetry is confined to single technical matters of symbol, structure and the rest, while the total effect of the poem is distinctly original. It is not a mere matter of blending. Where Arnold will call specific previous poets to mind—in the flower catalogues, for instance, so redolent of Spenser and Milton—his treading in the tracks of older poets is used for his own purpose, as a means of expressing his own unique attitude of mind. His flower passages are not only colorful and evocative, but usually drenched in evanescence, each color, each flower never stimulating the visual mind without some simultaneous kind of qualification:

> the *frail-leafed, white anemony,*
> Dark bluebells drenched with *dews of summer eves,*
> And purple orchises *with spotted leaves.* (My italics)
>
>   *(The Scholar-Gipsy, ll. 87–89)*

Arnold's traditional derivations, indeed, are themselves often used to enrich a certain tone of voice: the reader hears the phrase or accent of Milton or Wordsworth or Carlyle, but the association is neither simple nor direct. It remains Arnold's. It is an echo from remoter time or circumstance providing a plaintive overtone of assent —or ironically futile dissent—from what Arnold is saying in his own tone, and enriching its impact. Such near-allusions are used entirely for Arnold's own purposes; in *Thyrsis,* for example, there are faint echoes and a general suggestion of Keats' third verse in the *Ode to a Nightingale:*

> Yes, thou are gone, and round me too the night
> In ever-nearing circle weaves her shade.
>   I see her veil draw soft across the day,
> I feel her slowly chilling breath invade
>   The cheek grown thin, the brown hair sprent with gray;

and of Donne: [14]

> The mountain-tops where is the throne of Truth
> Tops in life's morning sun so bright and bare!
>   Unbreachable the fort
> Of the long-batter'd world uplifts its wall.

These glancing allusions effectually suggest that the traditions of English poetry itself must be gathered into the symbol of the dying sunlight in *Thyrsis.* They also must fade, along with youth, beauty, Clough and conscious existence itself, just as the symbolic daylight fails. The suggestion, once made, is denied in Arnold's customary way, but without great conviction, by the end of the poem; while in *Sohrab and Rustum* the lines dimly reminiscent of Milton [15] serve entirely to reinforce and anglicize the epic implications:

> When the dew glistens on the pearled ears,
> A shiver runs through the deep corn for joy—
> So, when they heard what Peran-Wisa said,
> A thrill through all the Tartar squadrons ran
> Of pride and hope for Sohrab, whom they loved.

Arnold's principal technical skill lies in this mastery of the English tradition and traditional devices: he is not, in the technical sense, an inventive poet. His strength lies in such matters as the sensitive selection of form for subject. From the brutal abrupt verities of Empedocles' chanting to the varied pace of the blank verse in *Sohrab and Rustum* there is no failure in this. Nor is there on the more limited scale of adapting line movement to image (the memorable wave movements in *Dover Beach* and *The Forsaken Merman*). But the most pervasive and effective techniques in Arnold always concern tone, particularly the long, fading vowels at the end of lines (as at the start of *The Forsaken Merman*), and his remarkable balance between repetition and variation. His own kind of vowel music is probably the most functional matter in Arnold's verse, for the uniqueness of his work depends basically on tone of voice, and its consistent appeal depends heavily on the experience of articulation in the mind. The modern reader finds a voice, in reading Arnold, for the expression of his own emotional reactions, and a tonal mirror which relates much more personally to him—in this century—than does the Romantic lamp. In this, Arnold provides a bridge between the English poetic tradition and the modern mind. He has brilliantly used old, traditional techniques and allusions to speak with his own voice; balancing this is his deep concern for the modern issues of his time—a concern expressed emotionally rather than intellectually—and a sense of involvement with his time and a feeling for its climate. In his sensitivity to evolutionary thought, in his suggestions of the future Freudian road human inquiry was to take (". . . how our own minds are made,/ What springs of thought they use,/ How rightened, how betrayed . . ."), in his awareness, like Carlyle and Ruskin, of the "unmeaning taskwork" which kills, Arnold as a *poet* (quite apart from his criticism) is contemporary and modern.

I mentioned earlier the consistent and prospering status accorded Arnold's poetry in the decades since his own time. If one seeks a view of his work from the perspective of a century, the first conviction to emerge is that Arnold has been successful precisely *because of* a spiritual range far narrower than that of the Romantics. The consistent impression his poetry gives is of passivity, of unassertiveness; beside the Romantics he is eloquently inert. Like them, he often begins—or appears to—by moving from attitude to attitude in reverie (most obvious in poems like *Stanzas from the Grande Char-treuse* and *Rugby Chapel*). Unlike them, he remains largely on the level of worldly introspection, moving occasionally, as in *The Schol-ar-Gipsy,* to daydream used didactically, but never to genuine vision. Arnold's delicate balance of conflicting positions, the dependence of poem after poem on elaborate tensions, his seeming semi-commit-ment to withdrawal and his spiritual throwing-up of the hands in ag-nostic supernaturalism, his apparently retrogressive classicism and stoicism—all these things must have seemed even more irrelevant than Romantic vision to a Victorian mind seeking positive guidance. "To see life steadily"—the objective perspective Arnold seeks, itself works, in the Victorian world, against the possibility of commitment, and thus the guidance, the Victorians sought.

But if Victorian complexities made Romantic vision seem irrele-vant, thinking Victorian readers still believed in the possibility of a different *kind* of assertion, and it was this which Arnold, in his po-etry, failed to give. Such is the difference, however, between Victorian and modern conceptions of that possibility that Arnold's poetic de-nial of it works to his later advantage and gives him a sort of pre-science. Seeking commitment, Arnold remains in his verse, though not in his criticism, in an essentially modern position of stasis. He re-treats to the shelter of the varying, subjective self as the only possibil-ity for "truth," and even the possibility is unfulfilled for him. Among the many reasons for his continued high status as poet, this shift in general philosophic view seems to me to be the most opera-tive. It recognizes, as the Victorians could not, an inevitable and ter-rible truth in a mind moving only within a confined, repetitive circle of static tensions. If Arnold leaves that circle, it is only when excep-tional forces move him: *Rugby Chapel,* perhaps his only really asser-tive poem, is made so only because Arnold is drawn out of his nor-mal encirclement by the force of his feeling for his father. *Sohrab and Rustum,* with comparable imaginative and artistic force, is so only because Arnold is drawn out of himself by the animation of a plot which first attracted him as vehicle for his own inner feelings. But this happens seldom.

He provides three distinct kinds of poetic output: first, there is the poem where Arnold leans too obviously upon "the only solid guide," using classical subjects as direct vehicles for what are essen-tially *intellectual* conflicts of outlook. Poems of this nature are *Empe-docles on Etna* and *Mycerinus,* and they are poetic failures through lack of Arnold's emotional involvement. Second, there is the bulk of his poetry, which presents with muted emotion Arnold's spiritual and intellectual struggles, his conflicting tensions and ultimate stasis. They are basically unfulfilled struggles which—and this is Arnold's most striking contrast with Tennyson—*omit the process* of struggle; among them are attempts, like *The Scholar-Gipsy* and *Thyrsis,* to move in the direction of Romantic experience, but they only emerge as shadows and echoes of it. This kind of poem is Arnold's most characteristic; it shows most clearly his mental state, and it articulates most movingly and responsively the modern dilemma. The poetry of the Romantics had been indissolubly linked to an infinite universe; this central work of Arnold's sees, metaphorically speaking, that universe with its divine infinitude as mere limitlessness, and man its alien prisoner, wandering without purpose or direction.

But there is a third kind of poetry in Arnold, which he never fully developed, and of which *Sohrab and Rustum* is the only extended example. Here, Arnold's ultimate reality is not an uncomprehending and uncaring universe, but man himself. Arnold is drawn into a mode of expression analogous to drama, in which the focus of his interest is the struggle of other human beings. The introspective, subjective prisoner which is his own mind is animated by, assimilated into, other human actions and thoughts. It is not escape, for it uses Arnold's own permanent doubts to contribute to a certain view of humanity. Despite what I view as its happy poetic results, in *Sohrab and Rustum* Arnold seems to have made an uncharacteristic suggestion that spiritual troubles may to some extent be sublimated to the human drama of living. Arnold, in fact, half-suggests a road he never travelled. The ultimate extreme of that direction is dramatic poetry of primary historical or psychological interest—in other words the sphere of Robert Browning.

NOTES

[1] See Chapter III of J. H. Buckley's *The Victorian Temper* (Cambridge, Mass.: Harvard University Press, 1951) for a fuller and lively discussion.
[2] To cite many examples would be to catalogue all the really functional

areas of the novel. But one is the invitation to the reader to reject Nelly Dean's deliberately provocative view of Cathy's death as "repose that neither earth nor hell can break . . . where life is boundless in its duration, and love in its sympathy, and joy in its fulness." It is hard to read that even out of context without a mental snort of protest. It is the technique of Coleridge's *Christabel,* where the normal, comfortable, worldly explanation is carefully brought up by the poet and then dropped, the crucial alternative explanation being left up to the reader. Here, the force of our rejection of Nelly's saccharine view simply moves us to accept what the author wishes to stress, that Cathy faces a restless waiting within a larger cosmic order until the earthbound Heathcliff can join her.

3 As if to stress the diverse connotations of the term Romantic, *Wuthering Heights* is not included in the list of "Chief Romantic Works" in Bernbaum's *Guide to the Romantic Movement,* though the list does include such works as Southey's *Life of Nelson* and *History of the Peninsular War,* and Lamb's *A Dissertation on Roast Pig.*

4 *The Alien Vision of Victorian Poetry* (Princeton, New Jersey: Princeton University Press, 1952), p. 154.

5 For a detailed study of Arnold's comprehensive relationships to specific Romantic poets, see Leon Gottfried's *Matthew Arnold and the Romantics* (Lincoln: University of Nebraska Press, 1963). Its concluding chapter, "Between Two Worlds . . .", is especially relevant here.

6 Book Third, Chapter VIII, "Natural Supernaturalism": "Such a minnow is Man; his Creek this Planet Earth; his Ocean the immeasurable All . . . ."

7 *The Function of Criticism at the Present Time* (1864). It is one of a number of interesting inconsistencies in Arnold's prose criticism that, fifteen years later, in his introduction to the poems of Wordsworth, he applauded Wordsworth for having, in effect, such a "thorough interpretation" and the values derived from it. "The greatness of a poet," says Arnold in praising Wordsworth in his introduction, "lies in his powerful and beautiful application of ideas to life,—to the question: How to live."

One could argue, of course, that Arnold's understanding of Wordsworth, and perhaps of Romanticism, grew between middle and later life. I tend to view this, and comparable inconsistencies in Arnold, more as evidence that his prose criticism, which often seems so self-assured on its surface, sometimes shows at a deeper level some of the paralyzing uncertainty which expresses itself most fully in his poems.

8 *Matthew Arnold* (New York, 1939), p. 32.

9 *Lines composed a few miles above Tintern Abbey* . . . July 13, 1798.

10 See, for example, Walter Houghton's "*Empedocles on Etna,*" *Victorian Studies,* I (June, 1958), pp. 311–336.

11 *1853 Preface.*

12   As some rich woman, on a winter's morn,
        Eyes through her silken curtains the poor drudge
        Who with numb blackened fingers makes her fire
        At cock-crow, on a starlit winter's morn,
        When the frost flowers the whitened window-panes,
        And wonders how she lives, and what the thoughts

> Of that poor drudge may be—so Rustum eyed
> The unknown adventurous youth . . . .

[13] The best brief treatment of the "world" behind Arnold's symbolic language is, I think, Chapter I of A. D. Culler's *Imaginative Reason*: *The Poetry of Matthew Arnold* (New Haven: Yale University Press, 1966).

[14] Cf. Satyre III:

> On a huge hill,
> Cragged, and steep, Truth stands, and hee that will
> Reach her, about must, and about must goe . . . .

[15] Cf. *Paradise Lost*, I, 663–667:

> He spoke: and to confirm his words, out-flew
> Millions of flaming swords, drawn from the thighs
> Of mighty Cherubim; the sudden blaze
> Far round illumin'd hell: highly they rag'd
> Against the Highest . . . .

III
BROWNING

III

BROWNING

1. FOREWORD ᘒ There is hardly a single poem in the work of Arnold and Tennyson which does not reveal aspects of its creator's world-outlook, in a sense that a reading of one of the famous dramatic monologues of Browning does not. *The Bishop Orders his Tomb at St. Praxed's Church* is a striking imaginative recreation of Renaissance attitude and atmosphere; but it totally absorbs Browning himself, and for all we can deduce from it, the mind which made the poem may hold almost any philosophic view, or any religious view between outright unbelief and some form of Christianity. When Arnold (especially) and Tennyson write dramatic monologues, they do not—cannot —disappear in this way. Their inner conflicts are absorbed to some extent by situation and character, but rarely— very rarely—completely. It appears ironic that Arnold, advocate as critic of the "great" all-absorbing action, tends strongly in his poetry to use dramatic situation as the most transparent front behind which his own mental tensions stand revealed. Even in *Tristram and Iseult*, which provides some exception to this, and where Arnold seems absorbed within the Celtic legend, the legend itself is made to stress his familiar themes of isolation and un-

fulfillment, so that the poem and its myth appear almost personal.

Arnold's own awareness of this tendency in his poetry reveals interesting matters in his critical attitude to it. The signs are that he felt this repeated presentation of his personal conflicts, so thinly veiled by "action," great or not, would prove embarrassingly confined and unhelpful to thoughtful readers seeking help for allied problems of their own. I think that in general Victorian readers did find this so, and for guidance were liable to turn to Tennyson and (some of them), later, to Browning. Something of Arnold's realization of his general failure as "guide" in his poetry, and his total irrelevance as prophet, underlies his critical insistence on "great action" and his judgement of *Sohrab and Rustum* as his "best"—that is, among other things, nearest to being inspiriting.

But Arnold's appraisal of his work, seeing much of his poetry as agonizingly unhelpful in the Victorian dilemma, was based on the philosophic needs of his time. In his mind, as in those of many of his readers, existed an often obsessive need to move towards absolute truth. For example, one aspect of Arnold's interest in "touchstones" was that they seemed to offer a means of reaching, or almost reaching, absolute truth in the assessment of literature. Since the ideal of absolute truth existed, it was in part the task of the poet, who could come closer than other men to it, to teach, solve, and inspire, as Wordsworth and Carlyle had seemed to do for many. Arnold was not to know that a later age, abandoning the grail of "truth" except as a convenient term for tentative personal conclusions about isolated personal experience, would increasingly value his poetry for the very characteristics he himself appeared to indict. The next century would understand only too well the tensions holding his mind philosophically paralyzed. It would appreciate only too fully his unique tone of half-repressed pathos evoked by that mental condition. The twentieth century would, in fact, value his poetry almost in direct relationship to the negative qualities of its personal revelation and its tone. Hence in *Dover Beach* continues to be found the core of Arnold's appeal. But those Victorians still willing to believe in reassurance found more encouragement in Browning.

One of several ways in which this is surprising is that Browning's natural leaning as artist was directly opposite from the subjectivity of Arnold and Tennyson. The narrations of both these poets are usually steeped in their personalities. At his artistic best, Browning was a poetic ventriloquist allowing no hint of his own voice. It is clear from a survey of his whole output that to speak directly of his own state of mind was difficult for him.

Browning himself, in his *Essay on Shelley*, drew a famous distinction between the subjective and objective poet, but concluded that neither sort is commonly found in pure form: "A mere running in of the one faculty upon the other, is, of course, the ordinary circumstance." [1] This is true of most nineteenth century poets, certainly, and in considering most of them there is no pressing critical need to assess the degree of subjectivity where it is not obvious. We read Wordsworth (to take one example) because he provokes a certain poetic response, and yet Wordsworth as a philosopher is integral to the experience his poetry offers. Rarely, fortunately, but at certain times Wordsworth indeed appears as a philosopher who happens to write in verse—in *The Prelude*, XIV, ll. 63–129, for instance. And how far is it the poet himself speaking through his various personae? Is William, sitting upon his old grey stone and dreaming his time away, literally Wordsworth himself, or a more objective creation designed to evoke both poetic emotion and—simultaneously—philosophic idea? This question is probably unanswerable, nor does it matter much in considering Wordsworth. The ideas and attitudes of Wordsworthian personae are in fact consistent enough to imply a total, integrated outlook, and the poet's characters seem to exist not only for what he called "immediate pleasure," but at the same time for a consistent philosophic purpose beyond themselves. And this outlook, more accurately a philosophic-religious one, is beyond doubt the poet's own.

Browning's characters, however, share no such common basis. Whatever purpose they seem to have beyond themselves is usually historical or psychological, and above all individual, and it shows too little consistency or interconnection for any definite outlook to be inferred from it. It is, therefore, perhaps the thorniest general problem in this poet's work to assess how far his characters speak with his very self and voice. Any consideration of Browning which looks towards his cast of mind must face this problem. It is not solved by surveying the assorted reactions of Browning's literary critics, for they show almost every variation possible.

There is, for instance, the view common half a century ago, stressing Browning's high objectivity. Stopford Brooke, writing in

1902, remarked that the voice in his poems is "rarely the voice of Browning, nor is the mind of their personages his mind. . . . Browning has stripped himself of his own personality." [2] At the other extreme it is fairly common to find more recent critics, such as John Bryson in 1959, asserting (equally without real explanation or support), "And then we hear Browning's own voice" in the middle of *Fra Lippo Lippi*.[3] J. M. Cohen, a more sophisticated critic, attempts a compromise: to him, Browning's characters are "mouthpieces to express various attitudes to life . . . all, no doubt, his own at certain times and under certain circumstances." [4] This at least offers useful insurance against Browning's inconsistencies when the poet is viewed as essentially subjective, as Cohen generally sees him.

The most unequivocal and still useful statement on the matter is probably that of W. C. DeVane, who sees Browning's career in two phases, with the division in 1871—the earlier Browning objective and dramatic, and the later speaking in his own voice, usually argumentatively on matters which concerned him deeply.[5] This distinction, which DeVane draws in large and general strokes in introducing the *Parleyings,* is broadly valid. It cannot, however, be sustained if applied rigorously to mean that the pre-1871 work is simply and plainly objective and dramatic, in Browning's sense of those terms; it is largely so, but it poses the familiar puzzle of continual variation between that extreme and another which is highly subjective.

The truth seems to me to be this: if Browning's work is taken as a whole, it consists of multifarious shadings between two extremes. There is direct, autobiographical self-revelation on the one hand, and on the other the creation of self-contained dramatic character which does not represent Browning himself. Because it is a matter of variant shading, assessment of it becomes a problem with each individual poem. Even then it is hard to be precise, for there is nothing absolute to be assessed, only something relative to a context of perpetual variation in the rest of Browning's work. Granting all this, however, it is true that basically Browning writes two different *kinds* of poetry: it is less a matter of stages of development than of a mind quite definitely compartmented. He wrote personal, subjective poetry about transcendental subject-matter. He also wrote, more naturally and successfully, a much larger mass of objective poetry. In this work his own mind is largely absorbed and hidden, and such poetry presents dramatically a multiplicity of differing views which are often, however, *only incidental* to dramatic situation or psychological interest. Failure to make some such basic distinction opens the way to confusion about an already complex poet. If one takes, for instance, any one "voice" or character from one of the "objective" dramatic monologues, and cites it as direct revelation of the mind of Browning, his many other voices will provide masses of both confirmation and denial. They do not integrate into a total view, and confusion follows confusion.[6] That, of course, is not to say that feelings and attitudes expressed by dramatic characters do not represent what their creator knows well, but they are not direct and literal statements of his personal philosophy. Without careful consideration of the grounds for their subjectivity, it is not useful to quote the statements of Browning's characters as those of the poet himself.

I would add a word on the rôle of *The Ring and the Book* in this regard. Certainly it is Browning's most important work, and artistically it represents him best. But these facts simply illustrate that the poem is crucial to a total view of Browning's work, and that is not my concern here. To view Arnold and Tennyson as Romantics *manqués,* as poets of faith or attempted faith, leads to the consideration of the bulk of their work, including their best work. To view Browning so leads to a few poems, and usually not those by which he made his reputation. There is admittedly a risk of invidiousness when the subject of a book leads to the minor work of a major poet, especially when it must stand beside the principal work of two major contemporaries. It is a risk, however, which has to be taken, for Browning throughout his life did write subjective poems concerned with transcendental experience and vision. They are usually among his weakest work, but this in itself is important, as I shall suggest, to the understanding of Browning's psychology where matters of philosophic and religious belief are concerned.

Aside from the poetry itself and the questions it provokes, there is a good deal of more directly autobiographical evidence on Browning's outlook. Simplest of all, perhaps, is a view of his personal demeanor, offered by his contemporary Carlyle. Enlarging upon the "great contrast between him [Browning] and me," Carlyle commented: "He seems very content with life, and takes much satisfaction in the world. It's a very strange and curious spectacle to behold a man in these days so confidently cheerful." [7] Besides the general impression of an ebullient and occasionally over-assertive personality, the exterior confidence of Browning is confirmed by his letters. They are usually not deeply revealing of his inner philosophy, but where they do touch on religious matters, they usually provide repeated assertions of what sounds like orthodox belief. One letter claims to fear "wrath of men . . . as I fear the fly I have just put out of the window; but I fear *God*—and am ready, he knows, to die this moment in taking his part against any piece of injustice or oppression, *so* I aspire to die!" [8]

His personal history in matters of formal religion bears this out. He had begun, in his early intoxication with Shelley, in Shelleyan "atheism," but in his early twenties, according to DeVane, he returned to orthodoxy.[9] But what sort of orthodoxy? Cohen claims that Browning reconsidered, much as he does in *Christmas Eve,* his own youthful Nonconformity, Catholicism, and "a dilute ethical Christianity based on the free criticism of the Bible." Cohen concludes that "His own choice—or his wife's which for the moment he adopted as his—remained an etiolated version of that Nonconformity from which he had once half-heartedly rebelled, and of which he gives an acid picture in the chapel description with which *Christmas Eve* opens." [10] Cohen is a sympathetic critic of Browning, but in dealing with what he terms the "pedestrian Sunday-school moral-mongering" of *Christmas Eve* he faces up to the decidedly pallid quality of the poet's wanderings in the area of formal religion. For the moment, we may simply bear that characteristic in mind, together with the suggested "adoption" by the poet of his wife's religious position.

So much for the formal surface. Was Browning, in any deeper sense, a Christian? There is a good deal of conflicting evidence.[11] But the doubts surrounding his formal Christianity do not seem to me to matter very much. He does frequently express in his work an optimistic belief in a positive universal order, and there is no real doubt or critical disagreement about that. It was, certainly, philosophy rather than formal religion that drew him most powerfully. The "theory of life" which helped win Browning a belated but devoted following late in his career has been inferred from his poetry and set out many times by critics and interpreters early in this century, and since there are no vital general disagreements one version is as good as another for stating the established view. The "at peace, firm-fixed" Browning seen by Stopford Brooke is—though I believe it is possible to see beyond it—assuredly there in the poetry: "Browning was certain of his hope, and for the most part resolved his discords. Even when he did not resolve them, he firmly believed that they would be resolved." Writing in 1902, Brooke had been able to distinguish Browning from other poets of the previous fifty years by "how steadily assured was the foundation of his spiritual life." [12] Indeed, as Brooke saw it, the very variety of subject and treatment in Browning's work was his way of relieving what would otherwise have been the monotony of an unvarying basis of thought over a period of sixty years.

Brooke went on to summarize what he calls the theory of life sustaining his "firm-fixed" poet. Reduced to essentials, it comes to this: life is a period of trial and growth for future lives; present life on earth is necessarily limited, though that does not prevent—in fact it invites—aspiration towards the higher life; the human task is to work and strive within the imposed limits of finite life, never losing the aspiration to move beyond it. The worst sin is contentment, a sinking back into the world of finite limitations for its own sake.[13]

While it may be possible to question the basis for any of these assertions individually, Brooke is merely illustrating in detail the standard view of Browning's optimism. Such a set of presuppositions as he cites does not differ in essential theory from the Romantic outlook. Like the latter, it enforces consequent assumptions: the roles of evil and death in Browning's poetry do not differ in principle from their Romantic ones.[14] Death is the gateway, as it is in Shelley, through which aspiration becomes reality. Evil becomes positive, an instrument for provoking growth. As DeVane reads Browning, "Evil is not really evil; it is only apparent. God has placed it in the world so that man may develop his moral nature. God is thus like a father who while building a house has given his son a few worthless boards to saw in order to make the boy think he is helping." [15]

There are, of course, important differences between Browning and the Romantics, above all in the road by which the affirmation of theory is arrived at. Evil had been real enough to Wordsworth, and he had found it, by his own experience, to function constructively in the end. Browning, by comparison, is far more abstract. To him, evil is an illusion, but, as DeVane remarks, he "insisted that man must not *know* whether it was illusion or not. That is, ignorance became a necessary part of his theory of an all-loving god." [16]

Despite an apparent general similarity, there are not only differences of origin between Browning's and Romantic theories, but also differences of application. Browning had to face certain essentially Victorian problems, such as the implications of evolution. It is perhaps revealing that he evades the specter of a purposeless universe by appearing to accept Darwin's mechanism, but then tacking on a God at the end—*or rather at the beginning*—of it. In one letter, he writes:

> In reality, all that seems *proved* in Darwin's scheme was a conception familiar to me from the beginning: see in *Paracelsus* the progressive development from senseless matter to organized, until man's appearance (*Part* v.). Also in *Cleon,* see the order of "life's mechanics,"—and I daresay in many passages of my poetry: for how can one look at Nature as a whole and doubt that, wherever there is a gap, a "link" must be "missing"—through the limited power and opportunity of the looker? But go back and back, as you please, *at* the back, as Mr. Sludge is made to insist, you find (*my* faith is as constant) creative intelligence, acting as matter but not resulting from it. Once set the balls rolling, and ball may hit ball and send any number in any direction over the table; but I believe in the cue pushed by a hand.[17]

Despite such difficulties, Browning's philosophical-religious outlook, though sometimes qualified, is sustained and steady in his work. By and large it can fairly be concluded that there is a standard, established view (including his own) of Browning's outlook, and its core is a steady optimism. The painstakingly-inferred theories of life by early commentators may be summarized by the view of DeVane in the twenties. He described Browning's famous lines in Pippa's song, "God's in his heaven— / All's right with the world" as the poet's "axiomatic faith" which "he spent the rest of his life defending." [18] In the later fashion such a view is apt to be qualified, as it was, in 1959, by John Bryson, who notes Browning's "trial, doubt, and self-examination." These, however, are merely seen as milestones on the poet's journey to optimism: "He believed that the world contains much more good than ill, and he was not afraid to proclaim that belief in assured and sometimes strident tones. He was confident in an age when many were unsure. . . ." [19]

There remains no real disagreement. There are other things in Browning, but his center, in life and work, is normally seen as a firm optimism. It remains, before asking whether this may be seriously questioned, to examine the basis for it in his poetry.

2. BROWNING'S RELIGIOUS POEMS ஃ There are certain poems in the Browning canon—and despite the claim of his early general "objectivity" they are not all late in his career—which deal quite

explicitly with religious and philosophical problems as such. These poems would appear, in theory at least, to throw the frankest light on Browning's cast of mind.

Christmas Eve is apparently Browning speaking in his own person—speaking of what seems personal experience, though given a half-suggestion of dream as frame (Section XXII). There are also musings upon this experience, and conclusions which attempt to clarify a religious position. In its loose narrative point of view, in its account of worldly incident leading to vision, and in its inferred didactic conclusions, the poem seems to be the sort of nature-religious, anecdotal affirmation so often met in Wordsworth's *Prelude*. It is, however, given Browning's own form and style. The poem also carries considerable urgency in its tone, though its poetic form, involving some laboriously undignified rhyming, works against this. The experience in the poem is that of a relatively young man; the poem appeared in 1850, when Browning was still in his thirties, and it was probably written a few years before that.[20]

The work begins as narrative with the speaker seeking shelter from a storm, and entering a chapel on Christmas Eve: the suspicion the congregation shows towards the stranger, the superficial pleasure it feels at the carelessly-tossed out religiosity, are recorded by the poet —"My gorge rose at the nonsense and stuff of it" (III)—and he leaves the chapel. Outside, all is "pure and different." In the atmosphere of the intermittent moonlight and scudding clouds, the speaker's reaction becomes more liberal: "The zeal was good, and the aspiration." He goes on to consider his own church, to which he had been led by

> these very skies,
> And probing their immensities,
> I found God there, his visible power. (V)

The church appears to offer a sort of language by which the immanent love of God can be recognized and acknowledged. Browning makes a number of claims for such divine love, and they are based solely on intuitive conviction. God's love and wisdom are both infinite, and He

> Would never, (my soul understood,)
> With power to work all love desires,
> Bestow e'en less than man requires. (V)

There is direct, though isolated, affirmation of Browning's personal faith in the meaning of this divine love, and in his ability to find God:

> And shall behold thee, face to face,
> O God, and in thy light retrace
> How in all I loved here, still wast thou!   (V)

And the passage ends with what is an image in small of the whole poem. On the one hand Browning affirms liberal acceptance of the religious attitudes of others, even such as have just disturbed him so much in the chapel; on the other he makes an affirmation of faith, presumably of at least equal strength, in his own religion:

> . . . Oh, let men keep their ways
> Of seeking thee in a narrow shrine—
> Be this my way! And this is mine!

The apparent dichotomy is left philosophically undefended.

The poem then moves into a presentation of vision. It is introduced (VI) in a generally Romantic manner by a picture of the night sky with a moon-rainbow and "steps of light" of increasing intensity. Discussion of this vision will be deferred for later consideration of Browning's Romantic heritage and methods. Here it is necessary only to note that it is a vision of Christ, which the poet follows to Rome, seeing St. Peter's crammed with the Catholic devout at Christmas service; then to a dissenting professor's analytic and sceptical lecture at Göttingen. From each of these the speaker feels apart, but he views them with tolerance because God ". . . himself discerns all ways/ Open to reach him" (XI).

The concluding part of the poem is so ponderously didactic that the lesson Browning would urge, while hardly convincing, is unmistakable. He outlines (XIX) a tempting, tolerant, basic universal religion with a viewpoint almost anthropological, but this optimistic position is followed by the speaker's being swept up in the "horrible storm" and deposited back on the college step, where, as holder of such a view, he belongs. Apparently, then, real value can only lie in deep personal commitment:

> Needs must there be one way, our chief
> Best way of worship: let me strive
> To find it, and when found, contrive

My fellows also take their share!
. . . and I exult
That God, by God's own ways occult,
May—doth, I will believe—bring back
All wanderers to a single track.   (XX)

This, in contrast with the storm, leads to the protagonist's being lapped into the folds of Christ's robe "full fraught/ With warmth and wonder and delight." And the poem ends back in the little chapel, with the speaker now genuinely full of goodwill towards all fellow-worshippers, including the absent Pope and the Professor.

The poem, despite its length and subject, its specificity and subjective nature, is far less revealing than these things would lead a reader to expect as an expression of Browning's religious position. Leaving artistic questions aside, it is for one thing highly diffuse, and it is difficult to decide on which of the poem's many facets ultimate stress should be placed. Above all, perhaps, it seems to be an attack on that lifeless kind of tolerance which vitiates genuine religion; but Browning devotes much of his poem to pointing out the redeeming strains in what he ultimately rejects—both Catholicism and scientific scepticism. The poem is in part, in fact, a defence as well as rejection of Catholicism, just as it also expresses an understanding of the scientific intellectual dissent which Browning rejects. It is—probably above all—a statement of personal faith, presumably in the Nonconformist Christianity he may well have adopted from his wife.[21]

It is also vision and embellished personal experience, but these seem subsidiary. Ultimately, it is the poetry of argument, to which vision and other personal experience are brought in as buttress. The final impression the poem gives is that Browning's impetus has been a determination to restate and confirm his own intuitive conviction by constructing around it a supporting frame of experience and imagination—not the other way round. The emphases given the poem's various facets, considered relatively, suggest that a Romantic horse of transcendent experience has been pulled by a cart of predetermined theology. The poem's fragmentation in pure subject matter renders it, as personal exposition, unconvincing. This impression is deepened by artistic considerations; there is a rhythm varying between jogging monotony and sudden abrupt shifts in kind, and an undignified and perverse ingenuity in pursuit of rhyme.

Easter Day, the contemporary and companion poem to *Christmas Eve,* is a relatively similar and equally uncomfortable combina-

tion of vision and argument, though it does come closer to some of
the basic philosophic-religious positions Browning was making his
dramatic protagonists take in his better-known works. The opening
lines ("How very hard it is to be/ A Christian!") are followed by a
lengthy monologue, made to an unseen observer, on the problems of
belief. Browning, in a manner rather like Carlyle's, attacks any general expectation that belief can be easily won:

> At first you say, 'The whole, or chief
> 'Of difficulties, is belief.
> 'Could I believe once thoroughly,
> 'The rest were simple. What? Am I
> 'An idiot, do you think,—a beast?
> 'Prove to me, only that the least
> 'Command of God is God's indeed,
> 'And what injunction shall I need
> 'To pay obedience?   (II)

The monologue goes on to ridicule rationalistic methods of arriving
at faith. From the fourteenth section of the poem it turns into an account of a vision of three years before, a vision of Judgement Day.
The vision is again introduced by phenomena in the night sky,
which, this time, is burning. The poet is judged and condemned for
having preferred the world to "heaven and infinity," and hence, with
ironic justice, is given the world. As in the Romantic view, earthly
beauty simply implies the fuller, more perfect one that lies beyond
it:

> 'All partial beauty was a pledge
> 'Of beauty in its plenitude:
> 'But since the pledge sufficed thy mood,
> 'Retain it! plenitude be theirs
> 'Who looked above!'   (XXIV)

Ultimately the speaker pleads to be allowed to go on living and hop-
ing for the love of God:

> 'Only let me go on, go on,
> 'Still hoping ever and anon
> 'To reach one eve the Better Land!'   (XXXI)

And with this he returns from his vision, and the poem ends with his
return to the difficulties of being a Christian ("as I said"), and concludes:

I fear

And think 'How dreadful to be grudged
'No ease henceforth, as one that's judged.
'Condemned to earth for ever, shut
'From heaven!'

But Easter-Day breaks! But

Christ rises! Mercy every way
Is infinite,—and who can say?

Again, the poem acknowledges the difficulty of belief which necessarily must do no less than connect finite with infinite, but ultimately it turns into a statement, supported by vision, of determination to exist in hope. It is less diffuse than *Christmas Eve,* but like that poem it gives the uncomfortable impression that vision is only subsidiary support to a predetermined and optimistic position.

But these are relatively early poems, and even had they proved more integrated and convincing, they can represent no more than a stage in Browning's religious development. It was almost thirty years later when, again putting aside the objective dramatic form of his famous poems, Browning once more appeared to speak directly of religion in *La Saisiaz* (1878).

The poem was provoked by the sudden death of a close woman friend, Miss Egerton Smith, who was at the time with Browning and his sister in Switzerland. The poem is embarrassing throughout for its heavy-handed failure as art, due chiefly to the use of long couplet lines and a maddeningly jogging meter. Browning attempts an unfortable wedding of abstract argument with a casual vernacular, the whole jerky effect being intensified by his always strong inclination towards questions and exclamations. The form of the poem dramatizes how very far Browning seems to have been from vision here.

To turn to subject matter: the opening finds the poet ascending a mountain to consider the meaning of so sudden a death as has just shocked him. It is not necessary to think of Wordsworth's comparable ascent at the end of *The Prelude,* but it is clear that Browning's starting point is largely the same as Wordsworth's conclusion; Browning, in fact, says in the first few lines:

Stationed face to face with—Nature? rather with Infinitude

and the prefatory verses to the poem, fittingly, contain both its starting point and conclusion at once:

Body may slumber:
Body shall cumber
Soul-flight no more.

The poet reminisces on the vividness and "aliveness" of the immediately previous days spent with his friend, and on the contrasting suddenness of death, which prompts the same kind of questioning as had the Judgement Day vision in *Easter Day*. The questions are piled high: ("Does the soul survive the body? Is there God's self, no or yes?"). There is a direct attempt to face up to ultimate questions by self-examination, but Browning's replies are based on highly abstract reasoning. And even if intellectual reasoning is accepted as a proper instrument to answer theological questions, its quality here is at best unconvincing:

> I have questioned and am answered. Question, answer
> presuppose
> Two points: that the thing itself which questions
> answers,—*is*, it knows;
> As it also knows the thing perceived outside itself,
> —a force
> Actual ere its own beginning, operative through its
> course,
> Unaffected by its end,—that this thing likewise
> needs must be;
> Call this—God, then, call that—soul, and both—
> the only facts for me.
> Prove them facts? that they o'erpass my power of proving,
> proves them such:
> Fact it is I know I know not something which is fact
> as much.

This sort of verse is quite without emotional impact; its complexity carries the tone of adolescent debate. Even if Browning's arguments here were given the clarity of good prose, they would still be unconvincing. A great deal of the latter part of *La Saisiaz* consists of this kind of verse, often as a mass of argumentative qualifications. Out of it all, after a prolonged debate between Fancy and Reason and with Browning's cautionary "only for myself I speak," there comes, inevitably, hope; it is again put forward abstractly and with careful qualification: "So, I hope—no more than hope, but hope—no less than hope." This hope is founded not at all on the extended arguments to which the bulk of *La Saisiaz* has been devoted, but simply upon personal conviction: ". . . if no one else beheld,/ I behold in life, so—hope!"

Browning's final direct poetic word on such matters is in the *Parleyings with Certain People of Importance in Their Day* (1887). Here again, using the poetry of argument, Browning speaks in his own voice with no mask of dramatic character. In the *Parleyings,* he addresses certain figures who had influenced his youthful mind, presenting to each his developed ideas in various fields of human activity and thought, and providing a defence of those ideas. The scheme was to form a record of Browning's mental journey towards his favorite doctrines, as well as a justification of them, and thus would result in a kind of Browningesque *Prelude.* Of the seven *Parleyings,* the one of overriding importance to the matters under discussion here is that with the philosopher Bernard de Mandeville—a *Parleying* in which Browning attempts to justify the optimistic philosophy of life.

It is a substantial work of great significance in assessing the standard view of Browning as inspiriting prophet of optimism. He here reaffirms, for instance, his insistent idea—which is also a Romantic one—that what appear to be failure and disaster at short range will lead in the end to understanding and spiritual growth. It is a Wordsworthian tenet, and it is fundamentally the view of evil which DeVane has stressed in reading Browning.

But the general foundations on which this conclusion has to stand are in Browning's case very sandy indeed. The heart of the *Parleying* with Mandeville is an argument (in which Mandeville is called on to assist Browning) with Thomas Carlyle—that later Carlyle whose vision had been largely destroyed by Victorian realities.

In brief, Browning insists that evil is the ncessary means of moral progress. But this is simply one corollary of his own asserted belief, which he goes on to try to justify. To reduce his argument to its simplest level, it amounts to the insistence on emotional and intuitive—as opposed to intellectual—recognition of man's relationship to God and the universe. His justification of this, as in all these poems in which he speaks directly of philosophical matters, starts from, and throughout is based upon, his own stated inner conviction, here summed up in the cry

> Sense, descry
> The spectrum—mind, infer immensity!

DeVane admirably sums up Browning's argument. The poet, he says, connects man with God "by means of the emotional and moral consciousness. . . . It is his final answer to Carlyle's pessimism. . . . he finds hopefulness in man himself. As man is against evil, so is God, for man is the image of God, in little; and thus God can be comprehended somewhat, in human terms. He answers Carlyle indirectly by setting up his own beliefs." [22]

Browning's statement of belief, here made late in life, does not differ essentially from the position taken in the previous poems I have considered. Here it carries, however, other factors making his assertion somewhat suspect. His very choice of Mandeville as audience and ally is enough in itself to make his case absurd. Mandeville's *The Fable of the Bees* had been a sardonic piece, defending evil on the paradoxical grounds that society is only possible through the selfish urges of humanity, not its virtuous ones. The tone of the *Fable* frequently carries a self-conscious satisfaction on its author's part at the shock-value of his thesis. DeVane is a sympathetic critic of Browning, but he shows clearly that the poet utterly misunderstood the emphasis of the *Fable*. He did so, moreover (charges DeVane) because his spiritual hunger for optimism led him, despite a powerful intellect, to striking misinterpretations if they suited his own ends:

> It is obvious from every bit of evidence in the case that Browning did not understand the true purport of Mandeville's teaching. He read Mandeville . . . at an extremely critical period of his life. He was returning from atheism to orthodoxy, and the tendency of the reaction was to make him read orthodoxy into all things. He had begun his search, a search that was to continue the rest of his life, for evidence of a loving and gracious God who utilized evil in this life to make it bring forth moral good . . . . It was just at this period when he had decided that he believed in light and truth, that the poet's attention was caught by Mandeville's paradoxical and striking sub-title, *Private Vices, Public Benefits*. Here was more evidence that a benevolent God turned evil to good. It is as one . . . like himself . . . that Browning summons Mandeville to the *Parleying*.[23]

What led Browning to misread Mandeville's *Fable* is not to be attributed to simple-mindedness. Rather, in his mind lay a deeper and perhaps subconscious motivation for distorting Mandeville into an optimistic ally; he could not face the possibility of having to envisage Carlyle's advancing pessimism as truth. Moreover, the very selection of Carlyle as his opponent in the *Parleying* appears to reflect his own dread of finding himself, like many Victorians, bereft of belief. Browning and Carlyle had been sociable, but between them lay a gulf of puzzlement and misunderstanding. Finally, Carlyle in his middle and later years was not only pessimistic, but also a renegade from that sweeping Romantic faith he had earlier expressed in *Sartor Resartus*—that same faith the young Browning had touched in his early delight in Shelley.

Carlyle may have been more honest with himself in losing that pitch of certitude than Browning was in his continual assertion of it. Certainly his poems enforce it again and again, through vision, through seemingly personal experience, and above all through argument. Such "optimism" underlies the cliché of Pippa's "all's well with the world." But Pippa's song, so far from epitomizing Browning's optimism, ought with more justice to haunt him like an ironic ghost. If we take the poems of religious focus in order of composition, they progress from relative certainty (in *Christmas Eve* and *Easter Day*) to something much more abstract and qualified in *La Saisiaz* and much more suspect in the *Parleyings*. The fact that these poems of Browning's transmit almost no emotional authority is not as important as the fact that the content fails so often *as* argument. While they are in general fairly clear, the later poems especially lapse into excessive abstraction, complex over-qualification, and occasionally memorable incoherence, usually at crucial points of argument. We cannot, of course, expect poems of personal belief to rest upon anything but their own statement, and a book like Newman's *Apologia* attests to the powerful sincerity which a writer's simple recognition of this can communicate. But Browning, speaking equally directly of matters of faith, appears to have no such realization—indeed the bulk of these poems is given to intellectual argument (the very thing he affects to surmount) and didactic example. The poems have a curiously split quality: Browning primarily insists on the supreme authority of faith, and of a hope which exists despite obstacles, but the bulk of each poem is given over to argument, vision and example consistently enough to suggest that his deepest feelings recognize the need of his overt message of faith for such support. "Despite this evil, despite this religiosity, despite this disaster," he seems to be saying, "I feel faith." But the bulk of these poems is given to the "despite this" rather than to the nature of faith and hope. Again and again, Browning is capable of first implying that faith needs no argument, and then constructing a ponderous argument to sustain it. In his direct treatment of philosophic and religious concerns, faith and hope are always insisted on and used as keystones, but it is hard not to sense that Browning's repeated claims for them result from motives far from simple.

3. POEMS OF FAME AND LOVE &ও The evidence for Browning's optimism is incomplete until certain of his better-known poems are examined. The philosophic and religious poetry already considered forms a small part of his output, and its very directness is uncharacteristic of his habit as poet. Cohen is right in sensing that Browning was uncomfortable in trying to speak so nakedly of his own experience and thoughts.[24] Possible reasons for his discomfort have been suggested, but they are partial and disproportionate unless Browning's attitudes are also judged as they appear through more objective poems, poems more difficult for the inference of his views, but of far greater artistic merit.

First it is necessary to clarify his natural way of poetry-making, and second to seek in his work those aspects which promise most fairly to delineate his state of mind. Besides, much of his status as guide to doubting Victorians stems, ironically, from this successful "objective" dramatic work and not, as one might logically expect, from his more subjective, direct presentations of personal outlook. Those who formed the staple of the Browning Society and others who looked up to the poet as teacher would hardly be likely to seek guidance in, say, Browning's love poems (which do concern themselves with the meaning of the extra-worldly instant of time in the Romantic manner). Neither would they seek it even in a poem like *Abt Vogler* (almost a Romantic poem in its mystical presentation of aesthetic experience). They may have accepted the insistent lessons of poems like *Christmas Eve* and *Easter Day*, though it is hard to imagine their reading them with joy or being deeply convinced by them, and certainly not by the abstruse ineptitudes of *La Saisiaz*. If the average Browning admirer found reassurance in his work, it is most likely that he did so through poems of hearty muscular belief like *Prospice*, and especially through poems with Christian themes like *Saul*. This last would indeed be ironic, for in *Saul* and similar poems dealing with Christianity Browning's focus of interest is not primarily religious in the genuine sense, but lies in the dramatic and human exploitation of themes which happen to be biblical.

One may draw some parallel, as well as a sharp distinction in popularity, between Browning's relationship to the Victorians and that of Byron to his readers earlier in the century. Almost all Byron's work may be put aside in considering those aspects of Romantic poetry which I have taken to be central (no one is likely to turn to *Beppo* or *Don Juan*, or even *Childe Harold* as an entire poem, for dramatic assertions of religious outlook on Byron's part!). Byron had only related to Romantic vision and its affirmation in a minute part of his work: where he did so, the passages are, as I said earlier, curiously isolated from their context, and their affirmation seems unconvincing and second-hand. Browning, whose work shows more consistent attempts at philosophic integration, shows within that work a comparable unconvincingness. Like Byron, he is most stimulated by human action in this world, especially as history and the art and architecture of the past record it. And while Browning, in much of his more celebrated work, is equally irrelevant to Victorian problems of belief, his own religious position has often been inferred from poems like *Saul* and *An Epistle of Karshish* because their plots have a Christian basis.

To do this is hopelessly over-simple, as appears both from his early development and from his approach and methods in his most characteristic dramatic monologues, including those with apparently religious themes. His earliest sustained poems, while dramatic or pseudo-dramatic in form and style, had not been objective: what is obviously the poet's own feeling shows through action and character. In *Pauline* and to a lesser extent in *Paracelsus,* there is evidence of individual experience of an aspiring sort, and of an almost Shelleyan Romantic yearning, but in style, diffusion of effort and confusion of structure the poems, *Pauline* in particular, relate more to Spasmodic than Romantic work. Browning's stress is consistently on the individual soul, as it was to remain in so much of his work: he wrote in the Preface to *Sordello* that "little else" but the development of a soul was "worth study." Such a stress on the soul is, of course, cardinal for the Romantics; but for them it is a means to an end, a means for human integration with the divine. Browning, for all his preoccupation with the soul, is primarily interested in its humanity; like all the major Victorian poets except Hopkins, he is incapable of integrating it positively and passionately with the universe in which consciousness exists. The Romantic religion had given Romantic poetry philosophic and artistic unity and a convincing affirmation, while Browning's often-expressed religious belief and general optimism give his poetry neither. Obviously many possible reasons, from shallowness of belief to alternations of mood, could be hazarded for this. The most likely, I shall suggest, is that Browning was psychologically suspicious of his own optimism; externalizing his art in various forms, turning it away from himself, provided some relief from this pressure.

Stung by Mill's view that *Pauline* showed "a more intense and morbid self-consciousness than I ever knew in any sane human being," Browning decided, about 1833, that his poetry would henceforth be dramatic. Several times during his life he defined this as the utterance of imaginary persons rather than his own voice. Attempting such work in the gradually increased objectification of *Paracelsus* and *Sordello,* he also tried to concentrate his "soul's study" into the discipline of shorter poems, creating the brief dramatic monologue which was to loom so large in his output, and of which poems like *Porphyria's Lover* and *Soliloquy of the Spanish Cloister* are prototypes.

Porphyria's Lover, though an early and imperfect poem, reveals at the simplest level a good deal about Browning's interests and methods. Its sensational theme—a sex murder—caters to his intense interest in human reaction in abnormal situations, and his treatment of it within a brief poem shows Browning as the episodic dramatist or short-story writer *manqué.* (It had been his relatively unsuccessful attempts at drama that had in part led him to the dramatic monologue.) The first lines of the poem are devoted to providing, with intense compression, the dramatic components of setting (the storm in the night with the suggestion of its spite); action, with a suggestion of the ominous ("when glided in Porphyria"); and stage-effects (the dripping clothes, damp hair, and symbolically soiled gloves). The event is narrated by the murderer, with its background given in general and abstract terms (ll. 21–25), and the murder itself described with chilling matter-of-factness ("I am quite sure she felt no pain"). The final line of the poem, "And yet God has not said a word," is important. Its very isolation draws attention to what the poem scrupulously avoids; there is no interest at all in the philosophic implications of the crime; the poet's interest remains entirely in the event itself, and particularly in the abnormal psychology of the speaker. Though it would be technically possible to interpret the last line so, the poem does not contain any comment by Browning on divine indifference; it is as far as it is possible to get from that kind of "philosophic" poem. *Porphyria's Lover* is, for its brief length, a diffuse poem, to which Browning attempts to give swift movement and forceful unity by a regular rhyme scheme. This is a tendency we shall see again in him—to attempt to compensate for internal difficulties, especially of thought, by manipulations of form. The *Soliloquy of the Spanish Cloister* is a far more skillful poem in its management of tone, but it is essentially the same kind of poem; its focus, entirely confined to human personality, is on the difference between appearance and psychological reality. Again, the poem is a dramatic episode, complete with scene and stage properties, the object of which is to reveal the psychological portrait of the speaker Browning creates.

In this kind of poem Browning confines his thought to the physical "actual" world and to human reactions to it. Within that limitation, however, he accords his energetic imagination enormous range. His interest in psychology, in history, in atmosphere, with developments in structure and technique, leads him through the whole series of famous dramatic monologues and culminates in *The Ring and the Book*. None of these poems departs much from its essentially objective kind. Outside this, Browning, like Tennyson, was also able to fulfill his imaginative versatility in a whole range of additional work demanding almost no introspective thought at all, from rousing patriotic narrative (*Incident of the French Camp*) to children's verse (*The Pied Piper*) and superficial nature poems like *Home Thoughts from Abroad*.

It might be expected, however, that when Browning came to deal with religious themes, he would offer both the guidance troubled Victorians sought and some convincing revelation of his own attitudes to problems of existence. And while some readers unquestionably were convinced they had found the first of these in Browning's "religious" poems, it is hard to see how they could possibly have discovered the second.

In *Saul*, for instance, his interest is still essentially on dramatic matters—on narrated events, on exotic scene and metaphor. It is true that David concludes, as the biblical source demands, with the possibly inspiriting advocacy of a religious lesson ("The submission of man's nothing-perfect to God's all-complete"). There is a statement, so frequent in Browning, of the ultimate value of human aspiration ("'tis not what man Does which exalts him, but what man Would do!"); there is David's insistence on the infinity of divine love. But while it might comfort troubled readers to find these things in a poem which is evocative and at times dramatically moving, they are quite subordinate to the demands of its legend, and there is nothing, beyond the ebullience of Browning's public personality, to suggest that they are put forward as serious, subjective religious statements by the poet. And even if one assumes they are, they remain merely isolated assertions, unconnected, so far as any record of it is concerned, with the poet's experience. This is not an artistic defect, but it is a didactic one.

The same view holds for the magnificently dramatic poem *An Epistle of Karshish*. As art it is almost unexceptionable; as a portrait of a pagan mind unwillingly struggling not to be too impressed by the vicarious impact of Christ, it is entirely convincing. The poem's detail is unforgettably evocative, from the opening Arab formula of address, to the plants and herbs, the colors and sounds of the ancient East. The character and mental struggle of Karshish form a psychological *tour de force*. The shock to western readers of an "outside" view of the Crucifixion, "a tumult . . . when the earthquake fell," is intense. The strangeness of atmosphere of the meeting with Lazarus is compelling:

> I crossed a ridge of short sharp broken hills
> Like an old lion's cheek teeth. Out there came
> A moon made like a face with certain spots
> Multiform, manifold, and menacing;
> Then a wind rose behind me. So we met
> In this old sleepy town at unaware,
> The man and I.

Additionally, the structural manipulation of Karshish's psychological attempts to escape, his "scientific" explanations and his insistent returns, despite his will, to the subject which enthralls him are superbly functional and integrated. But the poem remains one about the psychological impact of religious doubt in an empirical mind of an unfamiliar culture. It is, in its plot, about religion, but it is not, in any profound sense of the word, a religious poem at all. The idea that Browning is here insisting that doubt is a part of faith, and making a case for the acceptance of the two as one, is not sustained by the emphasis of the poem, which is upon an almost scientific examination of the psychological phenomenon in Karshish's mind. Theologically, the poem merely testifies that the Christian legend is a compelling one—something which an unbeliever may well be more ready to say than a believer.

An Epistle of Karshish and *Saul*, therefore, are not to be legitimately differentiated, except artistically, from a poem like *Porphyria's Lover*. The first two merely happen to have religious themes, which can be, if the reader wishes, taken as propaganda to plead the case for conventional Christianity; but there is no need to take them so.

A somewhat different kind of "religious" poem is exemplified by *Rabbi Ben Ezra*. This, from the beginning, certainly is highly assertive. It also seems to be an unusually subjective dramatic poem for Browning, who has chosen a speaker remote from the average reader's knowledge (unlike David in *Saul*). Thus associations which might have supported the poem as objective story or event are not readily available; the "voice" exists in isolation and tends to be taken as that of the poet, who appears to be using only the slight gesture towards anonymity which an insignificant mask provides. Ben Ezra, moreover, is given no dramatic personality at all (unlike Karshish). Even if, then, we concede a matter of some doubt, that this kind of religious poem does convey an unusual suggestion of personal involvement on Browning's part with its assertive content, it remains worthwhile to scrutinize that content closely. The poem, dated 1864, uses a general form, meter and style reminiscent of the chant in Arnold's *Empedocles* and of Fitzgerald's *Rubaiyat*. Readers comparing Browning's poem with those, however, will find that such technical similarities only serve to highlight its immense differences in philosophy from either. Ben Ezra refers to the doubt of his time and briefly raises the question of what to believe; but he merely remarks that he "prizes" the doubt (since to suffer is to be human and who would wish to change that?), and he answers the question of what to believe in the rest of the poem. That answer is, in brief, complete trust in God, despite experience ("welcome each rebuff"); it suggests that life is a kind of rehearsal, with the terminology of evolution used on this occasion as an argument *for* faith:

> Thence shall I pass, approved
> A man, for aye removed
> From the developed brute—a god, though in the germ.

The essential faith, however, lies in the belief that one will arrive at it—"I shall know, being old."

The poem's whole assertion is buttressed by near-Carlylean turns of phrase ("Trust God; see all, nor be afraid!") and by echoes from formal Christianity ("thy soul and God stand sure"). The divine potter and human clay in Browning's well-known concluding metaphor, existing as eternal realities outside time and ultimately beyond "this dance/ Of plastic circumstance," certainly approach Romantic conceptions.

But, again assuming that Browning is making a relatively subjective statement here, the poem's assertion is far less than convincing. It is a comforting spiritual world that Ben Ezra inhabits; the subject of doubt is raised, but there is no hint of any struggle with it, and the only statement on the question, before it is dismissed, is that doubt must be accepted. The Rabbi not only protests too much—the poem, for its length, being fairly repetitive—but he protests *in vacuo;* there is, again, nothing in the poem to connect the speaker's assertion with his experience. The assertion seems to parallel Romantic assertion, but it arises from no specific individual experience as far as one can tell, and apparently from no experience at all. Theologically, the poem asserts a position similar to Newman's, that faith is an intuitive matter not subject to intellectual argument, but if Newman had taken that position in isolation, with no account of his spiritual struggles in the *Apologia* or elsewhere, it may well have looked as irrelevant to the human condition as Ben Ezra's does here.

In brief, while Browning's "religious" dramatic poems generally deserve to be influential as art, and were in fact almost certainly influential as "teaching," they perform the latter function only through re-telling, in an original way, and reanimating Christian myths (as in *Saul* and *An Epistle of Karshish*), or through the insistence, repetition and rhetorical power of their "lesson" (*Rabbi Ben Ezra*). In no sense do they work through any revelation of the poet's religious experience, for their whole emphasis is dramatic, and of this world.

Moreover, other clearly subjective poems by Browning, those I have called the poems of Romantic impulse—and particularly the love poems—show that the nature of what they attempt and a view of comfortable, optimistic acceptance such as Ben Ezra articulates can hardly co-exist. There is in Browning a fervent longing for fulfillment of soul which is often frustrated and defeated, and which blank acceptance does not even appear to qualify, let alone answer. But before moving to such poems from the hearty assertion of the Ben Ezra kind, I should like to consider the poem *Abt Vogler,* which is a half-way house between the two. It leads logically to the love poems and personal lyrics of 'Romantic impulse" in that it deals with what is clearly Romantic experience—here an aesthetic experience such as Keats had written of in the *Ode to a Nightingale;* it harks back to the "religious" position of *Rabbi Ben Ezra* in its conclusion, where the problem of the return to the untransformed world is dealt with.

It is an understatement to say that *Abt Vogler* shows Romantic tendencies. For a little more than half of its length it presents, by the Romantic means of creating emotional echoes of it, the experience of making artistic beauty in music, and rising through the musically-stimulated imagination to a mystical contact with divinity. To its fifty-sixth line it is a poem of genuine Romantic affirmation, and perhaps the only pure example of this in Victorian poetry.

The entire poem, in fact, can hardly be studied too carefully in the context of Browning's handling of his Romantic heritage. Among his whole output, it is perhaps the most revealing emblem of his mind. Nothing else in his work rivals the first fifty-six lines of this poem in showing so fully, in creating so brilliantly, the intensity of Browning's desire, held so passionately in a part of his mind, for Romantic faith. No poem shows so dramatically the two sides of his mind: from line fifty-seven the poem is an attempted answer to the old problems posed by Romantic experience. It is a religious answer, expressed with repetitive insistence and the full force of Browning's personality: we can put aside for the moment the relationship of answer to question, first considering the two parts of the poem in somewhat greater detail.

The theme of the first part of the poem is the old Romantic one of the experience of artistic creation (Abt Vogler ruminates as he pours music from the organ), and then the rest of the poem moves on to present the aftermath of such creation and consider its meaning. As such—and in certain of its phrases—the Romantic opening part of the poem inevitably brings to mind certain related Romantic poems—the *Ode to a Nightingale,* the Coleridge poems with which I began, much of *The Prelude;* in its visual brightness ("Raising my rampired walls of gold as transparent as glass,") and its evocative Eastern phrases ("And pile him a palace straight, to pleasure the princess he loved!"), it suggests *Kubla Khan.* The meter, so suggestive of the soaring and descending blasts of an organ, is here highly integrated with the subject-matter, a kind of unity which some other Browning poems notably lack.

From the start, the first part of the poem is a Romantic *coup.*

The sweeping metrical movements create excitement, the inanimate keys are seen by the speaker's rarified and intense imagination as alive and human, and the fire and light images further intensify the upward movement until

> Up, the pinnacled glory reached, and the pride of
> my soul was in sight.

And nature itself appears to the speaker to become involved in the gigantic creative spasm, which, the poem makes blindingly clear, is nothing less than Romantic transcendence, where the Romantic duality of finite and infinite touch and (in a final blaze of glory) become one:

> Nature in turn conceived, obeying an impulse as I;
> And the emulous heaven yearned down, made an effort
> to reach the earth,
> As the earth had done her best, in my passion, to
> scale the sky;
> Novel splendours burst forth, grew familiar and
> dwelt with mine;
> Not a point nor peak but found and fixed its
> wandering star—
> Meteor-moons, balls of blaze; and they did not pale
> nor pine,
> For earth had attained to heaven—there was no
> more near nor far.

Many of the other statements and implications of this part of the poem are thoroughly Romantic. Browning is at one with Keats (*Ode on a Grecian Urn*) in the idea (l. 40) that through art past and present blend and are stilled in perfection. There is the conception, as in Milton and Wordsworth, that artistic creation—music—is the direct human echo of divine creativity:

> Painter and poet are proud in the artist-list enrolled:—
> But here is the finger of God, a flash of the will that can,
> Existent behind all laws, that made them and, lo, they are!

Browning, in explaining the nature of artistic creation, slips into the entirely Wordsworthian technique of the sudden shift from the earthly to the cosmic, all-revealing image:

And I know not if, save in this, such gift be allowed
                                    to man,
That out of three sounds he frame, not a fourth
                                    sound, but a star.

He also intersperses, in a near-Shelleyan manner, the conception of
the dead as more truly alive than the living, using, again, the techniques of both Shelley and Wordsworth in reversing normal standards of expectation:

Or else the wonderful Dead who have passed through
                          the body and gone,
But were back once more to breathe in an old world
                          worth their new
What never had been, was now; what was, as it shall
                          be anon.

All these elements and others cohere magnificently, and develop as
the music develops to an integrated and steadily mounting pitch of
emotional excitement until the final line of the section is felt as inevitable.

And there! Ye have heard and seen; consider and bow the head!

From line fifty-seven, after the music and vision have ended, we
have a different kind of poem. The fine imagery, meter, and sound of
the previous lines simply vanish. Browning is, of course, facing the
old Romantic problem of returning from the infinite universe of
spiritual fulfillment to the finite world of sense. It is the dispiriting
anti-climax which Keats had so often combatted. But that sense of recent motion, of dazed but transformed, live emergence from one level
of existence to another is quite lacking here. Once the moments of
creative climax are over, Browning's poem becomes static, repetitive
exposition shot through with suggestions and near-echoes of the arguments and conclusions of formal philosophy. There is Browning's familiar idea of evil as set-off to good (which brings Leibnitz to
mind); there is the philosophic commonplace that sin is *nothing*, so
God cannot be its author:

The evil is null, is naught, is silence implying sound.

It is, of course, a central Romantic idea, and it is found also in
Spinoza, Hegel, Emerson and others. Why then should Leibnitz (and
perhaps Pangloss?) leap to mind when it is met again here? Because

Browning's lines—in the latter part of the poem—are so different from those of the first part, and generate resistance and scepticism in the reader. By the very repetition and insistence of his protestations, and by the change from the emotional echo of vision to abstract insistence (for it is hardly argument), Browning protests too much, and above all he does so inertly and *in vacuo*. Certain lines in the poem suggest, for example, an idea very close to Romantic Platonism:

> On the earth the broken arcs; in the heaven a
> perfect round,

but the suggestion simply occurs and is suddenly stumbled on by the reader; it is not adequately prepared for earlier in the poem, and it rests on no previous basis in the earlier assertion. The two neatly-compartmented halves of the poem render it not simply static in the Arnold fashion, but anti-climactic. The poem is at first a Romantic triumph; it then simply returns to the world of prosaic propaganda. There is no sense of loss, none of struggle, no sense of the speaker's being moved and changed by what he has seen and felt—there is only simple transformation. Romantic poems dealing with the failure of vision, like Coleridge's *Dejection,* and several passages in Keats, Wordsworth and Shelley usually transmit a sense of reaching, of the value of aspiration itself, of human, animated struggle and loss. Here, there is only quiet, self-contained, unquestioning acceptance and moralizing.

Though the difference is primarily one of philosophical attitude, it affects Browning's poetic technique. It is always difficult, of course, to move from the area of vision to that of philosophic pronouncement, but the Romantics had illuminated the latter with the former. The luminous light on the leaves in the lime-tree bower in Coleridge's poem is the light in the poet's mind after experiencing his vision. The impact of Romantic experience shapes the poetry itself, even when the poet must speak in the most general, concrete, or even negative terms of the passing or failure of vision. Hence as Wordsworth's Snowdon vision passes and he infers its general meaning, what he says is made to suggest itself as a stream from God, flowing down such a mountain as has played a part in direct vision. Vision, held in the mind, and poetic structure connect. Or as Keats enters and leaves the visionary world of the nightingale, it is by an involuntary movement through the no-man's-land of trance—"Do I wake or sleep?" There is nothing comparable in Browning's poem—just two almost unconnected extremes. The poem's progress from one half to the other, in fact, is the exact opposite of that of *Adonais*. In Shelley's poem, out of death comes a larger, supremely authoritative view of cosmic life. In Browning's, out of a climax of artistic vision comes pure resignation to its loss. There seems a flash of self-revelation on Browning's part in Vogler's lines:

> To me, who must be saved because I cling with
> my mind
> To the same, same self, same love, same God;
> aye, what was, shall be.

—"cling with my mind . . ."—the image sums up the kind of underlying, perhaps subconscious, certainly repressed desperation one senses again and again in reading Browning. It enforces violent escape into repetitive optimism because its implications are too intolerable to face. If this attitude does not provide a key to Browning's entire cast of mind, at least it helps to explain the dichotomy in a poem like *Abt Vogler*.

Browning's love poems are more fully revealing of this "divided" Browning, charting with some precision the contending forces within him. Like *Abt Vogler,* they are often records of aspiration and even glimpsed vision, but when the limits of these are reached, they often express frustration, puzzlement and near-despair, rather than *Abt Vogler*'s acceptance.

The love poems are generally brief personal lyrics, and since few dramatic characters are involved, they appear as simple vignettes recording moods of the poet's. As a group they are simple to classify: there are a few conventional love poems, such as *Life in a Love,* and one or two in which the focus of interest is dramatic or psychological (*A Light Woman*). But at the center of the group are works one can only call poems of Romantic longing, and they deal, in a way which brings Donne to mind, with the role of love in bridging the gap between finite and infinite realities. The poems vary somewhat in the aspects of love they treat, but the poet's attitude varies only negligibly whether the poem was written early or late in his career. What Browning is concerned with in *Cristina,* published in 1842 and a prototype of this kind of poem, he is still concerned with, and in essentially the same way, in poems such as *Summum Bonum* and *A Pearl, A Girl*, dated 1889. If there is any real change, it does not lie in that shift from early inspiration to later argument, and from early character-creation to his own direct voice later, which we find in the bulk of his poetry. It is simply a minor change from complex to simple style and subject matter. In other words, the point Browning reached early, in delineating the role of love as bridge to infinitude, never developed beyond quite restricted limits as his life went on, and here at least he resembles Arnold in confronting a blank wall beyond which he cannot pass.

Cristina (1842), like so many other poems of the kind it represents, is concerned with what Browning sees as the all-revealing moment of love, which exposes, literally in a trice, the ultimate meaning of whole lives—in other words gives the finite its true relation to something larger; it is the moment "When the spirit's true endowments/ Stand out plainly from its false ones." The one moment of communion reveals spiritual truth, and the meaning of life itself becomes clear:

> Doubt you if, in some such moment,
>   As she fixed me, she felt clearly,
> Ages past the soul existed,
>   Here an age 'tis resting merely,
> And hence fleets again for ages,
>   While the true end, sole and single,
> It stops here for is, this love-way,
>   With some other soul to mingle?

Of course, the moment of blinding vision must end: that is the law for "this world":

> Oh, observe! Of course, next moment,
>   The world's honours, in derision,
> Trampled out the light forever;
>   Never fear but there's provision
> Of the devil's to quench knowledge
>   Lest we walk the earth in rapture!

But the union is made; the two lives which have been joined in prefigured revelation of their purpose may go on to pass their remaining finite days alone, though these are irrelevant:

> And then, come the next life quickly!
>   This world's use will have been ended.

Cristina is an interesting and provocative poem, but it gives the impression, like more simple love poems of Browning's, that it is essentially the exposition of a theory which fascinates him, rather than his direct experience. The poem is clearly Romantic in impulse, and asserts a belief which accords spiritual meaning to earthly life. But its momentary vision, again, is recounted rather than presented; the reader is told about it; he is not impelled to feel something—even an echo—of its force. And finally its conclusion does not follow from the experience described in the poem in anything like so direct a way as it does in genuinely Romantic poems. It is, rather, a quiet statement of personal belief concerning after-life, which appears disjoined from the momentary vision earlier in the poem—largely through the lack of emotional impact in Browning's treatment of that vision.

A number of other poems—*Meeting at Night, Now, Summum Bonum,* and (in a direct autobiographical way) *By the Fireside*—are presentations, externalized to varying degree and given roughly dramatic form, of this same idea of love as the all-revealing glimpse of souls to be joined in eternity. *Prospice* is the statement of Browning's view of death, with like assumptions as its basis. Sometimes such assumptions are merely presented visually: *Meeting at Night* begins simply in broad panorama:

> The gray sea and the long black land;
> And the yellow half-moon large and low.

It ends in the literally flashing moment of the only reality:

> A tap at the pane, the quick sharp scratch
> And blue spurt of a lighted match,
> And a voice less loud, through its joys and fears,
> Than the two hearts beating each to each!

Browning uses this technique of narrowing down from broad vistas to the central core of experience in *Love Among the Ruins* (1855), a longer and extraordinary poem which perhaps shows the impact of the scale of time which evolutionary thought enforces. The scene is set on the open sheep pastures where a great city once stood, and the poem continually shuttles back and forth from past to present, from the broadest scenes in past ages to the particular intense moment, from the old city and the armies and the feelings of their men, to the overwhelming present reality which implies so much more:

a girl with eager eyes and yellow hair
Waits me there
In the turret whence the charioteers caught soul
For the goal,
When the king looked, where she looks now, breathless,
dumb
Till I come.

The poem's imaginative scope and unusual form give it an original
effect, but what it says amounts to no more than the assertion of its
final line:

Love is best.

And its meaning is precisely that of *A Pearl, A Girl* (1889):

I am wrapped in blaze,
Creation's lord, of heaven and earth
Lord whole and sole—by a minute's birth—
Through the love in a girl!

or that of *Summum Bonum* (1889):

Truth, that's brighter than gem,
Trust, that's purer than pearl—
Brightest truth, purest trust in the universe
—all were for me
In the kiss of one girl.

If *Love Among the Ruins* differs significantly from the earlier
Cristina or the love poems published so much later, it is in showing
an intermediate Browning compensating for the repetition of his
message by a wider-ranging imagination and a complex verse form;
this uses run-on long lines with short ones in such a way as to produce the effect of a particularly jangling internal rhyme, proving
quite inimical to his subject matter. While the piled rhymes may be
considered partly functional in echoing (as the present echoes and
contains the past in the poem), it remains impossible to articulate
the verse, even in the mind, without embarrassment. The device may
be compared with Arnold's attempts at mathematical symmetry of
form, which at least are fairly subtle, but in the case of *Love Among
the Ruins* it is disastrous in that the eccentricity completely domi-

nates the poem. It is remarkable how critics have found this kind of distraction unexceptionable in Browning.[25]

A far better poem, the most enlightening (and, I suspect, honest) of all Browning's love poems is *Two in the Campagna* (1855). Its far more simple verse gives the poem the authority of direct statement as the poet's mind reveals itself naturally. The poem involves the same theme of present seen against remote past, and is shot through with a view of life as a huge evolutionary process. The speaker, sitting with a woman in the open Campagna outside Rome, feels his thoughts wandering and reaching out, like a spider's web, amid the whole system of nature which embraces past and present:

> For me, I touched a thought, I know,
>   Has tantalized me many times
> (Like turns of thread the spiders throw
>   Mocking across our path) for rhymes
> To catch at and let go.
>
> Help me to hold it! First it left
>   The yellowing fennel, run to seed
> There, branching from the brickwork's cleft,
>   Some old tomb's ruin, yonder weed
> Took up the floating weft.
>
> Where one small orange cup amassed
>   Five beetles—blind and green they grope
> Among the honey-meal; and last,
>   Everywhere on the grassy slope
> I traced it. Hold it fast!

If this natural system, which grips plants, insects, and thoughts, is seen with eyes open to the scale of evolutionary ideas—and the phrasing of the poem leaves no doubt that it should be—then what place, the poet asks, is there in love for individual feeling? Is not love only a primeval mechanism, a life-force that merely uses us for its purpose?

> Such life here, through such lengths of hours,
>   Such miracles performed in play,
> Such primal naked forms of flowers,
>   Such letting nature have her way
> While heaven looks from its towers!
>
> How say you? Let us, O my dove,
>   Let us be unashamed of soul

As earth lies bare to heaven above!
How is it under our control
To love or not to love?

The poem, again, develops as a dichotomy, and in its second
half it puts, against this idea, the familiar human, individual, Romantic longing of the soul for complete fulfillment through absorption with a fellow-soul. Love is a part of human longing for infinitude, but even as the lover vents this longing he is also repelled by
his awareness of the emotionless finite system which directs and uses
it. The moment of fulfillment is seen here in true perspective, defeated—as for the Romantic—by the inevitable return to the conditions
of the untransformed world:

I would I could adopt your will,
See with your eyes, and set my heart
Beating by yours, and drink my fill
At your soul's springs—your part my part
In life, for good or ill.

No. I yearn upward, touch you close,
Then stand away. I kiss your cheek,
Catch your soul's warmth—I pluck the rose
And love it more than tongue can speak—
Then the good minute goes.

Here (as in *Cristina*) is one of the few places in Browning
where the problem of Romantic deprivation is at least recognised. It
is one step beyond the simple acceptance throughout the latter part
of *Abt Vogler*. Here, for a brief moment, Browning does not turn
from the negative consequences of his own longing, and his verse
moves close to Arnold's (especially in its concluding tone) in taking
on a plaintive immobility:

Already how am I so far
Out of that minute? Must I go
Still like the thistle-ball, no bar,
Onward, whenever light winds blow,
Fixed by no friendly star?

Just when I seemed about to learn!
Where is the thread now? Off again!
The old trick! Only I discern—
Infinite passion, and the pain
Of finite hearts that yearn.

In the love poems, Browning expresses his deep longing for unity, for lasting fulfillment of his momentary vision of love. Beside it, he puts an assertion of its all-encompassing meaning, and he envisages its philosophical implications. But he merely asserts these things, again, in relative isolation. They emerge, often, from described or recounted, rather distant experience, with little attempt to make the reader feel their effects vicariously. For the most part, he avoids treating the difficulties which his constant subject, the glimpse of the fulfillment of love, brings in its wake in a finite world. Usually he just withdraws from such considerations.[26] Where he does not withdraw, in one or two poems he sorrowfully records the difficulty, as in *Two in the Campagna;* he never wrestles with it, as Keats had done.

4. SISYPHUS LOST: A SUMMARY 🙠 These love poems, recording as they do an essentially Romantic longing or "reaching out" on Browning's part for some kind of supra-worldly authority, point the way to consideration of the whole area of his Romantic inheritance and its impact on his mind.

From his earliest formative years Browning had been drawn towards Romantic affirmation and style, and in Shelley especially he had found these at their most intense and personal. In his *Essay on Shelley* Browning had insisted that the distinction between the dramatic, objective poetry which was his own natural sphere, and subjective poetry, was fundamental, a matter of simple difference in kind. In discussing "subjective" work in the *Essay,* not only does he show an extraordinary understanding of a sort of poetry he was himself immensely drawn to but could not write successfully; he also provides, apparently without particular intention, a penetrating definition of the nature of Romantic poetry, and his terms reflect the supreme position, as critic, he accords it:

> The subjective poet . . . gifted like the objective poet with the fuller perception of nature and man, is impelled to embody the thing he perceives, not so much with reference to the many below as to the one above him, the supreme Intelligence which apprehends all things in their absolute truth,—an ultimate view ever aspired to, if but partially attained, by the poet's own soul. Not what man sees, but what God sees—the *Ideas* of Plato, seeds of creation lying burningly on the Divine Hand—it is towards these that he struggles . . . . He is rather a seer, accordingly, than a

fashioner, and what he produces will be less a work than an efflu-
ence.[27]

Accordingly, his own early long poems are clearly a sustained attempt in this Romantic key—in their subjects, style and inchoate vision. There has been a considerable shift in critical view of *Pauline*
and *Paracelsus*. Half a century ago, when Browning's reputation as
sage and teacher was high, critics like Stopford Brooke would wade
solemnly and ingenuously through the two poems [28] (and *Sordello*)
in quest of Browning's "theory of life." Recent critics tend to dismiss
these poems as immature and confused work, of little consequence, in
a would-be Romantic key which the poet has no chance of sustaining—Spasmodic work, in fact. This, I think, is undoubtedly nearer
the truth. J. M. Cohen says flatly that "Browning till thirty-five was a
minor Romantic," [29] and he goes on to add that the Browning of
Paracelsus was still "not sufficiently plain" to merit comparison even
with the principal Spasmodics! [30]

Certainly the entire tendency of Browning's early work is towards this kind of would-be Romanticism (whether labelled Spasmodic or not), and it is a tendency which continues well into his
middle period, and never really dies, as the later love poems show.
His attempts at the poetic transmission of vision, while Romantic in
impulse, are very different from those of the Romantics themselves.
Many years ago, Stopford Brooke, in comparing Browning's imaginative experience with mountains with that of Wordsworth, concluded
that Browning, so far from sensing a Wordsworthian harmony or interplay between humanity and the natural world, was apt to stress
their separation.[31]

In general this is true; Browning, in *La Saisiaz*, we recall, sees
the mountains as "Infinitude" which he must confront but with
which he is not, in any constructive spiritual way, connected. Strictly,
there is no vision, only the conclusion to which vision might have
conduced had there been any. Where Browning does deal with vision
he is apt to be most convincing when it is the result of artistic experience—that is to say, experience initiated actively by human means—
as in *Abt Vogler*. When he writes, in *Christmas Eve* and *Easter Day*,
of religious vision comparable to that of the Romantics, he is scarcely
convincing. His other-worldly authority in those poems is an awk-
ward presentation of vision as vanguard to Christian myth. In both
poems the advent of Christ is preceded by natural phenomena—the

moon-rainbow in *Christmas Eve* and the cloud-fire in *Easter Day*, which is described as a "Waking dream." The truth is that both visions are formed of precisely separable constituents, and *Christmas Eve* provides sufficient example. There is precise, detailed description of changes in skies and clouds, followed by a brief shift into abstract, mannered Romantic rhetoric:

> Another rainbow rose, a mightier,
> Fainter, flushier and flightier,—
> Rapture dying along its verge,   (VI)

and lastly personal reaction and suggestion:

> Thus at the show above me, gazing
> With upturned eyes, I felt my brain
>   Glutted with the glory, blazing
> Throughout its whole mass, over and under
> Until at length it burst asunder
> And out of it bodily there streamed,
> The too-much glory, as it seemed,
> Passing from out me to the ground,
> Then palely serpentining round
> Into the dark with mazy error.   (VII)

> All at once I looked up with terror.
> He was there.
> He himself with his human air.   (VIII)

The central, remarkable feature of this presentation of religious vision, which stands out even further when placed against the full Romantic equivalent, is that the poet remains quite outside it. Browning's direct visions, as these poems describe them, are impersonal wonders, like a divine firework-display, at which he stands open-mouthed with the reader to see what will happen next. There is no interplay of human and natural forces, no sense of the poet's imaginative apprehension being enlarged, elevated, and integrated with what it experiences even while it occurs. Browning's divinities, in *Christmas Eve* and *Easter Day*, announce themselves by celestial conjuring tricks.

In his philosophic conclusions, he comes closer to the Romantics. His constantly-expressed views of death or of the role of evil, as we have seen, do not differ essentially from theirs. What is different here is that Browning omits of necessity that whole area of Romantic experience (sometimes making the sort of display-substitute referred to above) which had both led to Romantic conclusions and given them their imaginative force. Browning constantly gives an impression that he is not working from his own experience. His often-expressed belief in some imprecise form of Christianity, which appears to carry philosophical assumptions about the roles of love, death, and evil akin to Romantic ones, has an oddly automatic quality about it, and provokes comparison. If one puts the greatest loss in Browning's life, that of his wife, against Wordsworth's darker experiences in *The Prelude*, the contrast is marked. While both poets come to see deprivation as ultimately positive, Wordsworth comes to do so only after suffering, despair, and above all time have given him that larger perspective which is characteristically Romantic (see Book XI, especially lines 275–356). Browning's famous letter written to his sister immediately after his wife's death,[32] touching and inspiriting though it may be, has, like much of his poetry on transcendental matters, an automatic, predetermined quality about it: there is no place for suffering, little for experience and none for struggle—only the instantaneous reaction:

> My life is fixed and sure now. I shall live out the remainder in her direct influence, endeavouring to complete mine, miserably imperfect now, but so as to take the good she was meant to give me.

It is a Romantic conclusion in its impulse, its affirmation, even a little in its phrasing; but it is quite different in its lack of any sense of human struggle. This is quite typical of Browning, and in his poetry his affirmation of philosophical conclusions, while resting upon a far slighter basis than the Romantic one, is compensatingly more repetitive and more insistent, not less.

The great Romantic poems had been created from imagination and vision, which themselves shaped the poetry into their own image. When vision fell away, the artistic creativity of the Romantic poet, which had been inseparably bound to it, fell away too. But Browning's best creative work occurs in his *Men and Women*, and in *The Ring and the Book*, when he has turned from direct philosophical and religious problems, and stepped aside (the phrase is important) into human situation and character. The essential Wordsworth is in the *Lyrical Ballads*: the essential Browning is in those dramatic poems where his creativeness is exercised on an intense but limited finite area in which psychology plays the main rôle. One can formulate almost a "law" about this: the enduring poems of Browning are created in precise proportion to his ability to avoid the direct treatment of religious and philosophical problems, and thus be free to immerse his own personality in dramatic character and situation.

The truth is that to look at Browning as many late Victorians looked at him, as prophet of reassurance, is to be led to anti-climax. DeVane reaches the heart of that matter in finding Browning quite capable of degrading the intellect "if it impeaches *what he wishes to believe*" (my italics).[33]

The point is vital, illuminating as it does a psychological escapism in Browning which makes his entire "optimism" suspect. It makes him a bad teacher and hollow prophet, but it does not make him a bad poet. Where he is a great one, it is (again) directly according to the degree to which he can set aside the Victorian obligations of prophet. If we consider the total output of each of the three great Victorian poets, we have seen in Arnold's a mind in constant if static tension; we shall see in Tennyson's a mind in continuous, more animated struggle; in Browning's we see a mind simply compartmented, almost at the turn of a switch, and the best poems it produces tend to depend on the poet's finding a psychological release in historical or other concerns. There is, in both extremes of Browning's work, a striking lack of that intensely personal conflict which appears in differing ways in Arnold and Tennyson.

Browning's artistic achievement in the "objective" dramatic and psychological poem so generally admired is immune from serious challenge. But in other kinds of poetry, apparently far more subjective, he deliberately stresses the didactic and the prophetic, sometimes making repeated and even frantic assertions the focus of a poem. This occurs in much of his lesser-known work and also in well-known poems such as *Prospice, Rabbi Ben Ezra,* and the latter part of *Abt Vogler.* Here he challenges direct comparison with Arnold and Tennyson and emerges as less convincing than either, because of psychological limitations. For his assertion is not to be trusted. If Arnold's final touches of optimism do not seem to follow from the bulk of the poetry which precedes them, we can reject them because of the doubts and inner travail of the spirit that Arnold's poems express. But Browning's optimism, for all its emphasis, appears simply rootless, occurring as an isolated, predetermined phenomenon supported, if at all, only by consequent argument.

Many useful observations have been made about Browning's

tendencies as poet, which come together to enforce the idea of his radical rejection of inward struggle. His whole leaning to the form of poem he made so much his own, the dramatic monologue, can be seen, for instance, as a kind of escape, however fortunate artistically it may have been. It invites the kaleidoscope of (to use the phrase loosely) the mind's "stream of consciousness," and thus is far nearer twentieth-century relative ideas of "truth" than Arnold's or Tennyson's.[34]

Similarly, Browning's relationship to his Romantic predecessors emphasizes, not that he is a bad poet (in certain extensive areas he is brilliant), but that in matters of faith and doubt he is unconvincing or evasive, and sometimes both together. It stresses, too, that the quality of his work increases in direct ratio to the extent he can avoid confronting the central Victorian problem of world-view; the reader concerned with that will find Browning, except on the most superficial level, an irrelevant artist.

But it comes down to this, the ultimate irony. Browning limited his imagination, either deliberately or unconsciously, in the philosophic area. That done, his creative imagination could range so much the wider within the concrete, finite, human drama of atmosphere and psychological motivation. If the problems of alienation and confusion are metaphorically the burden of a Victorian Sisyphus, Arnold and Tennyson made attempts at the task, Arnold's limited, Tennyson's sustained, and in the manner of their attempts and inevitable failure lie their meaning and value. But Browning could only be a great poet by turning away from the rôle: whenever he tried to turn back to face it, he saw only the impossibility of his own Romantic desires for fulfillment, and could only deny—perhaps even convincing himself—that the task was really there. He is, in the end, the poet of an optimism unconvincing because it was motivated by his being psychologically unequipped even to envisage defeat.

NOTES

[1] *An Essay on Percy Bysshe Shelley* (London, 1888), p. 12.
[2] *Browning* (London, 1902), p. 281.
[3] *Robert Browning* (London, 1959), p. 23.
[4] *Robert Browning* (London, 1952), p. 4.

5 *Browning's Parleyings: The Autobiography of a Mind* (New Haven: Yale University Press, 1927), pp. xiii–xiv.
6 For this reason, few English poets have provided so rich a ground for spectacular oppositions of view. Thus Edmund Dowden could define Browning much as I would a Romantic poet: "Browning's chief influence . . . is towards establishing a connexion between the known order of things in which we live and that larger order of which it is a part." (*The Life of Robert Browning* [London, 1915], p. 396.) DeVane, however, writing twenty years later, could point out that critics had been inclined to disregard all that, in fact to disregard "what Browning says, and to fasten intently upon how he says it," and upon his psychological appeal. (*A Browning Handbook* [New York, 1935], p. 36.) That such controversy is still very much alive is shown by so recent a book as Norton B. Crowell's *The Convex Glass: The Mind of Robert Browning* (Albuquerque: University of New Mexico Press, 1968). This book opens by also complaining of "the widespread notion that one is well advised to read Browning . . . without regard to what the poet is saying," and goes on to attack a number of critics, many of them post-1935, on such issues as Browning's idea of evil and his optimism.
7 Quoted by Henry Jones, *Browning as a Philosophical and Religious Teacher* (Glasgow, 1902), p. 45. DeVane, in citing this, goes on to suggest that it is Carlyle's verbal opinion: at all events, it is clearly the middle-aged or later Carlyle speaking.
8 To E. B. Browning, June 12, 1846.
9 *Browning's Parleyings*, p. 7.
10 *Robert Browning*, pp. 63–64.
11 See Cohen, for example, who cites Browning's irregular church-attendance, and his "thunderous 'No' to Robert Buchanan's categorical question: 'Are you a Christian?'" On the other hand he notes "the letter written to an unknown correspondent in 1876, who imagined herself to be dying, and in this there seems to be a fundamental affirmation of Christian faith." Cohen's own conclusion is that "Browning was clearly an eclectic, accepting some Christian doctrines, passionately hostile to such ideas as eternal punishment beyond the grave, which he, nevertheless, envisaged in *The Inn Album*."
12 *Browning*, pp. 13–14.
13 *Ibid.*, pp. 117–119.
14 This is often dramatized for us whenever—as happens often—critics and interpreters of Browning sound as though they are writing of Wordsworth: "Even the most miserable wretch has some goodness in him, something of God; and it is through that germ of goodness, that power of love, that he reaches up to God. Thus it is through the heart that man is to comprehend the God who is love." (DeVane, *Browning's Parleyings*, p. 35.) It is, moreover, DeVane adds, through the moral consciousness that man relates to God.
15 *Browning's Parleyings*, p. 31.
16 *Ibid.*, p. 34.
17 To Dr. F. J. Furnival, October 11, 1881. *Letters of Robert Browning, Collected by T. J. Wise*, ed. Thurman L. Hood (New Haven: Yale University Press, 1933).

[18] *Browning's Parleyings*, p. 33.

[19] *Browning* (London, 1959), p. 8.

[20] See Cohen, *Robert Browning*, p. 49.

[21] *Ibid.*, p. 64.

[22] *Browning's Parleyings*, p. 49. In my entire reference to Browning's last major work here, I have relied upon DeVane's account of the *Parleying* with Mandeville very frequently indeed, and in ways both specific and indirect, so that only the most general acknowledgement is possible.

[23] *Browning's Parleyings*, pp. 7–8.

[24] *Robert Browning*, p. 69.

[25] See Cohen, *Robert Browning*, p. 85, for instance. He sees only Browning's "ring of certainty that is corroborated by the certain beat of each rhyme."

[26] *A Last Ride Together* (1855) is a case in point. The poem suggests that an after-life is the most meaningful earthly instant "made eternity": it simply concludes with that suggestion—"what if [it be so]?" The kind of vision the poem ends by diffidently putting forward is near-Romantic, but there is no serious attempt to deal with the questions it implies.

[27] *An Essay on Percy Bysshe Shelley*, p. 13.

[28] See, for instance, Chapter IV of his *Browning*.

[29] *Robert Browning*, p. 3.

[30] *Ibid.*, p. 15.

[31] *Browning*, pp. 59, 61, 65.

[32] To Sarianna Browning, June 30, 1861. *Letters of Robert Browning, Collected by T. J. Wise*, ed. Thurman L. Hood.

[33] *Browning's Parleyings*, p. 188. DeVane is writing of the *Parleying* with Francis Furini.

[34] See Robert Langbaum, *The Poetry of Experience* (London, 1957). There is, says Mr. Langbaum, now no "publicly accepted moral and emotional Truth, there are only perspectives toward it—those partial meanings which individuals may get a glimpse of at particular moments" (p. 137). In this modern situation poetry naturally gravitates towards the dramatic monologue.

IV
TENNYSON

1. TENNYSON AND REPUTATION 🠊 In certain revealing ways, Tennsyon was a more consistent poet than either Arnold or Browning. Philosophically—the celebrated outbursts of despair in *In Memoriam* notwithstanding—his mind moved less violently than theirs. And his attitude to his art reflects that general steadiness which finds its biographical expression in his total and uncompromising devotion to poetry throughout a deliberate, almost stately career. The obvious contrast here is with Arnold, who in complaining of a lack of animation in his own work recognized, consciously or not, the mirror of his internal tensions, and who had abandoned the writing of poetry by middle life, finally expressing a wish to be remembered by the prose lectures of *Discourses in America*.[1]

Tennyson's relative steadiness is similarly reflected in the range of his poetry. It was set early and never changed sharply, and though it was broadened by the mild adventure of the *Idylls* and his experiment in blending the past with the topical (*The Princess*), such departures were not radical. Tennyson's final volume, in 1892, was little different, in the general kind of poem it offered, from his volumes of half a century before. G. M. Young, citing a line of Tennyson, could comment, "That is Tennyson at twenty. It might be Tennyson at eighty." Here the dramatic contrast is with Browning, who has been seen to provide spectacular shifts—sometimes obscured by the overriding success of the famous dramatic monologues, but nevertheless covering a range from a *Last Duchess* to a *La Saisiaz*, from a *Pied Piper* to the love poems.

Recognition of this air of steadiness in Tennyson deepens the irony that, among the three poets, it is his work that has provoked the wildest variation in critical reaction. For Arnold and Browning, such reactions are most clearly envisaged through the simplest sort of graph. Browning, once *The Ring and the Book* had focused his reputation, appealed a century ago, as he does now, to devotees of a certain imaginative taste, a sympathy with complexity and experiment, with psychological probing; in short to a taste running back to Sterne and forward to Joyce, Pound and the later Yeats, and perhaps most recently to the experimental theater. In the later nineteenth century Browning tended to provoke a simple *for-or-against* reaction, as he does still. Arnold's graph of critical standing as poet begins at a low point in his own time, and rises steadily in the twentieth century; evaluation of his poetry has risen proportionately as its emotionally-tinged expression of spiritual paralysis has stirred recognition. His work has been the emotional articulation of a common impasse, and as one critic has implied, it is Arnold's inability to speak to his age that lies at the foundation of modern interest in him.[2]

Seen against these, the celebrated vagaries of Tennyson's reputation loom even more spectacularly. There has been, of course, the Victorian adulation of him, culminating in the spate of books and articles on the theme Tennyson-as-oracle, and moving F. L. Lucas to remark that "He might have been, one would think, Aristotle and St. John in one."[3] There has been the reaction against such adulation—Tennyson seen as not much more than a meretricious, cloying versifier with nothing of consequence to say, an assessment dated by a recent authority as starting with the change in taste of the last three decades of the nineteenth century, and ending soon after the First World War.[4]

More than one factor, naturally, underlies such immense contrasts in critical assessment of Tennyson, but the major one is that throughout his career he wrote poetry dealing with personal belief. It is a problem we have met before, in confronting the Romantics. Tennyson is neither prophet nor guide for us, because we have, with an existential shrug, largely thrown the problems he wrestled with into the limbo of the insoluble. This situation does not arise when we read Arnold, who takes a recognizably modern position. In Browning, it arises directly in only a few poems, most of them seldom read and of doubtful artistic value, and most readers are content, and for good artistic reasons, to let the standard dramatic monologues and *The Ring and the Book* dominate. But Tennyson provokes a recent tendency to thrust aside his "philosophy" as the pursuit of an irrelevant and fruitless grail, and to compensate for that by re-emphasizing his most "poetic" touches. The position taken by F.L. Lucas, in his brief introduction to a selection of Tennyson's poems, will serve as an example. Lucas refers briefly to the Victorian worship of Tennyson, then to the reaction from it, and finally appears to avoid both extremes by finding the essence of *his* Tennyson in a series of quotable nature-vignettes like

> Ever the weary wind went on,
> And took the reed-tops as it went.[5]
> *(The Dying Swan)*

Such a view is not an isolated one, and much more ambitious and sophisticated estimates of Tennyson leave an allied impression.[6]

The danger, then, is that even the most open-minded critic, seeking to redress matters after the anti-Tennysonian reaction, can do so only through the grey-tinted spectacles of modern scepticism. He is impelled to stress the *how* rather than the *what* of Tennyson's poetry, and in that he is further abetted by a second factor, the poet's technical achievement itself. This, strongly influenced by the Romantics but in many ways going beyond them, has always encouraged and exaggerated upheavals in evaluation. Technical brilliance doubtless played its part in intoxicating the sober judgment of the Victorian Tennysonians who looked up to the intellectual throne. Subsequent reaction saw the poet's technical achievement as tinsel draped over specious, even fraudulent thought. In seeking to avoid both extremes, one must resist merely re-presenting the last in more sophisticated form; in other words reviving, rather condescendingly, discussion of Tennyson's thought before finally reaffirming him a considerable poet by grace of the unforgettable vignette, a latter-day Herrick who universalized the Lincolnshire countryside as Herrick had universalized the Elizabethan chimney-corner. This may be well-intentioned, but it is fragmentary and verges on irrelevance.

Of course many critics have succeeded in surveying Tennyson in a more integrated way. E.D.H. Johnson, for example, considers the poet broadly and finds the key to his work in an inner conflict between his "artistic sensibility" and his "public role." [7] This conception has been generally approved, and I have found that if Tennyson is read while bearing it in mind a deeper understanding of his work seems to result. Tennyson indeed does write most impressively when animated by conflict—there is no doubt about that—but I am convinced that it was a more complex fabric of oppositions than Johnson's formulation of one major strand—and quite probably my own —manage to demarcate. [8]

I see Tennyson's conflict in different terms from Johnson; primarily, it appears to me to lie between Tennyson's Romantic vision, influenced deeply by the older poets, intermittently but never completely ratified by his mystical experience, on the one hand, and—obviously—the "modern," anti-religious, anti-philosophical conditions of the Victorian world (*provoking* social demands on its poets) on the other. It is a preconception which can shape, with some profit, a reading of Tennyson; it is, of course, an inevitable preconception given the approach of this book. I am submitting that in Tennyson, as in Arnold and Browning, the Romantic heritage of intense affirmation in poetry is a principal key to insights valuable in understanding the canon. Such insights may be variously regarded, but if there is consistency to them they will help in inferring the "outlook" of Tennyson, and his cast of mind is a crucial matter. It is crudely expressible by "physical" metaphor: to create a sculpture of Tennyson, representing the dominant spirit of his poetry, how is the model to be posed? So far (to continue that deliberately simple metaphor) we have arrived at an Arnold locked in self-combat to the point of paralysis; and a Browning self-compartmented—escaping psychologically from the problems he failed to resolve in poems like *Christmas Eve, Easter Day* and *La Saisiaz,* into either a self-contained affirmation which protests too much, or to the varied canvas in time, place and personality of the great dramatic monologues.

Despite the usefulness of preconceptions, however, an approach to Tennyson through the Romantic door must start with caution. Tennyson, for several reasons, is not a Romantic poet; neither is he primarily philosopher nor "vignette" poet. He is, not less than Arnold or Browning, a poet of conflict. If his conflicts are indeed as broad as I have suggested, it may be useful to avoid predigested criticism by re-examining directly a group of "quintessential" poems: I propose the best-known of the 1832 and 1842 volumes. From such a preliminary survey should emerge some sense of the rich suggestibility of his verse, and its features, laid open to the approach of this book, should yield directions for emphasis.

2. QUINTESSENTIAL POEMS ࿐ I should like to begin with a brief overview based on a re-reading of eight poems: *The Lady of Shalott, Oenone, The Lotos-Eaters,* the *Morte d'Arthur, Ulysses, Tithonus, The Palace of Art,* and *The Two Voices.* These are probably the best-known of Tennyson's volumes of 1832 and 1842, and all are poems which have contributed heavily to his reputation. My comments will doubtless be elementary, as well as conservative in the sense that they could be developed or qualified, but I have two particular reasons for making them at this point. First, they raise certain characteristics central in Tennyson's poetry, characteristics which I hope later to investigate further; second, every one of these poems, as we shall see, involves Romantic concerns.

The Lady of Shalott is a ballad-like poem, hung upon a slight shell of plot: the fairy Lady is tempted by an unaware Lancelot to look at the actual world outside her tower, operating the curse which destroys her. The poems works as an integrated whole, with powerful effect. It seems an obvious Romantic continuance, of the genre of *Kubla Khan,* though it more particularly reflects *La Belle Dame Sans Merci.* Its achievement is above all to create for the reader a certain imaginative experience, the vision of a world which momentarily dominates the consciousness and seems more authoritative than the everyday. This need not be escape; it is undeniably enrichment. To this end of emotional impact everything in the poem contributes. There is no need to be exhaustive here; the incantatory vowel-sounds at the line-endings, the clipped repetition of the refrain, the traditional associations of Arthurian character and scene, the high colors —crimson, yellow, brazen and so on, are all simply obvious musical and visual stimulations of the same kind as work in Keats' poem. The detail, however, seems precise rather than sensuous: we "see" "the aspens quiver" (to exemplify Tennyson's choice of diction) largely because the visual pattern of movement is "acted out" by the repeated trochees of subject and verb.

The poem transmits some sense of ulterior questioning, but its "meaning," a reader is made to feel, should not be pursued too explicitly. Whatever it may be, it is subservient to the work's imaginative and emotional effect. The poem scarcely seems to invite the allegorical and intellectualized view, for instance, that it explores "the maladjustment of the aesthetic spirit to the conditions of ordinary living." [9] Even if it is allegorical in that way, its underlying meaning is very simple, requiring no further definition than to say it lies between a "magic" area of existence and the destructive allure of a "real" one.

Oenone, an emotionally heightened narrative, is obviously concerned with the experience of deprivation, and if that recalls Romantic parallels they are stressed by the nature-setting in which Oenone is placed, and by the intensity of her relationship with it. The effect of sustained emotional intensity seems due in part to a variety of vowel music and a pervasive refrain. But the poem never becomes remote from its roots in the physical world: the scenery has the same naturalistic precision as that in *The Lady of Shalott;* it is *right,* and we see what is presented. *Oenone,* in fact, appears extraordinarily rich in evoking the physical, even for Tennyson: the appearance of Paris is visually blinding, and the detailed splendor of the goddesses is almost Pre-Raphaelite. There are certainly echoes of Keatsian verse also.

Again, the "meaning" does not appear abstruse. It is even possible to take the poem as mere setting to the episode of the goddesses, which leads, in the speech of Pallas (ll.142 ff.) to a moral fable advocating "self-reverence, self-knowledge, self-control," [10] but it seems too arbitrary so to elevate an incident from the whole poem. It is a dramatic monologue, yet its center rests not on Oenone herself, but on all human sorrow and alienation. It is probable, then, that the poem essentially deals with the Romantic paradox of beauty and pain, and if so it reflects (translated into equivalent Keatsian terms) an *Endymion* stage of development rather than the reconciliation of the *Ode on Melancholy.*

The Lotos-Eaters is apt to strike the returning reader with echoes of his schooldays, since its intimidating wealth of technical resources have seemed to make it irresistible, as supercharged "poetry," to high-school syllabus-makers.[11] It is true that the vowel-music, the movements of lines and verses between acceleration and deceleration, the repetitions and the rest are formidable, and it is fascinating to see their workings. But the poem is not, finally, one of "escape," as I was taught in school. It is true that much of it—most of it—is devoted to presenting the emotional and sensuous appeal of "escape," but a re-reading of the poem with the quest for "meaning" in mind gives curiously mixed reactions. Verse which counsels soporific escape is in many places remarkably animated, and there are many specific and carefully-wrought ironies: the conception of "no toil" appears hollow indeed when forced by rhyme against "the fruitful soil." In short, there is a battle within the poem.

The *Morte d'Arthur* tells a story most people know in one form or another, and clearly here the "meaning" is meant to be applied universally. The poem constantly echoes other literature for restatement and re-emphasis, and it has a frame which claims for it a modern relevance. While it does create, in its theme and its scenery, the atmosphere of the epic, and while it exploits a ballad-like incantation, it is not a remote poem, and it constantly appeals to the reader's experience in the "real" world of sense. The imagery is exact, striking; in places arrestingly modern; the description dazzling (the hilt of Excalibur), and the realistic detail uncompromising (Arthur's face "striped with dark blood"). The poem is a blend of the remotely traditional with the omnipresent consciousness of the contemporary and immediate. If this is a way of making the "meaning" of the poem significant for a modern reader, what is that "meaning"? As far as it rests in idea at all, it appears to be in Bedivere's dilemma, where the tradition of his disobedience is presented in terms of rationality *versus* faith, or worldliness *versus* forces beyond the world, symbolized by Arthur's destination.

A related conflict is suggested by both *Tithonus* and *Ulysses,* which treat their ancient themes with an arresting modernity, or rather universality. The poems, like *The Lady of Shalott,* cannot be confined within a bond of intellectual meaning. As far as it may be done, *Tithonus* dramatizes the gap between a human longing on the one hand and the unbending conditions-of-existence on the other. It is a protest against, and ultimately and more importantly a reconcilement with, the finitude of earthly existence. In that, the poem has a Romantic affiliation, but it inverts a familiar Romantic formula: here it is not the passion of youth longing like Endymion or Alastor for extra-worldly fulfillment, but age and degeneration longing for rest in death, and for acceptance in the round of nature. If *Tithonus* is to be given a philosophical meaning, it lies with the lesson learned in Keats' *Lamia* by Lycius—the futility of seeking to distort or break natural conditions as a means of fulfilling desires. But again, "meaning," in that sense, is a small part of the poem. It exists far more powerfully as an integrated emotional creation of the dual extremes which human consciousness must contend with. If the poem may be said to turn on its major features, it turns on its extensive suggestions of ambivalence between Aurora the goddess and the coming of dawn in nature; and on the opposition—indeed deep irony—of setting the wearied age of Tithonus in so extensive a symbol of hope and promise, an irony summarized in the one identity which is both tears and dew. The poem is a dramatic monologue, but not at all in the Browning manner; the stress is not in the least on Tithonus as a person; like Ulysses and Oenone, he exists to focus an imaginative experience.

Ulysses also has its Romantic affiliations: it looks to "that untravelled world" and to a desire for knowledge "beyond the utmost bound of human thought." Its moral is essentially Carlylean, and the aging Ulysses himself an eloquent adaptation of his traditional image, sharply de-glamorized. He is the voice of dignity and resolution, using a language almost stark in its simplicity and universality. The poem's symbolism may still be Romantic—the voyage, the untravelled world, the sailing beyond the sunset—but its essence lies in the clipped resolution of the final line.

The Palace of Art and *The Two Voices* differ from the other poems mentioned here in that they are direct treatments of conflicts; they do not depend upon traditional narratives and their associations as metaphors to express them. *The Palace of Art,* philosophically, is Tennyson's recognition of the obligations imposed by his own second Chamber of Maiden Thought. Clearly the conflict is between escape into aestheticism and the facing of worldly pain. The resolution of the poem is equally clear: only by facing up to the world as it is can the speaker be freed from guilt. In view of this, however, the work is oddly proportioned, for its negative side, didactically speaking,—the lure of the Palace—occupies some two-thirds of it: in that, it recalls the weight given to the lure of "escape" in *The Lotos-Eaters.*

The "meaning" of *The Two Voices* is focused directly throughout the poem, as it is by its original title, *Thoughts of a Suicide.* It is a direct presentation of the speaker's conflicts of mind, and in general style it bears a close resemblance to the long chant of Empedocles in Arnold's poem. The verse, like that of *The Palace of Art,* is spare in form, and its phrasing at times ("A noise of tongues and deeds,/ A dust of systems and of creeds") operates on a level of suggestion which Arnold and Fitzgerald were later to develop. The elements of conflict are specific, and may be represented on one side by the doubts (and a language) stemming from evolutionary concepts, and on the other by a personal if qualified hope of human purpose stemming from quasi-Romantic aspiration, intuitive moral impulses, and mystical experience. The work is given a resolution which, artistically speaking, is reminiscent of the moral tag at the end of *The Ancient Mariner*. The speaker, reacting to the sight of a churchgoing family, sees it as a symbol of love and hope, and the poem ends affirmatively on that note. It is a Romantic, but hardly a convincing, ending. The symbol given so much weight appears arbitrary; the reassurance it brings is confined to the last section of the poem, fully six-sevenths of which is again devoted to conflict, and, as in a number of poems by both Arnold and Browning, it seems in no way a consequence of the bulk of the poem it concludes.

Every one of these eight poems, as I have suggested, involves Romantic facets in some form—in extra-worldly conflicts, in desires for imaginative escape, in aspiration or a Romantic view of death. *Oenone* leaves the co-existence of beauty and deprivation unresolved, and *The Lady of Shalott* merely dramatizes a conflict; but of the other six poems (if we accept, as I think we must, that *The Lotos-Eaters* ultimately counsels not escape but the reverse) all make some attempt, with varying conviction, to come to terms with the world, ranging from the insistence on faith in the *Morte d'Arthur* to the dignified determination of Ulysses. In attempting this, *The Palace of Art* and *The Lotos-Eaters* are preoccupied with relatively early stages of Romantic development comparable with those in poems like *Endymion* and *Alastor*.

The general effect of this group of Tennyson's poems, however, is quite different from that of Romantic poetry. Not a single poem attempts to "echo" vicariously the stages of transcendental experience itself. What positive affirmation there is in these poems rests rather on the general, untranscendent human condition itself, as in *Ulysses,* or on mystically-based conviction briefly and abstractly described as intuitions or "gleams"; and this element is infrequent and slight. As in *The Two Voices,* it is stated almost incidentally, not insisted upon; and wherever it does occur, it is within poems which have other major concerns to stress.

Those concerns, broadly speaking, are the doubts and conflicts which all but drown affirmation. In *The Lady of Shalott,* they lie between the magic and real worlds; in *Oenone,* between beauty and pain; in *The Palace of Art,* between aesthetic escape and the facing of pain; in *The Lotos-Eaters,* between hedonistic refuge and the dedication to continuing struggle; in the *Morte d'Arthur,* between rationalism and faith; in *The Two Voices,* between consciousness itself and the deliberate ending of it; in *Ulysses,* between rededication to life and relapse from it; in *Tithonus,* between natural acceptance of the world and unnatural retreat from it. Conflict thus appears to be the "subject" of all eight poems, though in six of them the struggles are veiled by metaphor, that is, presented through the situation of a protagonist after an implicit or explicit chain of events: such a situation pervades the entire poem, and the poem itself becomes a symbol in mental biography, sometimes a rather uncertain one (*The Lady of Shalott*). Nor is such conflict always even: in *The Palace of Art, The Two Voices* and *The Lotos-Eaters* the voice of disillusion or escape dominates the bulk of the poem—they are unbalanced, that is, and towards the darkness.

The poems appear divided also in the aesthetic and philosophic effects they create. Except for *The Lotos-Eaters* and *Oenone,* they seem spare beside Romantic intensity and luxurance. This relative economy in language and verse-form seems to stress how firmly they remain within the sphere of the senses in the finite world. Hence the description and detail carry a terse factual precision, creating an illusion of the way things "really" are. There is not only precise and realistic detail, but the psychological realism of conflict in *Oenone, The Palace of Art,* and *The Two Voices,* and to some extent in the figure of Bedivere. The poems seem at once realistic and modern, and the permeating veil of metaphor on which all but two depend allows them to penetrate more deeply than explicit statement of conflict would: rather than lessen the impact of conflict, the mask of metaphor itself enters the subconscious level of awareness. The poems are not fables, and if we do not accept the facile resolution of *The Two Voices,* only *Ulysses* and *The Palace of Art* offer anything resembling positive solutions to the problems they pose.

The final impression given by these poems is of universality rather than modernity. All, except the two poems of explicit conflict, use the traditions of the remote past for their metaphorical base.

What they stimulate, however, is the very reverse of historical or traditional remoteness. The experience and doubt they dramatize may be ancient and traditional, but their point of relation is to the present—to the reader while he reads. The conflicts are simply human and therefore timeless, the metaphor which expresses them ancient; but the application of the conflicts as the poems reveal them suggests that something of direct and ultimate importance has been said, which relates only to continuing life, and perhaps defines it. It is a paradoxical sensation which to an extent itself defies definition, but there are reasons for it, and I shall go on to try to locate them.

3. TENNYSON THE ROMANTIC & The brief and impressionistic rereading of Tennyson's "best" shorter poems which has preceded is somewhat deceptive as an indication of his Romantic inheritance. In his best-known shorter work he is a poet who has somehow freed himself of, or, more accurately, controlled the direct impact of Romantic poetry, which suffuses and almost dominates the rest of the *Collected Poems*. In other words, in his best poetry Tennyson was able to control and reshape his Romantic heritage; in his lesser work, if it does not control him, he at least accepts it piecemeal, indiscriminately.

The problem of controlling and individualizing the ideas and styles of English Romanticism is one we may suspect to have been crucial to the mid-nineteenth century poet. In making some full statement of personal struggle in the face of generally declining religious and philosophical belief, Tennyson leads us to his best work, and especially to *In Memoriam;* Browning, to poems like *Easter Day* —artistic disasters, in part through his failure to control Romantic directions; Arnold, only to an emotional reaction to his own inability to participate in active struggle.

To examine the extent and kind of Tennyson's Romanticism, then, it is necessary to move away from the well-known poems to a consideration of the general canon. And that is to be confronted by such a mass of example that the problem is to keep it within bounds. Before examining Tennyson's ways of individualizing his Romantic inheritance, I should like to show the striking extent to which it dominated his earliest work. This can be done through a close consideration of one lengthy poem, *The Lover's Tale*.

This poem, while unimportant as art, and rightly judged by Tennyson himself as "scarce worthy to live," has a special history, making it most revealing of the poet's reactions to the subject-matter and style of Romantic poetry, both early and late in his career. Tennyson tells us in a Preface that he composed the first three parts of the poem as it now stands—that is, roughly three-quarters of it— when he was in his "nineteenth year," [12] and that a "recent" pirating (the Preface is dated 1879) of the first two parts has made it desirable to publish the whole poem with a fourth part as conclusion, or "sequel" as he calls it, written in "mature life." The poem is thus an attempt at a complete work of 1459 lines, of which 1074 are youthful work, completed by a further "mature" 385 lines.

The poem's plot, concerning young love hopelessly frustrated by social obstacles, has probably its closest affinities with the Werther prototype. Here Julian, wildly loving his cousin and foster-sister, Camilla, has seen her married to his friend and rival Lionel, and the poem is basically an account, in retrospect, of Julian's sufferings. It is a plot which readily lends itself to verse echoing *Endymion* and *Alastor*—recent poems when Tennyson was eighteen—and it is in matters of expression that their influence is most marked.

The stylistic impression made by the whole poem is prefigured in its opening frame as Julian, in a suitable nature-setting, endeavors to approach his painful memories. Although this frame itself consists of less than 180 lines, it is a remarkable achievement in that it re-creates almost exactly the distinctive utterance of every major Romantic poet with the unaccountable exception of Blake, though it comes close to him at times. Within the frame alone, for instance, we have Shelleyan intensity—and diction, and image:

> Breathe but a little on me, and the sail
> Will draw me to the rising of the sun,
> The lucid chambers of the morning star,
> And East of Life.
>
> . . . when day hung
> From his mid-dome in heaven's airy halls.

The frame includes the precise atmosphere of the scenic panoramas of the Alastor-quest:

> And like the all-enduring camel, driven
> Far from the diamond fountain by the palms,

Who toils across the middle moonlit nights,
Or when the white heats of the blinding noons
Beat from the concave sand; yet in him keeps
A draught of that sweet fountain that he loves,
To stay his feet from falling and his spirit
From bitterness of death.

And, again within a few lines, we have the accent of Wordsworthian reflection:

> . . . I muse
> On those dear hills, that nevermore will meet
> The sight that throbs and aches beneath my touch,
> As tho' there beat a heart in either eye;
> For when the outer lights are darken'd thus
> The memory's vision hath a keener edge.

Then there is imagery for Romantic deprivation—here closely echoing Coleridge in *This Lime-Tree Bower My Prison:*

> It grows upon me now—the semicircle
> Of dark-blue waters and the narrow fringe
> Of curving beach—its wreaths of dripping green—
> Its pale pink shells.

There is, still within the confines of the frame, the Keatsian conception,

> Trust me, I should have died, if it were possible
> To die in gazing on that perfectness
> Which I do bear within me.

And there is Julian's self-portrait, strongly Byronic in egotism and tone:

> To me alone,
> Push'd from his chair of regal heritage,
> The Present is the vassal of the Past:
> So that, in that I *have* lived, do I live,
> And cannot die, and am, in having been—
> A portion of the pleasant yesterday,
> Thrust forward on today and out of place; . . .
> The grasp of hopeless grief about my heart, . . .
> The clear brow, bulwark of the precious brain,
> Chink'd as you see, and seam'd . . . .

These early hints in the frame are merely previews of what takes place in the poem proper. I am putting these imitations (for that is what they are) in terms of specific Romantic poets for the sake of brevity, but the derivative nature of the whole poem is far more general than that implies.[13]

While the poem is permeated throughout by such stylistic borrowings, its level of Romantic assumption is at least as great.[14] The youthful Tennyson was apparently intoxicated with the conception of vision in the Romantic poets, though he assimilated it in a way which suggests he had not been able to realize its implications. Here, Julian's "visions" are frequent, but strictly concerned with mundane matters: of another taking his place (I, 575–590); a vision of drowning, stimulated by the picture of a ship and presenting in metaphorical form the death that is life without Camilla (II, 164–205); and a vision, occupying the whole of Part III, of Camilla's funeral, and her return to life only to be claimed by another. Early in the poem (I, 157), Tennyson says that dreams are "our other life," and that is simply what the "visions" in this poem remain—in no sense a pointer to a larger one.

If the sheer weight of direct Romantic derivation suggests that here Tennyson has piled together his Romantic borrowings in an unselectively Spasmodic way, the impression is confirmed by the poem's totality. And the work is not rescued by the adult Tennyson. The first three parts of *The Lover's Tale* form a Spasmodic agglomeration of Romantic borrowings—natural enough to Tennyson's youth and the time of composition—on the soul-torment of thwarted love. It is, or aims to be, passionate; it is consistently introspective, and is comparable with, though mercifully shorter than, a fairly similar attempt by Browning in *Pauline*. While it is only fair to say that substantial rescue would be impossible, what Tennyson, years later, tacked on to the earlier three parts of his poem does not blend at all. In his *finale, The Golden Supper*, a narrator takes over (just as the editor does after Werther's suicide), and adds a story taken from Boccaccio; it is told, in contrast to the repetitive introspective meanderings of the first three parts, objectively and at dizzy pace. Julian, Romeo-like, goes to the "dead" Camilla's tomb intent upon a final kiss and his own suicide. He finds Camilla alive, and she is nursed back to health; Julian gives a banquet, inviting Lionel, Camilla's husband, and asks him who would, in his judgement, have claim on a servant rejected as dying and useless by one master and reclaimed to life by

another. Lionel chooses the rescuer, and his moral wisdom is re-
warded by Camilla's being brought in and returned to him.

The *Werther* technique of suddenly introducing an outside narrator may serve to point to one final and perhaps surprising facet of
the mature Tennyson here. His sequel remains strongly, and directly,
Romantic in style and content, though the influence in *The Golden
Supper* is predominantly Keats'. In the tomb, Julian's reaction to discovering Camilla alive is given the exact phrasing of *Endymion:*

> 'Do I wake or sleep?
> Or am I made immortal, or my love
> Mortal once more?'
>
> (IV, 78–80)

When Lionel and Camilla are reunited, it is with the Keatsian
suggestion that the height of bliss on earth is related to that beyond
death:

> And there the widower husband and dead wife
> Rush'd each at each with a cry that rather seem'd
> For some new death than for a life renew'd;
>
> (IV, 370–372)

and the feast itself is described with an intensity of sensuous imagery
like that in *The Eve of St. Agnes*. It is not, however, used in the
Keats manner to suggest levels of significance, but simply for its own
sake:

> Great garlands swung and blossom'd; and beneath,
> Heirlooms, and ancient miracles of art,
> Chalice and salver, wines that, heaven knows when,
> Had suck'd the fire of some forgotten sun,
> And kept it thro' a hundred years of gloom,
> Yet glowing in a heart of ruby—cups
> Where nymph and god ran ever round in gold—
> Others of glass as costly—some with gems
> Movable and resettable at will,
> And trebling all the rest in value—Ah heavens!
>
> (IV, 190–199)

It may be argued, of course, that in these matters an experienced
Tennyson is simply making the only *artistic* bridge he can to the Ro-
mantically-permeated work of his youth. But the immense differences

in subject matter, plot and pace between the early poem and its later conclusion make this unlikely. It is far more justifiable to see a mature Tennyson still largely saturated in Romantic thought and style, though not as uncontrollably as he had been at eighteen.

The Lover's Tale exhibits all the falsetto of Spasmodic poetry, and as a whole it fairly represents, at least in its first three parts, the fashions of its day. It does not, however, mislead in offering evidence that Tennyson's work is saturated in Romantic attitudes and styles. Unlike Browning's *Pauline*, it may not be thrust aside as simply a "stage" of the poet's development. Tennyson's collected poems provide consistent evidence that his work was always permeated by Romanticism, and that any assessment of the "Romantic" Tennyson based solely on the famous poems would underestimate his debt sharply, because in those poems he has, as I hope to show, worked out successful methods of disciplining, individualizing and in fact transforming Romanticism.

A really comprehensive attempt to list the elements in Tennyson's Romantic permeation would be voluminous and perhaps pointless, but my purpose demands at least some demonstration of its breadth. In referring to *The Lover's Tale* I have been intent primarily on stylistic influences, but Romantic thought and attitude is heavily evident throughout the canon.

The essence of Romantic poetry, I have argued above, is intense belief, which Arnold, to put it over-simply, could not attain; and from the possibility of which Browning simply turned aside to less risky concerns. There is a distinction here between Tennyson and the other two, obvious but often overlooked: he is as consistently assertive as a Romantic poet concerning the importance of his own mystical experience. Later I shall draw distinctions between that experience and that of the Romantics, but the point here is that it is almost impossible to read much of Tennyson's work without a sense of the sincerity of his belief. To go beyond the Romantic religion and to turn for a comparison to a more formulated sort, he believed as deeply as Newman came to believe. Here is Tennyson towards the end of his life, and in accents not unlike Wordsworth's, recounting his own experience:

> for more than once when I
> Sat all alone, revolving in myself
> The word that is the symbol of myself,

The mortal limit of the Self was loosed,
And past into the Nameless, as a cloud
Melts into heaven. I touch'd my limbs, the limbs
Were strange, not mine—and yet no shade of doubt,
But utter clearness, and thro' loss of self
The gain of such large life as match'd with ours
Were sun to spark—unshadowable in words,
Themselves but shadows of a shadow-world.

(*The Ancient Sage,* 229–239)

It is, as G. M. Young remarked, "Tennyson's own voice, telling of what he has known, and as such his age received it," and Young asserts that it was through such experience that "when he appeared as a philosophic poet with *In Memoriam* he was not only equipped for the great debate which was soon to open; he had anticipated it, had formulated at least a conceivable conclusion . . . and *one based on personal experience*" (my italics).[15]

The concomitant assumptions to such a faith are likewise Romantic, and simply need illustration. A number of Tennyson's shorter poems have their *raison d'être* as metaphors for Romantic aspiration. A typical example is *The Voyage,* composed before 1842, which presents through its earthly though heightened imagery a semi-fantastic sailing in pursuit of "one fair Vision." Despite the condemnation of the cynic who sneers "A ship of Fools," and who leaps, predictably enough, to his suicide, the voyage continues—endlessly, as it must while it is rooted in earthly life:

We know the merry world is round,
And we may sail for evermore.

The explicit Platonism of *The Sisters*—the later (1880) poem of that title—serves to show how the simplest philosophic formulations of the Romantic remained in Tennyson's work to the end of his career. The speaker affirms that "a man's ideal/ Is high in heaven, and lodged with Plato's God,/ Not findable here." He also finds in Platonism the old Romantic recognition, almost a formula, of the deceptive nature of what we prematurely assess negatively as pain, which seen more largely is constructive:

My God, I would not live
Save that I think this gross hard-seeming world
Is our misshaping vision of the Powers
Behind the world, that make our griefs our gains.

The broader dualism enforced by this Romantic thinking is a staple of *De Profundis* (published 1880) [16] addressed to a child:

> who wailest being born
> And banish'd into mystery, and the pain
> Of this divisible-indivisible world
> Among the numerable-innumerable
> Sun, sun, and sun, thro' finite-infinite space
> In finite infinite Time—our mortal veil
> And shatter'd phantom of that infinite One,
> Who made thee unconceivable Thyself
> Out of His whole World-self and all in all—
> Live thou!

The corollaries of such a dual outlook—the view of love and death, for instance—color Tennyson's poetry from beginning to end. In an early poem, *Love and Death,* with a Shelleyan clarity of complex metaphor, Tennyson had made Love say to Death:

> Thou art the shadow of life, and as the tree
> Stands in the sun and shadows all beneath,
> So in the light of great eternity
> Life eminent creates the shade of death.
> The shadow passeth when the tree shall fall,
> But I shall reign for ever over all.

And late, in *Rizpah* (1880), we find a blend of *Wuthering Heights-*cum-*Lucy Gray* treatment of death, given ballad style, in the mother's haunted perception of her dead son, the "voice in the wind." As late as 1889, *Vastness,* a poem largely given to expressing weariness bordering scepticism, still leads to a defiant conclusion: "the dead are not dead but alive."

This suffusion with characteristically Romantic assumptions shows in the least "philosophical" of Tennyson's poems. The artless and relatively early love lyric *Move Eastward, Happy Earth,* for instance, presents, quite incidentally to its lyric purpose, the close relationship between the individual's consciousness of his mood and the operations of the universe. The earth is to

> bear me with thee, smoothly borne,
> Dip forward under starry light,
> And move me to my marriage morn,
> And round again to happy night.

Similarly, love in *Maud* (1855) works in a fabric of cause-and-effect in an integrated universe:

> And as long, O God, as she
> Have a grain of love for me,
> So long, no doubt, no doubt,
> Shall I nurse in my dark heart,
> However weary, a spark of will
> Not to be trampled out.

The Wreck (1885), a rather jangly poem on incompatibility and adultery, implies in its ending a cosmic retribution, and therefore an order, no less inexorable than that of *The Ancient Mariner;* though the effect, for stylistic reasons, is didactic rather than haunting as it is in Coleridge.

There is, then, repeated insistence in Tennyson's poetry on the validity of Romantic thought or, more accurately, on a philosophy shaped by mystical faith. If there is significant development it is that the insistence becomes more pronounced in the later Tennyson. His middle years, often enough, are represented by general, shorter poems, like *The Sailor Boy,* which act as simple metaphors for belief, the need for which is taken for granted rather than insisted upon. It is precisely Tennyson's bitterest attacks on his day, like that in *Locksley Hall Sixty Years After* (1886),

> When was age so cramm'd with menace? madness? written, spoken lies?

which seem to provoke his most uncompromising assertion as a *finale:*

> Follow Light, and do the Right—for man can half-control his doom—
> Till you find the deathless Angel seated in the vacant tomb.
> Forward, let the stormy moment fly and mingle with the past.
> I that loathed have come to love him. Love will conquer at the last.

The most detailed and uncompromising statement of Tennyson's faith in his mystical experience is in *The Ancient Sage* (1885), a poem he described as "very personal." [17] The Sage, noting that

> nothing worthy proving can be proven,
> Nor yet disproven,

goes on to assert the idea of unity, and offers two instances, in some detail, of visionary contact with it. The first, in boyhood, occurred when the poet had been led to feel the connection between

> The first grey streak of earliest summer dawn
> The last long strife of waning crimson gloom,
> As if the late and early were but one—

and the second presented the recurrent visionary phenomenon when Tennyson would induce a receptive state in himself through the repetition of his own name.[18]

A reading of the Tennyson canon with Romanticism in mind inevitably suggests connections with particular writers, as distinct from the mass of generally Romantic conceptions and attitudes I have been indicating. An early sonnet such as *Poland*, for instance, reads (despite the strongly conservative political vein that ran through the poet's life) like an echo of Byron's or Shelley's liberalism. *Maud* (1855) expresses, for the first time in Tennyson's career in so sustained a way, a vein of political and social disillusion—resentment, rather—of a time "so sordid and mean"—which in tone is Carlylean, though it is the later Carlyle it reflects:

> when the rotten hustings shake
> In another month to his brazen lies,
> A wretched vote may be gain'd.
>
> Ah God, for a man with heart, head, hand,
> Whatever they call him—what care I?—
> Aristocrat, democrat, autocrat—one
> Who can rule and dare not lie!

A large number of Tennyson's shorter poems, varying in importance from *The Sailor Boy* or *The Islet* (both 1864) to the earlier *Ulysses* are metaphorical pleas for the Carlylean life of action. More than one critic has seen *Locksley Hall* as Tennyson's *Sartor Resartus;* [19] J.H. Buckley, for instance, remarks, "As if illustrating the pattern of *Sartor Resartus* . . . the hero turns from an Everlasting No, born of self-absorption and romantic malaise . . . to the Everlasting Yea of activity in a self-confident and energetic 'Mother-Age.' 'I myself,' he resolves, 'must mix with action lest I wither by despair.' " [20]

It is not unusual to come across a brief lyric of Tennyson's, often originating in mid-career rather than early, which impresses one as the exact voice of some Romantic poet. An example is *The Flower* (1864), a little "fable" on the shaping of minds by avarice and desire. Its opening stanza fairly represents the entire poem in its Blakean compression and terse metaphor:

> Once in a golden hour
> I cast to earth a seed.
> Up there came a flower,
> The people said, a weed.

If the multiple Romantic strains of *The Lover's Tale* may be seen as dominated by any one poet, it is, as I have said, Shelley. But in the rest of Tennyson's work it is Keats and, even more, Wordsworth who are brought to mind most often. The juvenile poem *Claribel* is essentially early Keats ("Where Claribel low-lieth/ The breezes pause and die,/ Letting the rose-leaves fall . . ."), and the early *Recollections of the Arabian Nights* is also the Keatsian stage of sensuous daydream for its own sake. But *The Voyage of Maeldune* (1880) is still exploiting a background of Keatsian sensuousness of suggestion:

> And we came to the Isle of Fruits; all round from the cliffs and the capes,
> Purple or amber, dangled a hundred fathom of grapes,
> And the warm melon lay like a little sun on the tawny sand,
> And the fig ran up from the beach and rioted over the land,
> And the mountain arose like a jewell'd throne thro' the fragrant air,
> Glowing with all-color'd plums and with golden masses of pear . . . .

The Bounteous Isle here, like the Islet in the poem of that title, and the island of the Lotos-Eaters if the totality of that poem is felt, becomes unbearable in its fullness, like the idea of fadeless beauty in *Lamia*.

It is, however, Wordsworth who is most consistently the source of echo in Tennyson. A few—there are many—select examples should include *Dora,* an early poem, and several poems from the 1864 *Enoch Arden* volume, which is deeply Wordsworthian, though that influence could be documented almost anywhere in Tennyson's work. *Dora* seems a conscious attempt at imitating Wordsworth, particularly *Michael.* A tale of family estrangement and ultimate reconcilement, it exceeds its progenitor in the terseness of its opening and ending:

With farmer Allen at the farm abode
William and Dora. William was his son,
And she his niece. . . .

        . . . and as years
Went forward Mary took another mate;
But Dora lived unmarried till her death.

It resembles *Michael,* too, in its ballad leaps in time, and its biblical overtones—"And all the land was dark."

Aylmer's Field, although its opening echoes the thought of Shelley's *Ozymandias,* is consistently Wordsworthian in the style and accent of its blank verse.[21] *Enoch Arden* itself has the terse ballad ending of the *Michael* genre, but Enoch's affiliations, in his lonely isolation outside his family, lie more with the leech-gatherer of *Resolution and Independence.* The Tennyson poem even tends towards an embarrassing trait of Wordsworth's (though not, normally, of Tennyson's)—the bathetic dignifying of the commonplace; here, Enoch's fish-basket becomes an "ocean-smelling osier."

Another "leech-gatherer" figure is the heroine of *The Grandmother,* a further ballad-poem on the theme of resignation to death. When Tennyson attempts the brief Wordsworthian lyric, as in *Flower in the Crannied Wall,* he tends to be too explicit (". . . but *if* I could understand/ What you are, root and all, and all in all,/ I should know what God and man is"). The idea of eternity in a flower could hardly be stated more overtly than it is here, but one suspects Wordsworth would have made so eloquent a symbol bear its own reverberant implications.

Though the subject of King Arthur had caught his imagination well before 1850, when *The Prelude* was published, it is both philosophic and poetic justice that Tennyson came to realize Wordsworth's suggestion (*Prelude* I, 168–185) of an epic on "some British theme" of a chivalric sort. *The Idylls of the King* have often been seen as "escapist" literature; that has fairly recently been corrected, and convincingly.[22] The degree to which they are Romantic poetry —while they are much more than that—also deserves recognition. The underlying philosophy of the *Idylls* is Platonic, and often finds direct voice: thus Arthur bewails:

"O me! for why is all around us here
As if some lesser god had made the world,

But had not force to shape it as he would,
Till the High God behold it from beyond,
And enter it, and make it beautiful?"
                    ("The Passing of Arthur," ll. 13–17)

This basic vision of the "otherworldliness" of Reality, completely Romantic in kind, sets up dual themes of appearance and
reality, actual and ideal, which continually find expression at major
turns of event in the poems.[23] As Gareth approaches Camelot, for
instance, he is confused at finding himself between these extremes,
and doubts

"whether there be any city at all,
    Or all a vision."

But the old seer to whom he complains is aware of the meaning of
the city, and of Arthur, and what is ambivalent to Gareth in his answers becomes clear enough to the reader who knows the basic concerns of the *Idylls*. The seer is aware of the confusions prompted by
the dual view of Camelot and all else:

"For there is nothing in it as it seems
Saving the King; tho' some there be that hold
The King a shadow, and the city real."
                    ("Gareth and Lynette," ll. 260–262)

He knows that vows to the King will force Gareth into an area of aspiration beyond his mortality:

"the King
Will bind thee by such vows as is a shame
A man should not be bound by, yet the which
No man can keep;"
                    (ll. 265–268)

and he ends with a kind of Platonic riddle:

"For an ye heard a music, like enow
They are building still, seeing the city is built
To music, therefore never built at all,
And therefore built for ever."
                    (ll. 271–274)

In much the same way, Guinevere's self-recriminations at her sin
are shaped by double-awareness. It is "but of the world—/ What

else? What hope?" ("Guinevere," ll. 624–625). Both the pull of the
world, the "warmth and colour" which she yearned for in Lancelot,
and that of a larger future reality, "that purer life," are implicit in
Guinevere's reaction to her crime. In a speech of great dignity and
dramatic impact (ll. 419–576), Arthur himself is forced to recognize
the destruction of the ideal purpose of his life by the worldly,

> "till the loathsome opposite
> Of all my heart had destined did obtain."
> (ll. 488–489)

The *Idylls,* in short, show the purpose of life as the following of
a moral pattern ("Else, wherefore born?" asks Gareth). As Tennyson
says in the concluding lines to the Queen, the *Idylls* are

> New-old, and shadowing Sense at war with Soul,
> Ideal manhood closed in real man.

It is the old Romantic battle, and Arthur's defeat in the world is put
into the perspective of worldly limitation, and we are left with the
familiar Romantic pattern of the rediscovery of what had been illusory defeat as present and future triumph:

> Then from the dawn it seem'd there came, but faint
> As from beyond the limit of the world,
> Like the last echo born of a great cry,
> Sounds, as if some fair city were one voice
> Around a king returning from his wars.
> ("The Passing of Arthur," ll. 457–461)

The final note, therefore, is affirmative:

> And the new sun rose bringing the new year.

Arthur as soul—a meaning which Tennyson insisted that he always intended—is an allegorical conception which works to make the
reader aware of the difficulties of recognizing the soul for what it is.
Accordingly, on the level of event, even the knights at the founding
of the Round Table experience various degrees of difficulty in recognizing Arthur for what he is. But Arthur as soul or spirit is not allegory at a simple level; the relationships implied are philosophical. As
F.E.L. Priestley puts it,

Tennyson is asserting through the *Idylls* the primacy of the Unseen, the ultimate reality of the Spiritual, which is manifested in a constant succession of phenomena, and gives permanent meaning to them. The phenomena are not merely shadows or illusions; they are "real" in that they are the temporal actualization of the ideal. Man's task is not to pierce through the evil of appearances and brush it aside; it is to recognize the relationship of appearance to an ideal reality he cannot fully know, and to work in the realm of phenomena towards more complete actualization of the ideal in so far as he knows it.[24]

I have been stressing the Romantic suffusion of the *Idylls*, and it should be noted how consistently Priestley, in discussing them, uses a terminology most relevant to Romantic poetry. But while *Enoch Arden* and most of my recent examples are little more than restatements of a Romantic inheritance, the *Idylls* are a transmutation of it. Their dominant concern, to cite Priestley again, is to actualize the ideal, to relate Romantic dualism to a present universe. *Enoch Arden* and the poems it may represent are "about" neo-Wordsworthianism; the *Idylls*, as far as they are reducible to a phrase, are "about" recognizably modern struggle. It is true that they form a long poem with a "meaning" beyond neat allegory; they employ a style most modern readers would regard as outworn; they are "epic" in structure and to some extent in proportion; and they are, like most of Tennyson's work, suffused with English Romanticism. Nevertheless, in them Tennyson has fused and transformed what he took from the Romantics, with all its marks of the age, into something timeless. This process lies at the heart of all his best poetry, and justifies considerable emphasis.

Tennyson is, of course, close to being a Romantic poet in many ways—even in what I have insisted upon as the Romantic's central criterion. He is an assertive poet in his positive belief, and (in contrast to the sporadic assertion of Browning) that is what he remained throughout his career. Moreover, his better artistic achievements express that assertion; he is not at his best as an artist, as Browning is, when he turns elsewhere. The authority and universality his best poems carry derive largely from his methods of presenting his belief, and even more from those by which he presents the mental struggles leading to it. His poetry is, on one essential level, articulation of those struggles made acceptable to the modern mind; he comes to terms with his time, and to some degree philosophically, though usually not stylistically, with ours. Tennyson, again in his best work, makes of those antithetical forces—loosely faith and the world of sensed phenomena—neither the impasse of Arnold, nor Browning-esque fragmentation, but simply an art, which secondarily expresses his own conflicts. In examining the process I shall draw my illustration chiefly (but not exclusively) from the well-known poems of 1832–1842 and *In Memoriam,* that is to say from what I have repeatedly called his best work.

4. CONFLICT IN METAPHOR ૨ﻌ The basis for Tennyson's assertion should perhaps be considered first. He himself tried to define it more than once; the result is apt to be more of a statement of his instinctive reaction to experience than a description of experience itself:

> Yes, it is true that there are moments when the flesh is nothing to me, when I feel and know the flesh to be the vision, God and the Spiritual the only real and true. Depend upon it, the Spiritual *is* the real; it belongs to one more than the hand and the foot. You may tell me that my hand and my foot are only imaginary symbols of my existence, I could believe you; but you never, never can convince me that the *I* is not an eternal Reality, and that the Spiritual is not the true and real part of me.[25]

The experience of such moments, according to this and similar accounts by Tennyson, appears to be of the same general sort as Romantic vision, but (unless there has been deliberate and uncharacteristic omission of vital matters) narrower. It is not, apparently, led up to by steps in a relationship with the natural world; there is not any overwhelming sense of universal unity, nor any consequential moral scheme. There is simply the statement of Tennyson's having perceived another level of reality; he is convinced that it is "real and true" and that the flesh obstructs it; it is not described, except for his saying that it is closer to his consciousness than his own body. It is referred to in baldly abstract and clichéd terms—"God and the Spiritual."

Let us now look at this experience in poetic form, incorporated in Arthur's speech concluding "The Holy Grail":

> "Let visions of the night or of the day
> Come as they will; and many a time they come,
> Until this earth he walks on seems not earth,

This light that strikes his eyeball is not light,
This air that smites his forehead is not air
But Vision—yea, his very hand and foot—
In moments when he feels he cannot die,
And knows himself no vision to himself,
Nor the high God a vision, nor that One
Who rose again: ye have seen what ye have seen."

This passage is close, in both content and terminology, to the prose statement quoted by Hallam Tennyson in the *Memoirs*.[26] It is direct, plain statement in somewhat Wordsworthian blank verse. Its main poetic device is the string of negative metaphors in which the various senses encounter undescribed phenomena not of earth. There is the same insistence on the "reality" of the experience, and an additional one on its accompanying sense of immortality. Perhaps above all—and running counter to Romantic parallels—there is no poetic attempt to "echo" the impact of the experience through images of light, sound, color or (except very faintly) a rising emotional ladder.

Tennyson, somewhat like Keats, had been attracted very early in his life to the phenomenon of dream as "more rewarding" than normal sensed apprehension. But in *Armageddon*, perhaps his first poem, we find what is obviously mystical experience, with some attempt, relying heavily on abstractions, to define it:

My mind seem'd wing'd with knowledge and the strength
Of holy musings and immense Ideas,
Even to Infinitude. All sense of Time
And Being and Place was swallowed up and lost
Within a victory of boundless thought.
I was a part of the Unchangeable,
A scintillation of Eternal Mind,
Remix'd and burning with its parent fire.

Tennyson omitted a poem called *The Mystic* from his works after the 1830 volume, along with others relating to vision. It is probable that he was embarrassed by the incongruity of presenting deeply personal experience by such means as Shelleyan imitation. The experience, however, does not remain absent from his work; it is there throughout the rest of his career, but almost always in his own characteristic form, once he had found the means to control its presentation. It is always put simply and directly; it usually stands uncompromisingly alone. In a late poem like *By an Evolutionist* (1888–9), in fact, the abrupt assertion is Browningesque:

But I hear no yelp of the beast, and the Man is quiet at last
  As he stands on the heights of his life with a glimpse of a height that
  is higher.

This particular assertion is nakedly open to the sort of sceptical reaction I have applied to Browning, but in Tennyson's greater work the mystical foundation and consequent assertion of belief are far more convincing. There, almost invariably, the assertion projects emotional integrity because the poet places it starkly against a full background of rational scepticism and disillusion.

This involves, among other matters, two consistent areas almost embarrassingly obvious when focused on; they are functional everywhere in Tennyson's poetry. The first is his doubt, in all its weight and variety of form—an area of personal experience which Browning, except in a rare poem like *Two in the Campagna*, treats only occasionally. The second is the corollary to doubt, the internal conflict set up as it assaults the poet's commitment to the "other" order of reality. The assaults of doubt form the dominant subject in the entire Tennyson canon. T.S. Eliot's comment on *In Memoriam* as "not religious because of the quality of its faith, but because of the quality of its doubt" could apply equally to almost all Tennyson's characteristic work.

If he was not born to scepticism, it certainly took early root in his mind. As a student he was sensitive to negative aspects in the intellectual currents of the time. At Cambridge, like other thoughtful young men, he rejected standard arguments, such as Paley's, for inferring a benevolent deity from the "perfect machine" of nature.[27] But he was not an uncomplicated sceptic, and there soon appears some sense of the contentions working within his scepticism. He was impressed by Malthus, and saw the natural world as a bitter struggle for survival which "appalled" him [28]—but that did not prevent his making a sharp attack on Discovery (or science) in the poem *Timbuctoo*.

These "sunless gulfs of doubt," as Tennyson was to call them in his sonnet *To the Nineteenth Century*, soon posed an artistic problem to the poet, though there never appears to have been any question in his mind about the need to represent them fully in his work. His position, prophetic of the entire attitude that was to shape his work for decades, is expressed very early in *Supposed Confessions of a Second-rate Sensitive Mind*. There it appears in the image of doubt as a sort of ordeal by fire, only through which tempered and

quintessential truth may be discovered and accepted on the evidence
of its own survival.

> It is man's privilege to doubt,
> If so be that from doubt at length,
> Truth may stand forth unmoved of change,
> An image with profulgent brows,
> And perfect limbs, as from the storm
> Of running fires and fluid range
> Of lawless airs, at last stood out
> This excellence and solid form
> Of constant beauty.

"Constant beauty," the old Romantic passion, here points up the
broad problem which Tennyson faced from the start. His whole inclination, as we have seen, was deeply Romantic, but the hypnotic allure of the Romantic world-outlook, honestly presented against a
background of Victorian disillusion, would only lead to where it led
Arnold as a poet—to the "damned vacillating state" which is Tennyson's concluding word of the early *Confessions*.

There is much evidence that this problem—of finding means to
integrate his own doubts into his work both honestly and artistically,
while speaking clearly to his time and yet avoiding "freezing" his poetry into balanced Arnoldian paralysis—was a perpetual one for him,
and not to be solved to his satisfaction by any one method. When he
tries the means readiest to hand in the popular styles of the time, he
usually fails as artist. The tone and posture of the speaker in *Maud*,
for instance, exploit the Spasmodic fashion; it is the falsetto whine of
old Romantic desires, played out against the realities of an ugly, kill-
ing present, but still excessively vocal:

> Till I well could weep for a time so sordid and mean,
> And myself so languid and base.

But Tennyson usually managed to control the problem of presenting disillusion better than he did in *Maud*. He could simply let
the theme of his poem speak for itself: hence the many themes of
loneliness, abandonment or deprivation, as in *Oenone, Mariana in the
South, The Lady of Shalott,* and the rest. Sometimes he manages to
make subtle shifts in the total implication of otherwise Romantic
poems. *Flower in the Crannied Wall* (1869), for instance, Wordsworthian though it is, suggests as a whole the pressures of a latent

agnosticism largely through the conditional emphasis of its ending.[29] Or sometimes Tennyson will simply write poems, like *Oenone*, leaving open the problem of fulfillment and deprivation (or beauty and pain), the poem itself simply presenting the extremes without seeking to reconcile them (the eloquent silence at the end of *Oenone* is itself the expression of half-despair). This is what the Romantic poet had sometimes done in moods of depression or at early phases of philosophic development. Even such obvious methods indicate correctly the general direction of Tennyson's presentation of doubt. It is always towards omission, spareness, understatement—in other words quite in accord with the bleakness of the mid-century's spiritual climate. In the poem *Despair* (1881), for instance, it stands by itself, unqualified by any real concession to optimism. The poem, marred by a jangling meter, suggests *The City of Dreadful Night* in its picture of the modern world:

What! I should call on that Infinite Love that has served us so well?
Infinite cruelty rather that made everlasting Hell,
Made us, foreknew us, foredoom'd us, and does what he will with his own;
Better our dead brute mother who never has heard us groan!

And against this is only

Ah yet—I have had some glimmer, at times, in my gloomiest woe,
Of a God behind all—after all—the great God for aught that I know.

There is another quality in Tennyson's treatment of doubt, probably less than obvious in any single work except *In Memoriam*, which appears at once from a perspective view of the canon. That is the sense of its honesty—the sense that an actual, personal weight of doubt is being expressed. For one thing, Tennyson does not shrink from recreating again and again the precise philosophical position taken in his other poems. Thus the afterpiece to *Tiresias* (1885), an afterpiece on Fitzgerald's death, repeats exactly the doubt of *In Memoriam:*

> What life, so maim'd by night, were worth
> Our living out? Not mine to me
> Remembering all the golden hours
> Now silent, and so many dead . . . .

And—it is one of the few really clear developmental steps in Tennyson—the later poems become increasingly preoccupied with an old but newly re-emphasized cosmic glimpse of earth as a speck in an un-feeling, empty and automatic space. *Vastness* (1885) is typical:

Many a hearth upon our dark globe sighs after many a vanish'd face,
Many a planet by many a sun may roll with the dust of a vanish'd race.
. . .
What is it all but a trouble of ants in the gleam of a million million of suns?

The broad variety of Tennyson's doubt is, of course, fully real-ized only by a reading of his work, but it is sometimes highlighted: less than a third of *The Palace of Art* deals with "the painful earth," yet within that confined area a mere three stanzas seem to form a complete poem in the Arnold manner, and through that chance re-semblance they seem further to indicate the narrowness of Arnold's range, even of despair, beside Tennyson's.

> A spot of dull stagnation, without light
>   Or power of movement, seemed my soul,
> Mid onward-sloping motions infinite
>   Making for one sure goal;
>
> A still salt pool, locked in with bars of sand,
>   Left on the shore, that hears all night
> The plunging seas draw backward from the land
>   Their moon-led waters white;
>
> A star that with the choral starry dance
>   Joined not, but stood, and standing saw
> The hollow orb of moving Circumstance
>   Rolled round by one fixed law.

Probably the most exact articulation of Tennyson's attitude in suffering the negative threats of the modern condition is to be found in the Epilogue to *The Charge of the Heavy Brigade at Balaclava* (about 1882). Here the Poet, justifying war-poetry after a young woman has objected to it, goes on to view the ultimate pointlessness of poetry in a modern world:

> But Song will vanish in the Vast;
>   And that large phrase of yours
> "A Star among the stars," my dear,
>   Is girlish talk at best . . .
> The fires that arch this dusky dot—
>   Yon myriad-worlded way—

The vast sun-clusters' gather'd blaze,
    World-isles in lonely skies,
Whole heavens within themselves, amaze
    Our brief humanities;
And so does Earth; for Homer's fame,
    Tho' carved in harder stone—
The falling drop will make his name
    As mortal as my own.

It is clear, then, that Tennyson could see vividly enough the dreadful irrelevance of human aspiration (including his own) to an evolutionary universe of no apparent purpose. The poem I have just quoted, however, ends thus:

And tho', in this lean age forlorn,
    Too many a voice may cry
That man can have no after-morn,
    Not yet of these am I.
The man remains, and whatsoe'er
    He wrought of good or brave
Will mould him thro' the cycle-year
    That dawns behind the grave.

This affirmative ending, seen against what precedes it, epitomizes the basic conflict within Tennyson's poetry. As an artist he was able to use his philosophical schism, between an inward commitment to "other" reality and the claims of a disillusioning world, as the impetus for artistic creation. The conflict is basic to him as man, and vital to him as artist; by what means does the poetic process turn his inner wrestlings into the most authoritative voice of his time?

One needs first to establish the earliest forms by which his conflict was expressed. The two paired juvenile poems *Nothing Will Die* and *All Things Will Die* form (in the order of Tennyson's arrangement) first a directly Romantic, rather Shelleyan, assertion,

Nothing was born;
Nothing will die;
All things will change,

and, second, Victorian denial. Similar balance, expressed in other terms, is in several early poems. In *Sense and Conscience* (the title is precise), Conscience, the need to face reality, is put to sleep, and the result is a sensuous experience, expressed through images forming the same sort of lush escapist daydream common in early Keats. Then Memory and Pain arouse Conscience, who is outraged, but the dilemma is left unsolved.

In *The Two Voices* the conflict is put less allegorically, and finds its central form. What is clearly Romantic aspiration, both philosophical and social,

> To search through all I felt or saw,
> The springs of life, the depths of awe,
> And reach the law within the law;
>
> .　　.　　.
>
> In some good cause, not in mine own,
> To perish, wept for, honoured, known,
> And like a warrior overthrown,

is explained by the opposing voice as a matter, almost, of chemistry —"the stirring of the blood." Much of the conflict in Tennyson's later poetry is even more explicit: the Doctor in *In the Children's Hospital* (1880) [30] asking, "Can prayer set a broken bone?" and musing that "the good Lord Jesus has had his day." Fuller and equally direct is *Locksley Hall Sixty Years After* (1886) which places a Romantic theism squarely beside an earth seen in empty cosmic perspective:

Earth so huge, and yet so bounded—pools of salt, and plots of land—
Shallow skin of green and azure—chains of mountain, grains of sand!

Tennyson's most complete and direct treatment of inner conflict —aside from *In Memoriam*—occurs in *The Ancient Sage,* published in 1885 but probably written about 1882. The poem is in a sense another *Two Voices,* since the Sage throughout is replying to a powerful and lyrical scepticism expressed in a scroll of verse; it points, for instance, to the fairness of earth and sky, asking:

> "And yet what sign of aught that lies
> Behind the green and blue"?

The Sage admits that "nothing worthy proving can be proven," and advises "cleave ever to the sunnier side of doubt," for human wisdom is highly limited: ("thin minds, who creep from thought to thought,/ Break into 'Thens' and 'Whens' the Eternal Now:/ This double seeming of the single world!"). The debate between Sage and the scroll of scepticism continues; first scepticism:

> For all that laugh, and all that weep
> And all that breathe are one
> Slight ripple on the boundless deep
> That moves, and all is gone,

and then the answer, which is faith within doubt:

> But that one ripple on the boundless deep
> Feels that the deep is boundless, and itself
> For ever changing form, but evermore
> One with the boundless motion of the deep.

The poem ends with the Sage, rather like a Victorian Wordsworth, reassessing the mystical intuitions of his own boyhood, and ultimately counselling reliance on them, and upon the hope that a disciplined morality may lead to "The Nameless."

If this kind of central, recurring conflict were always presented so nakedly in Tennyson's work, its artistry and emotional impact would be infinitely less. But he is able to compel the reader's participation in it in a variety of ways. At the simplest extreme he turns it into elementary allegory. The struggle between faith and reason, for example, becomes the narrated struggle of Bedivere in the *Morte d'Arthur*, between his rational desire to keep the brand Excalibur and his moral commitment to obey Arthur, with faith leading to the ultimate miracle. In this sense almost every significant poem Tennyson ever wrote (but for some Laureate obligations and dialect poems, and by no means all these) is metaphorical presentation of one facet or another of his basic conflict, whether we take the beauty/deprivation theme of *Oenone*, the escape/involvement of *The Lady of Shalott, The Lotos-Eaters,* and *The Palace of Art,* the life/death of *The Two Voices,* and so on. This metaphorizing, however, is not always simple. For one thing, in the process Tennyson will often manipulate the weight of the conflicting elements: thus the very distance and slightness of Romantic certitude in *Ulysses* are used to provoke and justify life and action in this world:

> Yet all experience is an arch wherethrough
> Gleams that untraveled world whose margin fades
> Forever and forever when I move.

In general, however, the metaphorizing of conflict creates a diffusive effect, veiling the obvious struggle in varying degrees of opacity. A poem becomes, often, a series of metaphorical oppositions which become as a total neither balanced nor static (a vital difference from Arnold) but which work to provoke the reader to accept the underlying conflict to an extent as his own, and to react to it. In such a way the agglomeration of Keatsian lushness, languid vowel music, and subtly varied pacing of meter in *The Lotos-Eaters* is Tennyson's way of using poetic resources to weight one side of the poem's battle between escape and involvement, to the deliberate point of making escape provoke satiety and ultimately repulsion. This artistic provocation is reinforced, as I suggested earlier, when the rousing pace of the final lines itself becomes an ironic rejection of the closing "O rest ye, brother mariners . . . ." Similarly a line redolent of the background and reputations of the heroes of Troy is followed at once by one given to the most unepic of goals, with the irony deepened by rhyme thrusting the incongruous pair even closer:

> To lend our *hearts* and *spirits* wholly
> To the *influence* of *mild-minded melancholy.*

This transmuting of his inner conflict into a series of oppositions and (often) ironies is consistent in Tennyson, and operates to control and animate each restatement of it. Sometimes his method is as simple as the ironic naming of Enoch Arden's ship the *Good Fortune*; sometimes it is as complex as the treatment of the dawn in *Tithonus*.

The most celebrated example of the complexity and provocativeness of Tennyson's use of metaphorical oppositions in presenting his conflict is the brief lyric "Tears, Idle Tears" from *The Princess*. It is enough first to point to the poem's central irony, the perception of dawn as it appears to the consciousness of a dying man:

> Ah, sad and strange as in dark summer dawns
> The earliest pipe of half-awakened birds
> To dying ears, when unto dying eyes
> The casement slowly grows a glimmering square;
> So sad, so strange, the days that are no more.

CONFLICT IN METAPHOR   201

It seems, on the surface at least, a simple irony, but its effects have been rich indeed. Consider the variety of reaction this and its attendant system of conflicting metaphor have provoked in critics of the poem.[31] One should simply reaffirm, perhaps, that irony and paradox, poetic devices dear to our own century, are not somehow fortunately blundered into by Tennyson, but arise from his consistent methods of metaphorizing a conflict he felt all his life.

So—to put it more broadly—it is not fortuitous that interpretation of his work should vary, as does that of "Tears, Idle Tears." Tennyson habitually expresses his own philosophical struggles by means of metaphor balancing concealment against an inviting richness of suggestion. The aim of this deliberately "incomplete resolution" is to force a reader to contribute part of the meaning from his own consciousness: in other words to enforce that interchange with his consciousness which art demands. It is not a matter of unclarity (though poetry usually needs to be less "clear" than prose designed to carry a one-dimensional intellectual meaning), but of imaginative provocation.

It is useful to examine an instance of how Tennyson's handling of conflict metaphorically by this "incomplete resolution" works in a whole poem. *The Lady of Shalott*, as we have seen, is a poem which creates for its reader a unified imaginative experience comparable to that of *La Belle Dame Sans Merci*. It operates, and impressively enough, as a story movingly told. But something, beyond the area of ballad, remains to perturb. There is a conflict in the poem which catches at a reader's own awareness of his world. The Lady, like the wife of Arnold's Forsaken Merman, is tempted from her enchanted home into the more "real" world outside (more "real," but still at a remove from the reader's), and she is destroyed. Her conflict is veiled and enriched, in Tennyson's familiar manner, but it is not resolved, and the poem as "lesson" must be left open; and what a critic chooses to stress ultimately reveals only his own predilections in relating to the poem. This is quite different from the effect of agonized static balance symbolized by the beach at the end of *The Forsaken Merman*, about which it is hard to imagine critics disagreeing. But *The Lady of Shalott* causes Lionel Stevenson to see it as counsel to escape from sterile creation (pictures of the world derived only at second-hand through a mirror) into the real world, which is worthwhile to the Lady despite her brief taste of it.[32] E.D.H. Johnson sees the Lady's world as a metaphor for the creative imagination, shattered by the real world of Lancelot's arrival—in other words as complaint about the destruction of creativity by actuality,[33] not (as Stevenson does) as counsel to leave the world of an unreal creativity for that of real life. Tennyson himself stressed that it was *love* for something that moved the Lady from "shadows" to "realities." [34]

What an approach from the direction of Romantic poetry suggests about this poem is that its manipulation of light imagery, in the Romantic manner, would hint that commitment is to be found somehow in the world of actuality and action, with the glittering appearance of Lancelot, the sun dazzling through the leaves, and the "blue unclouded weather" all contrasted with the "shadows" of the Lady's life, and the "falling light, "gleaming shape," and dead pallor of her passing. Yet it is the color, light, and activity, as allurements of the actual world, that are the means of her destruction. Thus a Romantic symbol, of light as commitment, has been developed by Tennyson into a paradox much more representative of his own state of mind.

Such differences in interpretation matter less for themselves than as evidence of Tennyson's methods of stimulating his readers. The stimulation occurs at deliberately varied distances from the reader, sometimes directly stated, more often simply metaphorized; most often metaphorized as infinitely provocative ambivalence or paradox. The result is that, in confronting a poem dealing with mental conflict, the reader himself undergoes a secondary one; then the vein of metaphor grows into symbol, and the reader experiences a vicarious echo of Tennyson's own relationship with the climate of his time. A reader becomes involved in the poem, as all good poetry must involve him, and in Tennyson the process is accompanied by first a vague, then a growing, and finally a firm recognition of a conflict he knows himself, the terms of which he is largely left to define for himself. The spheres of poet and reader become no longer clearly separable, but fluid.

All Tennyson's poetry is finally such "re-enactment" of inward struggle, in which the poet deliberately holds up his bare mystical remnant of Romantic certitude to the assaults of scepticism and disillusion, and chronicles the ordeals of its survival. That is a bleak enough philosophic conflict if directly expressed, and it remains so when the poetry is "clear" but thin and omissive, as are the later poems of conflict such as *By an Evolutionist* and *Parnassus,* and as Browning almost invariably is in treating self-conflict directly. But often, even within slight poems, Tennyson can express the shift and blend of his struggle, as in *The Islet* (1864), where he "imbues the landscape of 'the beauteous hateful isle' with a strange terror, his own half-frightened attraction to sensuous escape and his dread . . . of a lonely aestheticism." [35] In his best work the suggestiveness increases until Tennyson's conflict becomes universalized, with a permanent capacity to stimulate self-definition in a reader, at whatever stage of life he comes to read or re-read. That, of course, is art, but the best poems of 1832–43 and *In Memoriam* obviously depend upon the poet's equal control of resources broader than the metaphorizing of conflict with which I have been concerned here.

5. STYLE AS OUTLOOK   This depth of involvement for a reader must of course concern matters of style. Tennyson's style deserves exhaustive examination, but within the scope of this book it is possible only to discern stylistic directions the poet took in disciplining an expressive tendency demonstrably Romantic throughout his work. They make it at once "new" and his own, the mirror of his philosophic cast of mind, and a "voice" uniquely articulate to his time. I have been suggesting that in metaphorizing his conflicts Tennyson exploited a range varying from directness through differing degrees of ambivalence to full irony, and that he used such a range as a provocative force. His metaphorizing must above all engage the imagination; it must not create an effect of finality, or one of paralysis.

This distinction may be clearer if we consider, using examples, a specific poetic problem: the architectural proportions of a poem. Tennyson's problem is to impel in the reader a direct, "documentary" [36] confrontation with the elements and the order of mental schism. The poem *De Profundis* provides a simple hint concerning order. It is a moving and provocative work in the form of "Two Greetings" (its sub-title) on the birth of a child. One is religious and Romantic, the other scientific and evolutionary, the complete poem being in many ways a Victorian treatment of the concerns of Wordsworth's *Intimations*. The order is important. Tennyson does not repeat the Wordsworthian order of a basic insistence on the child's transcendental origin, modified by shades of the prison house. One suspects that an Arnoldian treatment would have presented the birth in terms of agnostic mystery or distant qualified longing, precisely balanced by inexorable images of the bleak modern world the child was to live in. One speculates that Browning would have greeted the birth with fierce affirmation of its divinity, and if he *had* assayed a second part at all, it would have been philosophic argument in justification. Tennyson, in arranging the poem as it finally stood from the two sections which compose it, simply presents two views, the evolutionary one first,[37] thus claiming topical common ground with the reader; the Romantic affirmation comes as a finale, appearing to survive and transcend the first, and giving the crowning impression of the poem.

The Palace of Art provides a fuller example of Tennyson's actual proportioning of contending elements. Something over two-thirds of the poem concerns aesthetic isolation; the predominant weight of the poem is given to the lure of the Palace. It is then curtly and savagely destroyed in the brief conclusion, presenting its collapse and the consequent lesson of worldly responsibility. This balance—or significant flouting of it—suggests that the ending operates on a more powerful and authoritative level altogether than the body of the work. Comparison may well be made with *The Scholar-Gipsy*, with its mathematical balance between a Romanticism felt at a remove in the Gipsy's recreation, and the lecture on the spiritual bleakness of modernity. The precise halves of *Abt Vogler*—assertion and philosophic argument—differ equally from Tennyson's practice here.

Comparable to this sort of proportioning is Tennyson's stance as creator of dramatic monologues. Many of his best poems, of course, appear to be as directly "subjective" as *The Two Voices,* or for that matter *In Memoriam,* while subjectivity in Browning is almost certain artistic disaster. In the dramatic monologue, however, Tennyson rarely or never achieves Browning's kind of objectivity; Tennyson's speakers are "thin" voices recognizable as tones of his own. In other words, Tennyson uses the dramatic monologue to achieve a certain dramatic distance as poet; it is another variety of ambivalence, neither near nor far. The impression remains in most of his dramatic monologues that it is the poet—at a distance, perhaps, but still the poet—who is speaking, not the character. If the rise of the dramatic monologue in the nineteenth century is indeed a logical feature of a collapsing moral and emotional orientation, as has been suggested (see p. 164) then Tennyson seems to try to control the process by consistently writing with a mild, only half-realized objectivity in certain "dramatic" poems.

To move to what is more purely "style" is to find seemingly deliberate reductions of Romantic practice. In several poems Tennyson's expression reflects the philosophical climate of the time in a bare, uncompromising diction of which the best example is that throughout *Ulysses,* and which lends itself to understatement:

> And see the great Achilles, whom we knew.

Where there are Romantic implications, such as the "near human" vitality of the natural world in which Oenone lives, they are made briefly and almost casually:

> The swimming vapour slopes athwart the glen,
> Puts forth an arm, and creeps from pine to pine,
> And loiters, slowly drawn.

Not that Tennyson, in his more celebrated work, eschews Romantic diction rich in sound and levels of suggestion, but any Keatsian height of lushness is usually exploited for wider effects beyond itself: the deliberate cloying beyond surfeit in *The Lotos-Eaters,* for example, and to some extent a parallel effect in *Oenone,* where the reader is made to feel some distrust of the over-rhapsodic past and is emotionally directed towards the painful present.

There is a corresponding simplification, often, in verse form, where Romantic fullness—at an extreme in the odes of Keats and Shelley—is slimmed down in certain poems, notably in *In Memoriam* itself. In *The Two Voices* the form does much to compel the inexorable, unanswerable tone of the poem. This is also true in *The Palace of Art,* where the effect towards the end is reinforced by the direct imagery of collapse, implying a former and more solid condition:

> Remaining utterly confused with fears,
>   And ever worse with growing time,
> And ever unrelieved by dismal tears,
>   And all alone in crime.
>
> Shut up as in a crumbling tomb, girt round
>   With blackness as a solid wall . . . .

In his use of the barest sorts of verse form Tennyson, again, uses an eloquent technical representation of the spirit of his time; it was a lead which Arnold was to follow in *Empedocles,* Fitzgerald to crown in *The Rubaiyat,* and which Housman would sustain at the end of the century.

Tennyson may be said to have abandoned the core of Romantic poetry in that he does not use poetic resources, as the Romantics had, to recreate an echo of transcendental experience. Rather, he uses poetry to involve his reader in the *recreated struggle* between faith and doubt. The actual assertion itself is reduced in Tennyson's work to a simple mystical statement, simply put, as we have seen; but additionally Tennyson often underscores the vagueness deliberately, as if to say that his emphasis as a man is not on mystical experience itself, but on a consequent struggle to retain belief in its meaning. The recurrently vague terms in *The Two Voices* are an example:

> "Of something felt, like something here;
> Of something done, I know not where;
> Such as no language may declare."

Thus the presentation of transcendental experience, despite its importance for Tennyson personally, is here casually underemphasized, in direct contrast to the practice of the Romantics. On the other hand, the sphere of actual sensed phenomena moves in the opposite direction, and is presented in terms giving the impact of detailed, exact "truth." Tennyson uses his poetics to present physical phenomena on two levels of sense. The brook in *Oenone* thus creates a visual image for the reader, while the cadences of the line reproduce the steps of the brook's downward movement:

> In cataract after cataract to the sea.

Indeed, there are many often-cited instances in the Tennyson of the "matchless vignette"—the phrase which the reader discovers as the inevitably *right* and all-expressive statement of his own experience: the wind which

> . . . took the reed tops as it went,

the haunting by the ghost in *Maud,*

> 'Tis the blot upon the brain
> That *will* show itself without,

the emigration in *The Brook,* which depends for its impact upon a moment's reflection,

> Katie walks
> By the long wash of Australasian seas
> Far off, and holds her head to other stars,
> And breathes in April-autumns,

and the coming of summer dawn in *The Princess,*

> Till notice of a change in the dark world
> Was lispt about the acacias, and a bird,
> That early woke to feed her little ones,
> Sent from a dewy breast a cry for light.

They leap out of context and the sensitive reader of Tennyson makes his own anthology of them, voluntarily or otherwise. They spring from a rigorous awareness of the natural world—I shall return to that later—and the remarkable control of a wide range of stylistic effect, from the eloquent generality of "took" the reed tops, to the sound of the wind rustling the trees in the last quotation above. The point here is that they are not merely memorable vignettes, but poetic attempts to "echo", to force the reader to undergo again, in a sense fuller than the word "imagination" usually carries, his previous experience of the world of sense. Only if that background is convincing, or compelling, can the vital foundation of recognition and acceptance be made, and the bare philosophic assertion which surmounts it become compelling also.

The very purpose of poetry—and an area essential to understanding Tennyson's work—lies in this special kind of relationship with the reader. The poetry reflects the facts of the world he knows, in its observation of nature as in its presentation of science, and it also relates to a recognizable spiritual climate. Its reader is induced to perform an act of recognition of common ground.

In consistently trying to broaden the area of sensibility which a reader might enter, Tennyson resembles Browning and differs sharply from Arnold, who largely confines himself to tradition. Tennyson exploits very fully the literary past as well as the contemporary world. He is, despite the conventional-seeming surface of his work beside Browning's, at once both a heavily traditional yet innovating, topical, searching poet.

Briefly to reflect on the traditional elements in Tennyson first brings to mind obvious matters, equally relevant to Arnold, demanded by the subjects and sources treated—the Greek choric formula in *Oenone* ("O happy tears, and how unlike to these!"), the Genesis view of creation at the start of *The Two Voices,* or the epic boast of the *Morte d'Arthur* ("The goodliest fellowship of famous knights/ Whereof this world holds record"). But there are less obvious and more indicative instances of the scope of Tennyson's exploitation of literary traditions. Thus the imagery of the *Idylls,* and particularly that of the *Morte d'Arthur,* owes much to Anglo-Saxon and Middle English poetry.[38] There are points where it seems almost translation—of the scenery of *Sir Gawain and the Green Knight,* for instance:

> Dry clash'd his harness in the icy caves
> And barren chasms, and all to left and right
> The bare black cliff clang'd round him, as he based
> His feet on juts of slippery crag that rang
> Sharp-smitten with the dint of armed heels.

The manner of the Old English *Wanderer* similarly seems to lie upon the surviving Bedivere's speech:

> And I, the last, go forth companionless,
> And the days darken round me, and the years,
> Among new men, strange faces, other minds.

And, although the actual debt here, as so often with such apparent echoes, is to a broader tradition embracing both, the home of the Phoenix in the Old English poem bears a marked relationship to the description of Avilion in Tennyson's *Morte d'Arthur:*

> the island-valley of Avilion;
> Where falls not hail, or rain, or any snow,
> Nor ever wind blows loudly, but it lies
> Deep-meadowed, happy, fair with orchard lawns
> And bowery hollows crowned with summer sea.[39]

Some of the scenery in Tennyson's poem is not to be differentiated, except in form, from Ossian:

And in the moon athwart the place of tombs,
Where lay the mighty bones of ancient men,
Old knights, and over them the sea-wind sang
Shrill, chill, with flakes of foam.

The influence of *Hamlet* on Tennyson's *Ulysses* [40] and *The Two Voices* [41] has been pointed out, and I shall refer later to further examples concerning *In Memoriam*.

In such ways, Tennyson looks back. His use of contemporary material, "his modernity" and prescience, however, are much fuller and more complex, and deserve consideration far beyond the standard citing of the well-known conclusion to *Locksley Hall*. If one of the functions of his "modernity" is to broaden the area of involvement with his readers, as I have been insisting, another was to test and try his own assertion against the most uncompromising assaults his epoch could bring. His poetry, again and again, evokes a sense of his having been able to assess contemporary ideas and attitudes as if from a perspective in the future. In a similar way, *The Two Voices,* a quarter of a century before *The Origin of Species* appeared, reflected a foreboding that the evolutionary machine worked through types rather than individuals:

> It spake, moreover, in my mind:
> "Though thou wert scattered to the wind,
> Yet is there plenty of the kind."

In a very early sonnet Tennyson had expressed a psychological interest, which he was to sustain, in the mental sensation of "re-living" an experience:

> As when with downcast eyes we muse and brood,
> And ebb into a former life, or seem
> To lapse far back in some confused dream
> To states of mystical similitude.
> If one but speaks or hems or stirs his chair,
> Ever the wonder waxeth more and more,
> So that we say, "All this hath been before,
> All this hath been, I know not when or where."

There is often, in fact, an impressive psychological realism in Tennyson's work. The poem *Sea Dreams* (1858) contains an effectively handled dream with convincing interpretation, but most prominent is the transition as the sleeper wakes after dreaming of a fleet of glass ships, almost foundering on a reef of gold, and

> ". . . fearing waved my arm to warn them off;
> An idle signal, for the brittle fleet
> (I thought I could have died to save it) near'd
> Touch'd, clink'd and clash'd, and vanish'd, and I woke,
> I heard the clash so clearly. . . ."
> "Nay," said the kindly wife to comfort him,
> "You raised your arm, you tumbled down and broke
> The glass with little Margaret's medicine in it;
> And, breaking that, you made and broke your dream . . . ."

And in *Maud*, Tennyson is aware of the mind's capacity, in moments of shock, to seize on the inconsequential as relief:

> That it should, by being so overwrought,
> Suddenly strike on a sharper sense
> For a shell, or a flower, little things
> Which else would have been past by!

If these matters do not appear as striking as they should, it is because we belong to a psychologically-saturated age. It is probably more impressive, then, to find an imagery in Tennyson which seems that of modern poetry reflecting visually a contemporary atmosphere: take the lines in the *Morte d'Arthur:*

> an agony
> Of lamentation, like a wind that shrills
> All night in a waste land, where no one comes . . . .

To read Tennyson's work, in fact, with the hindsight of later poetry in mind is constantly to experience recognition. He was also highly sensitive to the achievements of his contemporaries in advancing poetry, and some of the dramatic monologues of his later career, such as *Columbus* and *Sir John Oldcastle* (1880), are clearly Browningesque:

> and I saw
> The glory of the Lord flash up, and beat
> Thro' all the homely town from jasper, sapphire,
> Chalcedony, emerald, sardonyx, sardius,
> Chrysolite, beryl, topaz, chrysoprase,

Jacynth, and amythyst—and those twelve gates,
Pearl—and I woke, and thought—death—I shall die—
(*Columbus*) [42]

Tennyson's attempts at the extended dramatic monologue, however, may be held a failure in his search to broaden his range. He could never avoid self-consciousness, and the poems are diffuse and weak beside Browning's totally objective work. Here, perhaps only the fact that Tennyson made attempts in this direction is important.

He was often able to strike notes which were to become central in later poetic movements and styles. In *Oenone*, for example, is that combination of Romantic sensuousness and pictorial detail, deriving chiefly from Keats and Shelley, that was to become a staple of the Pre-Raphaelites:

Idalian Aphrodite beautiful,
Fresh as the foam, new-bathed in Paphian wells,
With rosy slender fingers backward drew
From her warm brows and bosom her deep hair
Ambrosial, golden round her lucid throat
And shoulder; from the violets her light foot
Shone rosy-white, and o'er her rounded form
Between the shadows of the vine-bunches
Floated the glowing sunlights, as she moved.[43]

In much the same way, some poems of Tennyson's 1880 volume come very close, in style as well as substance, to what Kipling (who was fifteen at the time) was to write. *The First Quarrel* is one; there is also *The Northern Cobbler*, whose ruin has been gin, and who keeps a quart bottle in his sight in order to defy it; he is made to exclaim:

Wouldn't a pint a' sarved as well as a quart? Naw doubt:
But I liked a bigger feller to fight wi' an' fowt it out.
Fine an' meller 'e mun be by this, if I cared to taäste,
But I moänt, my lad, and I weänt, fur I'd feäl mysen cleän disgraäced.

A further consistent means of drawing the reader closer to the poetry, and simultaneously leaning the balance of his naturally Romantic work towards worldly phenomena in accord with the climate of his time, is that strain in Tennyson's work which, for want of a better word, we should nowadays call realistic. It is allied to the general toning-down of the more riotous excesses of Romantic image and diction which formed the staple of *The Lover's Tale*. It is much more typical of the mature Tennyson that even poems on old themes like the *Morte d'Arthur* are given exact and precise detail:

> A broken chancel with a broken cross,
> That stood on a dark strait of barren land.

Or there is the detail in *The Lady of Shalott:*

> All in the blue unclouded weather
> Thick-jewelled shone the saddle-leather,
> The helmet and the helmet-feather
> Burned like one burning flame together . . . .

These are simple matters, but the range of the tendency is a varied one: it would include the conception of a deglamorized Ulysses, and Tennyson's ability to give visual images a two or three dimensional effect (the visual image itself, the splash of water and the sense of its movement, for example, in "In cateract after cateract to the sea"—a line which still retains the effortless impact of prose). It would include the precise rendering of physical sensation—the effect of drugs, for instance, in *The Lotos-Eaters:*

> but whoso did receive of them
> And taste, to him the gushing of the wave
> Far far away did seem to mourn and rave
> On alien shores, and if his fellow spake,
> His voice was thin, as voices from the grave;
> And deep-asleep he seemed, yet all awake,
> And music in his ears his beating heart did make.

And it would include the sudden brief simile, at once universal but personally precise,

> Like one that feels a nightmare on his bed
> When all the house is mute.
> *(Morte d'Arthur)*

This general sense of a documentary, scrupulously-observed "truth" parallels a similar impression in the prose of the early Ruskin. Ruskin, in viewing nature and art, attempted to revivify the Romantic impulse by looking with re-opened eyes and rigorous observation at the wonders of natural detail in a wave, the clouds, the conditions of foam, the marvelous variety of foliage, the exact plumage of birds, and so on. The Ruskin of *Modern Painters,* writing in prose, was essentially a young Romantic poet. The comparable vein in Tennyson may quite possibly derive from similar motives, conscious or otherwise, but Tennyson does demonstrably control and modernize his poetic record of such observation by the paring down of Romantic value-words and Romantic emotionalism. So the wind which

> . . . took the reed tops as it went

captures an exact, distinctive movement in nature with the plainest and most generalized verb: the effect is that *what* is seen matters, and style becomes incidental—or appears to. It is, in brief, an attempt to prevent anything from diffusing or complicating the artistic illusion —it is an illusion—of "pure" fact. The concrete, scientific facet of consciousness is recognized by the reader, and helps enforce his deeper involvement in the poem as a unit. The reader accepts the poet's voice as his own, articulating his own perceptions at a height of exactitude he himself cannot approach.

A more easily separable attempt to impel that sort of relationship lies in Tennyson's use of "frames" to his poems. At the simplest level, their function is to bridge the gap between reader and poem, as Wordsworth had done in the opening setting of *Michael* or, for that matter, in *The Prelude* itself. *Oenone* has that sort of nature-setting in the "vale in Ida." Tennysonian frames are not numerous, but their function is inescapable. The simplest example is the poem *The Epic,* which Tennyson wrote about 1838 as frame for the *Morte d'Arthur,* and the main function of which is to point up the relevance of the Arthurian poem to the modern situation.

There is, however, a more sophisticated function to the frame at the end of the *Morte d'Arthur,* for it presents the process of a quasi-Romantic imaginative experience, with the poem itself as stimulus. The speaker's first reaction, which he ascribes to the tone of the reading he has just heard or "perhaps some modern touches here and there," is emotional—rapt, in fact. This leads, when he goes to bed, to a dream-vision:

> I seemed
> To sail with Arthur under looming shores,
> Point after point.

It culminates, before the world of wakefulness and actuality can reclaim him, in the appearance of Arthur "like a modern gentleman," but one who "cannot die." He brings "all good things, and war shall be no more." On this note of faith and triumph the speaker is awakened by the peal of bells, which he finds are actual enough, for it is Christmas day. The progressive pattern of this frame is important: first emotion, provoked by art (the poem itself) leading to dream-vision; dream-vision leading to the sight of an Arthur beyond death, and the conviction of immortality; finally, an assertive faith rising from this. The progression makes the frame, in fact, a disciplined and scaled-down echo of Keats' insistence on the meaning of art. It is at a deliberate remove, but it is fulfilled and positive, and so carries an effect quite different from that of the quasi-Romantic frame which Arnold made to open *The Scholar-Gipsy*.

To this point I have been considering separable areas where content and technique are consistent enough to form recognizable methods of turning Romantic practice towards Tennyson's particular poetry of struggle. But much of what Tennyson does with Romantic practice, of course, is not to be categorized, for his relationship to the earlier poetry also involves individual concerns from which simple patterns do not emerge. A great many "Romantic" adaptations are not consistent, but, considered together, form evidence that his struggle to revitalize an outworn Romanticism was a continuing attempt rather than a finished achievement, and included failure and regression as well as success. In short, his struggle as artist mirrors his philosophic struggle as man.

To cite individual examples of Tennyson's adaptations of Romanticism is to select from a rich store. For instance, the word "infinite" is as apt in his work to be used negatively as positively; at times it carries its Romantic connotation, but at others it means unending cosmic vastness, as it does in *The Two Voices:* "Thou hast not gained a real height,/ Nor art thou nearer to the light,/ Because the scale is infinite." And the seasonal round of nature, a central symbol of Romantic affirmation, with which Coleridge had joyously blessed his son in *Frost at Midnight,* and into which both Lucy and Adonais had passed in endless fulfillment, is used to suggest only escape and inertness in the superb rhythmic deceleration of the stanza, "Lo! in the middle of the wood . . ." of the Choric Song in *The Lotos-Eaters*. Here Tennyson first inverts the Romantic symbol of the seasonal round from affirmation to its lack. Then, by ironic saturation of the weariness and inertness, he goes on to destroy his own inversion, but painfully and with ambivalence. Thus *The Lotos-Eaters* struggles finally to affirmation, but one made remoter, more rueful, more hesitant. It is Tennyson's own, and it is characteristically Victorian, not Romantic.

The forces of fate (which through Lucy's death had later revealed Romantic order to Wordsworth) become, often, gloomily ironic in Tennyson, and a metaphor for doubt. The gods, in the Romantic world-view, do not kill us for their sport, but Tennyson seems frequently to prefigure the detailed mockeries of fate in Thomas Hardy. When Annie opens her Bible to find a "message" about Enoch in *Enoch Arden,* she misunderstands its ambivalence, takes him for dead, and remarries.

I have in general been concentrating upon the poetry of Tennyson which has standing as his "better" work, omitting, for the moment, *In Memoriam.* Even in this poetry, however, there are striking artistic failures, and they are most apt to occur when Tennyson takes over Romantic practice without either individualizing it or placing it in a context sufficiently dramatic to absorb it. The clearest example is the resolution of *The Two Voices.* Here a familiar symbol of the Romantic sort, the love uniting the church-going family in simple dignity, remains what it essentially is—Wordsworth's leech-gatherer undigested. In Tennyson, the speaker, moved by the sight of the family, blesses it, and, like the Ancient Mariner, finds release from his burden—here the "dull and bitter" voice. There is even the comparison of the reassuring hint the family provokes with

> an Aeolian harp that wakes
> No certain air, but overtakes
> Far thought with music that it makes

—a fanciful rather than imaginative simile considerably weaker than its Romantic forbears. The moral of the event is akin to that of *The Ancient Mariner,* echoing the moral tag at the end of that poem even in its style:

> To feel, although no tongue can prove.
> That every cloud, that spreads above
> And veileth love, itself is love.

This resolution echoes Romantic poetry in practically every detail as well as in its principal affirmation. But its general poetic effect is different: for one thing it is subjoined to the main body of the poem, the conflict of the voices, rather than forming an integrated consequence. In this Tennyson resembles Arnold rather than Coleridge or any other Romantic.

There is another resemblance, this time to Browning, in *Locksley Hall Sixty Years After*. In this poem Tennyson—most exceptionally for him—uses rational argument to support his refusal of the finality of death. Its basis is more or less anthropological:

Indian warriors dream of ampler hunting grounds beyond the night;
Ev'n the black Australian dying hopes he shall return, a white.

The poem seems unusually dogmatic for Tennyson. There are bitter pessimistic strictures on the time, reflecting the later Carlyle in tone: ("When was age so cramm'd with menace? Madness? written, spoken lies?" "Equal born? O yes, if yonder hill be level with the flat"). The poem poses the old Romantic problem of the dissolution of potentially permanent beauty:

Dead, but how her living glory lights the hall, the dune, the grass!
Yet the moonlight is the sunlight, and the sun himself will pass,

and it finally asserts that "Love will conquer at the last." While its tone and dialectic contribute to the dogmatic atmosphere of the poem, its main cause is that Tennyson (again unusually for him, and veering close to Browning) presents a final position, rather than the internal struggle by which it was reached. *Locksley Hall Sixty Years After* is one of a number of poems which raise the question of Tennyson's "progress."

A variety of developments have been discerned:

. . . his work—read as a whole and, as far as possible, in chronological order—is the faithful record of his development from the wondering child of Somersby to the ancient sage of Aldworth, from the aestheticism of the Cambridge period to the moral realism of the *Idylls of the King,* from the social confidence of "Locksley Hall" to the disillusion of its sequel, from the doubt of *In Memoriam* to the quiet assent of the last lyrics. An understanding of even the least of these verses gains from a familiarity with the total product of Tennyson's imagination. Each piece, however, must finally be assessed on its own intrinsic merits.[44]

It is debatable whether a view of Tennyson's development in such broad strokes is tenable, for almost all its elements are strongly marked in that endless inner struggle he metaphorized at all stages of his career. The only generalization I should care to make about his progress concerns his last poems: there is certainly the note of "quiet assent" there, and in having *Crossing the Bar* placed at the end of editions of his work Tennyson authorized that final note. But his last lyrics, chronologically speaking, give a different impression—more dogmatically insistent, like *Locksley Hall Sixty Years After,* and also more Browningesque in their assertion.

Vastness contains a long list of contemporary shortcomings reminiscent of Arnold's "lecture" in *The Scholar-Gipsy.* The poem questions the worth of "all that is filthy with all that is fair," but unlike Arnold's poem it ends in succinct and positive affirmation:

> . . . the dead are not dead but alive.

In *To Mary Boyle,* life remains "the Mystery," but the poem again ends affirmatively. *Merlin and the Gleam* is an allegory of Tennyson's poetic career,[45] but it chronicles milestones in poetic subject rather than an inner or philosophical development. That is reflected by a general pattern, in *Merlin* as in so many of Tennyson's last poems, of mystery and decline leading to affirmation:

> Launch your vessel,
> And crowd your canvas,
> And, ere it vanishes
> Over the margin,
> After it, follow it,
> Follow The Gleam.

Romney's Remorse, a Browningesque dramatic monologue involving a sentimental situation—an aging artist returned to the wife he had abandoned—is concerned with the "chasm between / Work and Ideal." It ends, again, hopefully.

In these works and others, Tennyson's last volume but one, *Demeter and Other Poems* (1889), forms the pattern most consistent in him—doubt resolved by affirmation. In *Parnassus,* despite the "terrible Muses" Astronomy and Geology, creativity itself, rather than its finished product, remains worthwhile: "Let the golden Iliad vanish, Homer here is Homer there." *By an Evolutionist* leaves its speaker standing on the heights of his life with a glimpse of a height that is higher,

and *The Play* (which is life) counsels patience in awaiting its resolution by some fifth act, Earth being only the first.

This insistent conclusion to Tennyson's work brings him close to Browning, mostly since these poems state problems followed by resolutions seeming arbitrary because the area of personal conflict leading from one to the other is not presented, as it usually had been in the bulk of the poet's other work. Tennyson, towards the close, seemed to be assuming, as a context, the poetic product of his long life. It is Tennyson not as the earlier Agonistes, but as the Ancient Sage expressing a succinct oracular wisdom without, for once, documenting the struggle that had led to it. If these last poems are assessed on their own intrinsic merits, they are unconvincing, because they are simply summation. They should be regarded as pointers to a more crucial foundation which they themselves omit—a poetry itself a metaphoric reenactment of personal struggle to retain faith in a time grown hostile to it. That sort of poetry, universalized, becomes *In Memoriam.*

6. IN MEMORIAM   Whatever its inhibitions, the Victorian age was not prone to self-effacement in its literature, and among a flood of poetry there are several works of ambitious design. Only two of these, however, *The Ring and the Book* and *In Memoriam,* have gained a secure and universal standing beyond their epoch. Tennyson's poem retains an eminence never seriously threatened even during the height of the reaction against his work. Except for a few short poems, *Ulysses,* the lyric *Tears, Idle Tears, Crossing the Bar,* and probably *The Lady of Shalott,* it is perhaps the only work of his to have received anything like the critical attention it merits. My own concern with the poem here is not critical analysis in general, but a consideration of the relationship of *In Memoriam* to Romantic poetry. I have been suggesting that in other poems Tennyson transmitted a personal assertion, mystically-based but diminished from full Romantic force; that he did so by stressing the assertion itself far less than the background of conflict it had had to survive; and that, to do so, he used consistent methods of adapting Romantic practice.

The recording of doubt and the operations of self-conflict which Tennyson both metaphorized and expressed directly in his shorter poems are, obviously, the essence of *In Memoriam*. T. S. Eliot insisted that it is the poem's doubt, rather than its faith, that is pre-eminent. Such a judgement is a sophisticated response to a basic force in the poem, a force which ensures that the one quotation from Tennyson which everyone knows concerns nature being red in tooth and claw. The design of the work, the immensity of the single blow of Hallam's death, and the time-scale of roughly three years the poem covers all give the poem an illusion of precise limitation; but the tragic event is only trigger and catalyst for personal conflicts ranging over the poet's whole life. The very process crucial to the making of the poem—the arranging of lyrics composed over several years—makes clear its central nature. Such selection and assembly require a perspective view of personal experience, and it is certain that Tennyson sought to winnow out that portion of his own mental experience which seemed to him of universal importance. Thus moods of grief, partial recoveries and retrogressions, dreams and nightmares, imaginative fancies, reactions to significant revisits (to Cambridge and to Hallam's house), and interconnections of mood at different points in time are all dramatically absorbed into the poem, which is spiritual autobiography universalized.

Such direct manifestations of conflict, obvious enough, form the burden of the work. As in other poems already discussed, however, Tennyson often reinforces them by means of more subtle metaphorical oppositions aimed rather at emotional than intellectual perceptions. The structure of *In Memoriam*, composed as it is of self-contained lyrics, allows Tennyson to set one poem against another to reflect mental extremes. Thus in Poem 2, the gloom of the yew tree over the root-enwrapped grave, never blooming, and altogether a marvelous symbol of a mind obsessed with the finality of death, stands beside the tree of Poem 39, where "Thy gloom is kindled at the tips." Poem 54 leaves the speaker, who has expressed his trust that in nature "not a worm is cloven in vain," regressing to an outburst of despair:

> So runs my dream; but what am I?
> An infant crying in the night;
> An infant crying for the light,
> And with no language but a cry.

In Poem 124, a poem describing mystical experience, that cry is answered, and Tennyson replies to his earlier self that it came through neither Romantic pantheism nor scientifically, in fact not through nature at all ("I found Him not in world or sun,/ Or eagle's wing, or insect's eye"). Such pairings of opposed mental experience meld, across the poem's chronology, and form one of the work's major dimensions, as any good commentary, such as A. C. Bradley's, shows repeatedly.

As consistently functional throughout the work, and giving starkness rather than subtlety, are the bare economy of the verse form (not the same but of comparable effect with those of *The Palace of Art* and *The Two Voices*), and the broad topicality. This last, particularly in the constant development of the implications of evolutionary theory, is partly responsible for the work's perpetual impact of modernity. In its remorseless questioning of what modern readers often prefer to dismiss as unanswerable, *In Memoriam* touches our most sensitive and raw repressions. As we have seen, Tennyson had been asking such questions clearly enough in *The Two Voices* and elsewhere, but *In Memoriam* offers scope for their full development. Poem 45, on the formation of self-consciousness and hence memory, has affiliations reaching back to Wordsworth's *Intimations,* and which seem to reach forward as well to the "something other" of Martin Buber. This sense of insistent demand on the twentieth century imagination emerges stylistically also, and at times with striking, almost shocking success. Consider the bare final line, which Eliot so admired, as the speaker, in his instinctive pointless visit to the dead Hallam's house, turns back to face the world:

> He is not here; but far away
>   The noise of life begins again,
>   And ghastly through the drizzling rain
> On the bald street breaks the blank day.

It is a line of contemporary poetry, entirely and economically functional in its monosyllabic thump, its alliterative sameness. Far more moving than eloquence in its chopped illusion of the inarticulateness of stunned grief, it carries the Ruskinian sense of exact observation, aimed at a center of universal experience.

The positive faith of *In Memoriam* rests on the mystical experience which had formed the heart of the early poems *Armageddon* and *The Mystic;* it had touched *The Two Voices,* closed "The Holy Grail" Idyll, and became the foundation of *The Ancient Sage,* published when Tennyson was a man of seventy-six. Since *In Memoriam,* like Tennyson's other poetry, concerns above all the struggles which his faith in the meaning of mystical experience had to survive, and depends only in a subsidiary way on representing the experience itself, direct treatment of it occurs in only two poems of the major work. In Poem 95 it is stimulated by a reading of the dead Hallam's letters; I shall point out later how, in the whole context of Poem 95, this experience is presented by a seemingly deliberate reduction of Romantic methods. For the moment, however, it is enough to note that vision is treated according to Tennyson's practice in his other work. It is briefly dealt with in a short poem, it is at once subject to doubt, and it uses terms of pure abstraction, as Wordsworth had done, but, again, with a reduction from that poet's complex diction to the simplest possible; this gives what appears a deliberate effect of inarticulateness, of refusal even to try suggesting the details of impact: "touched me," "that which is," "that which I became."

Poem 124, a more general treatment of mystical experience, is more metaphorical,

> A warmth within the breast would melt
> The freezing reason's colder part,
> And like a man in wrath the heart
> Stood up and answered, "I have felt."
>
> No, like a child in doubt and fear:
> But that blind clamour made me wise;
> Then was I as a child that cries,
> But, crying, knows his father near,

but still depends ultimately on the same brusque cryptic abstractions:

> And what I am beheld again
> What is, and no man understands.

The art of so proportioning oppositions to create an active (though implicit) declaration of attitude rather than the stasis of precise balance is used, in *In Memoriam,* more ambitiously than in works previously treated, the wider scope of the longer work encouraging this. An example is necessarily complex, but the clearest is probably this: immediately before the famous (and by now almost clichéd) outburst of despair in Poem 56, there is a preparatory group of poems. These, Poems 50 to 55 inclusive, form essentially an appeal—with reflections arising from it—for present communion with the dead Hallam; "Be near me when my light is low. . . ." None of the six poems is ostensibly about faith, but into each is worked, as an undercurrent, a suggestion of it. Poem 50 has "Be near me when my faith is dry." Poem 51 questions Tennyson's desire for communion with Hallam lest his own flaws be revealed, but it asks, "Shall love be blamed for want of faith?" Poem 52 is a complaint of the inadequacy of the love the poet offers, but the Spirit of true love answers:

> "So fret not, like an idle girl,
> That life is dashed with flecks of sin.
> Abide . . ."

Poem 53 expresses the Wordsworthian conception of apparent disaster as positive, specifying here that even "wild oats" are constructive; it is simply an argument for faith. The near-refrain of "O yet we trust . . ." and "I can but trust . . ." in Poem 54 stresses the theme of a poem which puts faith against an evolving universe. Poem 55 extends the theme, and ends:

> I stretch lame hands of faith, and grope,
> And gather dust and chaff, and call
> To what I feel is Lord of all,
> And faintly trust the larger hope.

The effect, of course, is a developing overture on the theme of faith, set up at carefully extended length, to be shattered at a blow by the sheer violence of passionate distress of Poem 56, and slowly rebuilt, in the whole drama, from Poem 57 on.

In *In Memoriam* as a whole, shifts of balance, reflecting shifts in state of mind, operate at greater distances. In Poem 14 the poet imagines Hallam leaving the ship to return to him in life: much later, in Poem 103, the speaker has an allegorical dream of his being taken off, much like the passing Arthur, in a "little shallop," accompanied by maidens, to a "great ship" on which he joins Hallam.[46] Thus, early in *In Memoriam,* it is death which is the barrier separating the poet from his friend; later, by the third Christmas after Hallam's loss, it has become life which does it, and the significant shift in thought is subsequently sealed and exploited in Poem 117:

> O days and hours, your work is this,
> To hold me from my proper place,
> A little while from his embrace,
> For fuller gain of after bliss.

The use of literary tradition as a means of reinforcing the poem's imaginative claims on a reader is as functional in *In Memoriam* as it was in the shorter poems discussed. To cite an example, the shadow of *Hamlet* stands behind *In Memoriam* in several places, as it also had behind *Ulysses* and other works. Poem 5, on poetry as self-expression to relieve grief, reflects that modern psychological awareness met before in Tennyson. Its line

> In words, like weeds, I'll wrap me o'er

may possibly suggest Hamlet's "Words, words, words," his "inky cloak," and "customary suits of solemn black." If it does not, it should when his "Ay, madam, it is common" is also recalled by the bitter word-play of the very next poem (Poem 6) on the same subject of loss:

> One writes that "other friends remain,"
> That "loss is common to the race"—
> And common is the commonplace,
> And vacant chaff well meant for grain.
> That loss is common would not make
> My own less bitter, rather more.
> Too common!

And once that has occurred, the opening of Poem 18 on Hallam's funeral,

> 'Tis well; 'tis something; we may stand
> Where he in English earth is laid,
> And from his ashes may be made
> The violet of his native land,

can scarcely fail to provoke the wish of Laertes for his sister:

> And from her fair and unpolluted flesh
> May violets spring!

It is not so much allusion as the consistent, if glancing, stimulation of the associations of universal literature.

A comparable broadening of the reader's susceptibility is provided by the Christian frame in the Prologue to *In Memoriam:* it parallels the frames of the shorter works treated earlier. The Christian terms and metaphor of *In Memoriam* are always, it seems to me, referred to with a certain embarrassment, for it is true that they are quite superfluous to the philosophical position the poet takes. Tennyson makes it very clear, in Poem 36, that they *are* metaphorical. The poem expresses gratitude for a universal intuitive truth, merely formulated by Christ:

> Though truths in manhood darkly join,
> Deep-seated in our mystic frame,
> We yield all blessing to the name
> Of Him that made them current coin.

But even disregarding this, a deliberate attempt on Tennyson's part to stimulate a collective consciousness provides a more convincing explanation of the work's highly Christian Prologue than does any brusque, unexplained dismissal of it as "metaphorical." Tennyson, in the Prologue as elsewhere, chose the most universal terms he could in order to stimulate the participation, conscious or not, of his reader.

The Christianity of the frame which Tennyson gave his masterpiece may be an initial stimulus and challenge to a reading of it, but a more accurate sign of the overall nature of *In Memoriam* is given by its first poem. It is cast in strongly Romantic terms. The tribute to Goethe ("him who sings / To one clear harp in divers tones") is clearly to that poet's versatility, but also to the totality of his commitment and the integration of his world-view. Similarly, Tennyson makes the psychological observation that to suppress grief may suppress love also, but he is simultaneously setting up the old Romantic dualism: the poet's faith in an eternal reality is sustained by love, and opposed to it is time, the "victor Hours". The entire poem, indeed, chronicles Tennyson's attempt to "reach a hand through time," and it is important that Poem 1 sketches a basic Romantic faith which is to be subjected—as it is in almost all his poetry—to the inevitable trial by ordeal. In this case the trial covers the remaining 130 poems of *In Memoriam:* "I *held* it truth," he begins.

The entire work, of course, is not to be confined to the theme of Romantic assertion *versus* Romantic deprivation. It becomes broader, more universal and thus more modern, and ultimately different in total effect from any Romantic work. There are extensive sections around the middle of the work (Poems 43 and 44 for instance) given over to informal philosophical speculation on the nature of after-life, and they are highly tentative compared with their Romantic precursors on the subject. Nevertheless, the philosophic implications behind several other poems do repeat Romantic ones. Poem 6, for instance, ironically bitter at its start towards useless attempts to comfort "common" loss, and returning inconsolably to that of Hallam at its end, is given a center of much softer mood as Tennyson treats the actual sorrows of others, and recreates for a moment the larger unity of all that lives. And it is love for Hallam, that provokes, in Poem 18, the early glimpse of what is to be the overall progress recorded by the entire work, "And slowly forms the firmer mind." The funeral setting chosen for this glimpse is apparently paradoxical until it is recalled how repeatedly in Romantic work it is the most dramatic "Everlasting No" from which later growth springs. Additionally, the relationship between personal mood and external nature is as central to the Tennyson of *In Memoriam* as it had been to Coleridge—the celebrated pair of converse Poems, 11 (morning calm) and 15 (evening storm), having that relationship as their main subject. And if one bears in mind Romantic attitudes towards death, the ending of *In Memoriam* summarizes much of the essence of the work. It blends (as Poem 129 ends) an assertion echoing that of *Adonais*,

> Strange friend, past, present, and to be;
> Loved deeplier, darklier understood;
> Behold, I dream a dream of good,
> And mingle all the world with thee,

with a Wordsworthian tone and phrase at the start of Poem 130:

> Thy voice is on the rolling air;
> I hear thee where the waters run;
> Thou standest in the rising sun,
> And in the setting thou art fair.

Both poems are given a Victorian accompaniment of near-agnostic mystery, but it is only the search for rational confirmation, and not the assertion itself, that is qualified:

What art thou then? I cannot guess;
    But though I seem in star and flower
    To feel thee some diffusive power,
I do not therefore love thee less.

The well-known group of Poems (9 to 17) concerning the ship bringing Hallam's body home is an excellent example of the Romantic inversion of the two "realities"—the sense-observed and the imaginative consciousness. The directly-addressed, physically "real" ship is treated, in Poem 9, as a phosphorescent ghost, moving with unearthly steadiness,

Spread thy full wings, and waft him o'er.

So draw him home to those that mourn
    In vain; a favourable speed
    Ruffle thy mirrored mast, and lead
Through prosperous floods his holy urn.

All night no ruder air perplex
    Thy sliding keel, till Phosphor, bright
    As our pure love, through early light
Shall glimmer on the dewy decks,

while in the next poem (10), the ship which exists in Tennyson's tormented imagination is presented as stark, documentary actuality through verbs of the direct senses:

I hear the noise about thy keel;
    I hear the bell struck in the night;
    I see the cabin-window bright;
I see the sailor at the wheel.

The reader's everyday sort of reality becomes ethereal, that of the poet's imagination intense; it is, of course, akin to the reversal of everyday perceptions which Wordsworth had enforced in recreating his experience on Snowdon (see pp. 15–16).

In the same group of ship-poems occurs (Poem 11) what appears initially to be an ironic fancy, a last turn of the screw, in the illusion of life as the poet envisions Hallam's body moving with the motion of the ship:

Calm on the seas, and silver sleep,
    And waves that sway themselves in rest,

And dead calm in that noble breast
Which heaves but with the heaving deep.

But it is not the sort of irony Lear suffers with the feather at Cordelia's lips. Seen with Romantic eyes looking beyond worldly death, the movement becomes a symbol of the idea of death as entrance to larger life in nature. It is not, at that point in *In Memoriam,* exploited assertively, as Shelley might have used so eloquent a symbol towards the end of *Adonais.* Tennyson, using that deliberate control he consistently applies to Romantic techniques, merely leaves it, for the reader, as subconscious inference to be made overt later. But the implications it carries are not dissimilar to those carried by Wordsworth's sensations of dizziness in the skating reminiscence of *The Prelude.*

When Tennyson does transcend the limits of sensed experience, moreover, it occurs in a setting remarkably like those of Coleridge's Conversation—more accurately "transcendental"—poems. Poem 95, the most crucial treatment of mystical experience in *In Memoriam,* opens with precisely that atmosphere of evening evanescence which Coleridge seems to have adapted from Collins and Gray. But the resemblance to Coleridge extends far beyond a similarity in setting. Poem 95, in fact, is a remarkable instance of Tennyson's presenting his own transcendental experience by only the slightest adaptation of Romantic "patterns"—the series of clearly-defined steps of experience which both Coleridge and Wordsworth had recreated so often. This is so vital to my case that I should trace it in some detail; I will quote the relevant sections of the poem individually, but in order.

In the atmosphere of the evening hush, when the poet finally finds himself in solitude ("But when those others, one by one,/ Withdrew themselves from me and night,/ And in the house light after light/ Went out, and I was all alone"), he begins to read Hallam's letters, and is flooded with love for him:

> and strange
> Was love's dumb cry defying change
> To test his worth . . . .

We have, then, to this point, stimulations identical to those in Coleridge's and Wordsworth's transcendental experience: the hushed world, the solitude, the feeling of being overwhelmed by human love. When the transcendence occurs, Tennyson confines himself to simple abstractions of description, though there is the brief echo of Romantic practice in the light image "flashed" and the suggestion of height:

> So word by word, and line by line,
>   The dead man touched me from the past,
>   And all at once it seemed at last
> The living soul was flashed on mine,
>
> And mine in his was wound, and whirled
>   About empyreal heights of thought,
>   And came on that which is, and caught
> The deep pulsations of the world,
>
> Aeonian music measuring out
>   The steps of Time—the shocks of Chance—
>   The blows of Death. At length my trance
> Was cancelled, stricken through with doubt.

As the experience passes, there is the familiar Romantic complaint of its inexpressibility: "Vague words! but ah, how hard to frame/ In matter-moulded forms of speech," and the return is to the still peace of the initial scene:

> Till now the doubtful dust revealed
>   The knolls once more where, couched at ease,
>   The white kine glimmered, and the trees
> Laid their dark arms about the field.

All seems the same, until—time having ceased to be, or more pointedly, having lost its relevance—the breeze of dawn acts as a symbol confirming the meaning of what has taken place; it unites the elements of the scene and creates the new day:

> And sucked from out the distant gloom
>   A breeze began to tremble o'er
>   The large leaves of the sycamore,
> And fluctuate all the still perfume,
>
> And gathering freshlier overhead,
>   Rocked the full-foliaged elms, and swung
>   The heavy-folded rose, and flung
> The lilies to and fro, and said,
>
> "The dawn, the dawn," and died away.

The entire treatment here deserves close comparison to Shelley's use of the dawn as visional transition in *The Triumph of Life* (see p.

41). Here, the return is to the actuality of day; at the same time it is a new day, and Tennyson ends by making clear the infinite implications its creation carries when seen through the experience he has had:

> And East and West, without a breath,
> Mixed their dim lights, like life and death,
> To broaden into boundless day.

Those implications are of unity: they resolve both the Romantic dualism and the dualism here focused on Hallam's loss. Such a dual view, and the infinitely personal struggle of the poet rocked between its extremes, is the subject of *In Memoriam*, as well as of almost all Tennyson's major work.

7. TENNYSON: A SUMMARY 🙐 The Romantic influence which Tennyson showed directly and crudely in his earliest work is just as omnipresent in his full development, but there he controls and moulds it to the point of original creation, as he does (to cite one of the clearest examples) in Poem 95 of *In Memoriam*. One of the main attractions of Romantic work for Tennyson, I think, must have been its persistent recreation of transcendental experience such as he had himself known, and would continue to know, all his life. The Romantic articulation of it had been larger, more detailed, emotionally evocative and more deeply rooted in pantheism than Tennyson would have thought appropriate to his own sense of "otherness"; and the assertive world-view it had impelled was certainly at odds with his Victorian milieu. One dominant strand among the web of contentions within his own poetry, therefore, is his struggle to adapt Romantic poetics to a form that could honestly reflect his attitude towards his time. As has been seen, the results cover a gamut from spectacular success in *In Memoriam* to points of embarrassing failure even in major poems: the ending of *The Two Voices* again comes to mind.

Usually, however, Tennyson was able to adapt Romantic practice fairly successfully by re-proportioning its elements. The Romantics had above all asserted a sweepingly positive faith in a certain world-view; and they had brilliantly used their art to present a recreated echo of experience which had first led to and later confirmed their assertion. Tennyson greatly reduces both echo and assertion. The latter occurs consistently in Tennyson's work, but its style is bare, dogged and brusque beside the exuberance of a Shelley. There is normally a foundation of transcendental experience behind Tennysonian assertion, but where he treats it he resists the multi-dimensional Romantic attempt to recreate its impact, instead describing from outside, in terms deliberately bare yet vague. More often, Tennyson's poems present a mental conflict, rendered into metaphor again and again until it becomes background against which his bare mystical affirmation enforces a reader's respect.

It is generally true to say that the quality of his work varies directly with its relevance to this perpetual trying and testing of positive belief against the doubts of his time. The summit, obviously, is *In Memoriam* itself; the celebrated poems of 1832–42 relate closely to this conception, and so do the *Idylls*, the best-known songs, and *The Ancient Sage,* while poems directly saturated with Romanticism, from *The Lover's Tale* through various Wordsworthian repetitions of the *Enoch Arden* sort, are just as obviously of secondary value.

This paramount area in which there occurs (to borrow G. M. Young's phrase about *In Memoriam,* "conviction won from doubt," affects Tennyson so variously that it is hard to set boundaries for its demarcation. It leads the poet, for instance, to anticipate many of the directions taken by later Victorian poets. *The Vision of Sin* foreshadows *The City of Dreadful Night,* and a poem like Tennyson's *Come Not, When I Am Dead* [47] (1851) seems to embrace both Hardy and Housman.

His handling of his assertion, however, points to the central nature of his poetry. The brevity and brusqueness I have observed are neither affectations nor concessions to the hostile atmosphere of his time. They stem from Tennyson's awareness that his professions of faith—because a poem must focus first on mental conflict—must usually seem secondary, standing apart. The poems do not, usually, lead to an epiphany arising from the experience they treat: where that seems to happen, as in *The Two Voices,* it is often unconvincing. Usually they lead to the quiet statement of survival of an inner conviction which has been there throughout. It survives despite what the poem has been "about"—it is apart from that, and Tennyson knows it. It is this sense of self-awareness which makes the doggedness of stated assertion so impressive.

His poetic resources, as I have viewed them, are devoted not to making a statement of faith directly convincing, but rather to giving the struggle behind it vitality and universality, thus *indirectly* giving authority to any profession of faith. The view of Tennyson as essentially a "vignette" poet is infinitely slight, for his most striking nature-vignette exists for a purpose larger than itself and as part of a total position he takes. His "best" poems are in a sense new and supremely evocative symbols externalizing a total consciousness, with its moods, assertions and regressions, victories and defeats.

Comparisons with Arnold and Browning are simple, though perhaps irrelevant in the end. Tennyson is a poet of documented struggle, unlike Browning, and of dynamic struggle, unlike Arnold. He is, in contrast to Arnold, an assertive poet, and he is, in contrast to Browning, a convincingly assertive one. His poetry reflects a mind assaulted by doubt, but creates the impression that it is a whole human consciousness we confront, rather than the separate points of a general variability presented by Browning or the glancing tonality of Arnold. Metaphorically speaking, the assaults on conviction for which the Victorian age is celebrated often turned Browning elsewhere, and they froze Arnold's poetic creativity to a point where he abandoned the writing of verse. Tennyson was the only major poet of his age to use its schisms as *impetus*—and they are the impetus for almost everything significant he ever wrote.

A more constructive comparison, as far as the essence of Tennyson's work is concerned, lies with Newman. Tennyson's early and intense attraction to the Romantics, and his continuing attempt to shape his Romantic heritage into an instrument to express his own outlook, may be seen to parallel Newman's attempts to reform Anglicanism before his conversion. Beyond that, the parallels become intense. The frame of mind which Tennyson's work expresses is essentially, and despite the very different object of Newman's commitment, the "Here I stand" of the *Apologia*. It presents a comparable background of mental conflict, in terms sufficiently human and convincing to make its ultimate affirmation (whatever its nature) deserving of respect. The impression given by both works is that what they say is the author's own experience, and true. They are informed by a similar self-awareness: both men equally and calmly accept the inevitable gaps between the world they live in and the commitment they make. I have been insisting that Tennyson's poems are about struggle; his assertion of faith must stand alone, and he knows it. He writes, in metaphor, about the relations of his own consciousness to the condition of his time: his faith rests on his inner experience. The two do not meet except by an act of will, and he knows that also. In the same way Newman gives his account of his own spiritual development (with a bare simplicity itself recalling Tennyson's treatment of his mystical experience), states his commitment, insists on its self-sufficiency, and rightly enough dismisses rational argument as irrelevant to it. As in Tennyson, it is the sense of vital and honest humanity behind the artistic presentation of mental conflict that irradiates it.

It has been suggested that the Romantic artist thought of himself as speaking for—or at—his age, and that towards the end of the nineteenth century, after the Aesthetic movement, that conception had been emphatically abandoned.[48] Such a process is, I think, irrefutable, and Tennyson's place in it a definite one. He had no Romantic clarion call to make, but he still spoke his own mind, both directly and metaphorically in his work, and in doing that he achieved a fully developed relationship with his time, and reached out to his readers. In coordinating these achievements, he was unique in the poetry of his time, and this complicates any assessment of him. Diminution of Romantic commitment indeed reaches the point of exhaustion in the Aesthetic poets of the nineties, where it is made only to "experience itself." It is simple to assume that there the process ends in a just anti-climax, for the modern philosophical question mark seems to put Romantic—or any sort of non-solipsistic commitment—out of the sphere of serious consideration. But there are places in modern poetry—in the *Four Quartets* for instance—where a poet is doing what Tennyson was doing, dealing, in vastly different terms of course, with the possibilities of philosophical commitment through recreating his own consciousness as a representative one. The problems of *In Memoriam,* in fact, remain our own; and if we do not dismiss them agnostically, reading Tennyson, one could assume, should still be relevant, and even stimulating. Tennyson's expression, of course, works on assumptions seeming narrow and unintellectual beside contemporary ones, and the violent history of its critical discussion has left him too often, and, ironically, with the sense of matters having been "righted," as the poet of the memorable vignette.

That, at least, is regrettable. Carlyle, at a time when he was inclined to impatient doubting of the relevance of poetry at all to the concerns of the age, found in Tennyson's verse "a right valiant, true fighting, victorious heart." We should today scarcely use such embarrassingly fulsome phrasing, yet the poet it points to is far more essentially Tennyson than the poet of the wind that takes the reed-tops.

NOTES

[1] Arnold's last poetic volume, *New Poems,* appeared when he was forty-five; the rest of his poetry came between 1849 and 1858 or, in terms of Arnold's life, between the ages of twenty-seven and thirty-six.

[2] E. D. H. Johnson, *The Alien Vision of Victorian Poetry,* p. xiii.

[3] *Tennyson, Poetry and Prose* (Oxford, 1947), p. vii.

[4] John Killham, "Tennyson, a Review of Modern Criticism," in *Critical Essays on the Poetry of Tennyson* (London, 1960), p. 1.

[5] *Tennyson, Poetry and Prose,* p. xvi.

[6] For example, G. M. Young, in 1939, wrote an excellent piece, "The Age of Tennyson" (reprinted in Killham's *Critical Essays on the Poetry of Tennyson*). Spurning the excesses of the anti-Tennyson reaction, he considers the poet first as philosopher asserting mystical experience, and second as nature poet with a touch of perfect rightness of expression and a sort of Ruskinian truth of detail, both combining to produce an emotional thrill at certain moments. Clearly determined to approach Tennyson bearing in mind both content and style, he closes his essay by citing the blend of both in "a complete apprehension of his own idea" at the close of *In Memoriam.* Here, Young concludes, Tennyson has "done the utmost that can be asked of a poet, in one act embracing the whole range of his deepest personal thought, and rendering it in the loveliest and most natural imagery that poetry affords, the moonlit sea and the lovers sleeping by its shores."

Despite the determined breadth of the approach, it is hard to resist an ultimate impression that Tennyson's "personal thought" is here regarded with an unconscious condescension—that it was "personal" in the sense that it mattered to the poet but cannot matter much to modern readers (the essay's *raison d'etre* is to explain the value which Tennyson's own day placed upon him). Here, then, as more blatantly in Lucas, Tennyson seems, after all, to emerge as primarily the poet of "the thrill."

[7] *The Alien Vision of Victorian Poetry,* p. 31.

[8] For a treatment of Tennyson which approaches the poetry through various facets of conflict (or "strands" according to my metaphor), see Elton Edward Smith's *The Two Voices* (Lincoln: University of Nebraska Press, 1964).

[9] J. H. Buckley, *Tennyson* (Cambridge, Mass.: Harvard University Press, 1960), p. 49.

[10] "Tennyson's own philosophy of life," according to G. B. Woods and J. H. Buckley, in *Poetry of the Victorian Period* (rev. ed.; Chicago, 1955), p. 967. One wishes, as Tennyson must have wished, that it were that simple!

[11] I am not sure that this has been true in the United States, where Long-

fellow and Poe have held sway; it was true in British schools before the Second World War.

12 Some critics believe that he continued to work over the poem for at least four or five years. See Buckley, p. 265, note 5.

13 The major debt in *The Lover's Tale* is unquestionably to Shelley, and, less so, to Keats. Their voices, in image and tone, are heard so consistently that I cite only a few obvious examples. For Shelleyan "intensity" there is:

> The wind
> Told a love-tale beside us, how he woo'd
> The waters, and the waters answering lisp'd
> To kisses of the wind, that, sick with love,
> Fainted at intervals, and grew again
> To utterance of passion.
>
> (I, 531–536)

For an example of the idealized, ethereal maiden-figure imitated from Shelley, see I, 683–694. This passage might well be seen as linking Shelley with Pre-Raphaelitism, *via* Tennyson. Some of Tennyson's Shelleyan derivations are from quite specific sources: the Romantic quest theme (II, 11–21), for instance, is clearly based on *Alastor*. This sort of derivation from specific Romantic poems is repeated from various directions. The blank verse, for instance, occasionally slides into the Wordsworthian style (see I, 196–202). The use of light imagery in *The Lover's Tale*, to express, for instance, Julian's spiritual enlargement in growing up with Camilla, owes a direct debt half to the imaginative climax in *This Lime-Tree Bower My Prison*, and half to Wordsworthian style (see I, 390–416). And sometimes a particular phrase will leap back from Byron:

> Mute, blind and motionless as then I lay/ (I, 596)

cf.

> A sea of stagnant idleness.
> Blind, boundless, mute, and motionless!
> (*The Prisoner of Chillon*, 249–250).

14 There is, for instance, a lengthy paean on the infinitude of love (I, 456–473), owing a good deal to Shelley, but generally Romantic in thought, and ending

> Sooner earth
> Might go round heaven, and the strait girth of time
> Inswathe the fulness of Eternity,
> Than language grasp the infinite of love.

The Keatsian notion of death at the height of Romantic experience is repeated:

> Had I died then, I had not seem'd to die,
> For bliss stood round me like the light of heaven.
>
> (I, 484–485)

[15] "The Age of Tennyson," *Proceedings of the British Academy*, XXV (1939), reprinted in *Critical Essays on the Poetry of Tennyson*, ed. John Killham, pp. 38–39.

[16] But see details of composition in note 37, p. 237.

[17] *Memoirs*, II, 319.

[18] *The Ancient Sage*, ll. 229–239. The passage is quoted on pp. 182–183.

[19] See, for instance, W. D. Templemen, "Tennyson's *Locksley Hall* and Thomas Carlyle," *Booker Memorial Studies*, ed. Hill Shine (Chapel Hill, 1950), pp. 34–59.

[20] *Tennyson*, pp. 76–77.

[21] So much the boy foreran; but when his date
    Doubled her own, for want of playmates, he—
    Since Averill was a decade and a half
    His elder, and their parents underground—
    Had tost his ball and flown his kite, and roll'd
    His hoop to pleasure Edith, with her dipt
    Against the rush of air in the prone swing . . . .

[22] See F. E. L. Priestley, "Tennyson's Idylls," *University of Toronto Quarterly*, XIX (1949), pp. 35–49.

[23] One of the very few direct outbursts by the poet in the *Idylls* is a gnomic exclamation of human blindness to the dual significance of existence; it prefaces "Geraint and Enid":

> O purblind race of miserable men,
> How many among us at this very hour
> Do forge a lifelong trouble for ourselves,
> By taking true for false, or false for true;
> Here, thro' the feeble twilight of this world
> Groping, how many, until we pass and reach
> That other where we see as we are seen!

[24] "Tennyson's Idylls," *University of Toronto Quarterly*, XIX (1949), p. 46.

[25] Quoted by Hallam Tennyson, *A Memoir by His Son*, II, p. 90.

[26] The similarity is implied by E. D. H. Johnson; see his note, *The Alien Vision of Victorian Poetry*, p. 55.

[27] Buckley, *Tennyson*, p. 29.

[28] *Memoirs*, I, 314.

[29] See p. 188.

[30] Dated 1872 by Woods and Buckley, *Poetry of the Victorian Period*, rev. ed., p. 150.

[31] See, for example, Cleanth Brooks' "The Motivation of Tennyson's Weeper" in *The Well-Wrought Urn*, Graham Hough's "Tears, Idle Tears," and Leo Spitzer's "Tears, Idle Tears Again." All are reprinted in John Killham's *Critical Essays on the Poetry of Tennyson*.

[32] See "The 'High-Born Maiden' Symbol in Tennyson," *PMLA*, LXIII (1948), pp. 234–243.

[33] *The Alien Vision of Victorian Poetry*, pp. 13–14.

[34] *Memoirs*, I, 117.

[35] Buckley, *Tennyson*, p. 160.

36 I use "documentary" in the cinematic sense of "actual living experience directly observed."

37 The first section was written first (in 1852), the second finished in the seventies.

38 Tennyson's indebtedness here extends also to metrical matters. I am grateful to Professor B. F. Huppé for pointing out to me that the lines quoted on p. 197, for example, "Many a hearth upon our dark globe sighs after many a vanish'd face . . ." are metrically like the old septenary line, deriving from the Latin and forming the metrical base of Middle English poems such as the *Ormulum* and the *Poema Morale*. Cf. "Ich ém nu alder þéne ich wés, a wintre ént a láre" (*Poema Morale*).

39 Cf. *The Phoenix*, ll. 13–21:

> Þæt is wynsum wong,   wealdas grēne,
> rūme under roderum.   Ne mæg þǣr rēn nē snāw,
> nē forstes fnǣst,   nē fȳres blæst,
> nē hægles hryre,   nē hrīmes dryre,
> nē sunnan hǣtu,   nē sincaldu,
> nē wearm weder,   nē winterscūr
> wihte gewyrdan,   ac sē wong seomað
> ēadig and onsund;   is þæt æþele lond
> blōstmum geblōwen.

"That is a fair field, green forests spread beneath the skies. There neither rain, nor snow, nor the breath of frost, nor the blast of fire, nor the fall of hail, nor the dropping of rime, nor the heat of the sun, nor unbroken cold, nor warm weather, nor wintry shower shall do any hurt; but the land lies happy and unharmed. That noble land is abloom with flowers." Trans. R. K. Gordon, *Anglo-Saxon Poetry* (London, 1926, 1954), p. 240.

40 See Douglas Bush, "Tennyson's 'Ulysses' and *Hamlet*," *Modern Language Review*, XXXVIII (1943).

41 Buckley, *Tennyson*, p. 63.

42 Consider also:

> Here is the copse, the fountain and—a Cross!
> To thee, dead wood, I bow not head nor knees.
> Rather to thee, green boscage, work of God,
> Black holly, and white-flower'd wayfaring-tree!
>   (*Sir John Oldcastle*)

Yet the Browning style in Tennyson is rather an independent vein of experiment than direct imitation, for *St. Simeon Stylites*, which was probably written as early as 1833, shows a similar style:

> And tho' my teeth, which now are dropt away,
> Would chatter with the cold, and all my beard
> Was tagg'd with icy fringes in the moon,
> I drown'd the whoopings of the owl with sound
> Of pious hymns and psalms, and sometimes saw
> An angel stand and watch me, as I sang.

43 There are many such examples in Tennyson's work: see, for instance, the "Sleeping Beauty" portrait in *The Day-Dream* (1842).

[44] Buckley, *Tennyson*, p. 254.

[45] See Gordon S. Haight, "Tennyson's Merlin," *Studies in Philology*, XLIV (1947), pp. 549–566.

[46] The maidens, according to Tennyson, are "the Muses, poetry, arts—all that make life beautiful here, which we hope will pass with us beyond the grave." The sea, where the great ship rides, is of course eternity.

[47] Come not, when I am dead,
  To drop thy foolish tears upon my grave,
To trample round my fallen head,
  And vex the unhappy dust thou wouldst not save.
There let the wind sweep and the plover cry;
      But thou, go by.

Child, if it were thy error or thy crime
  I care no longer, being all unblest:
Wed whom thou wilt, but I am sick of Time,
  And I desire to rest.
Pass on, weak heart, and leave me where I lie:
      Go by, go by.

[48] Johnson, *The Alien Vision of Victorian Poetry*, pp. xi–xii.

V
AFTERWORD

1. The Romantic Approach: Some Possibilities ❧ In concentrating upon certain effects and their causes in poetry, I have been trying to "illuminate" the major Victorian poets by approaching their work through the assertive, transcendental poetry of English Romanticism. To that attempt no conclusion is necessary, for my conclusion is the stance emerging from my examination of each poet's work, and its validity will have to rest upon that examination.

Instead, I should like to end by making a brief and simple gesture inviting the reader to apply a Romantic approach more broadly than has been possible in this book. The writers I shall mention are quite arbitrarily chosen, for no other reason than that I like them and find their work responsive to a Romantic approach. Quite clearly, the slight afterword to a book such as this can neither advance nor even meaningfully touch upon the large amount of critical work that has been done in Romantic aspects of Victorian and modern literature.[1] Here, I merely put forward some minor but specific suggestions.

To move beyond Arnold, Browning and Tennyson,

then, is to find that much later Victorian poetry is less relevant to Romantic work than is often assumed. Since Romantic poetry, more than any other, demands a suspension of disbelief, it can also highlight the limitations of poets who have not that to bring to poetry at all. Thus the Romantic affinities of the Pre-Raphaelites, which at first seem so obvious in subjects and style, still do not carry Romantic vision, integration, outlook, or assertion.[2] This is not surprising when one considers the Pre-Raphaelite view of Keats as simply a "beauty poet"[3] (a view quite close, incidentally, to the early misunderstanding of the Romantics which Matthew Arnold had shown).

In general, then, the reformulation of Romantic poetry which I have used is of small value for clarifying much late Victorian work of Romantic diminuendo. It would not apply at all, I think, to the work of Hopkins, who remains, somewhat like Blake, a writer of individual assertion and original expression, though in this case through a received formal religion. Limitations of this sort conceded, however, the approach may provide useful results. I should like to treat two examples, Ruskin and Wilde, in slight detail as indicators of this.[4]

It is a commonplace that Ruskin's basically Romantic initial outlook and his thoroughly Victorian development reflect those of Carlyle. More important perhaps is the extent—less well-known—to which he is, again like Carlyle, a Romantic poet whose achievement lies, technically, in prose. In the *Praeterita* he points out himself how his feeling for mountains would have been impossible before the Romantic age: "—before that, no child could have been born to care for mountains, or for the men that lived among them, in that way" (I, Ch. 6). His early attempt, as I have noted, was to revivify the force of Romantic experience, by going to its traditional stimulus, nature, for a more intent examination of its workings through a deeper observation and more sensitive perception. At the same time, the sight of the Alps early in his life revealed that aesthetic experience was as simultaneously *moral* for him as it had been for Wordsworth:

> I went down that evening from the garden-terrace of Schaffhausen with my destiny fixed in all of it that was to be sacred and useful. To that terrace, and the shore of the Lake of Geneva, my heart and faith return to this day, in every impulse that is yet nobly alive in them, and every thought that has in it help or peace.[5]

The parallels with Wordsworth are in fact intense.[6] Ruskin, writing of the sky, makes Wordsworthian assumptions in Wordsworthian phrases; it provides a "lesson of devotion" and "the blessing of beauty," [7] precisely like the opening of *The Prelude*. He is quite certain, at this stage, of universal harmony, divine intent, and the moral meaning of nature, though his ensuing phraseology may also suggest the unawakened seeds of the self-contained aestheticism he was to inspire later on by way of Pater:

> . . . there is not a moment of any day of our lives, when nature is not producing scene after scene, picture after picture, glory after glory, and working upon such exquisite and constant principles of the most perfect beauty, that it is quite certain it is all done for us, and intended for our perpetual pleasure.[8]

In *Modern Painters*, Ruskin tells us that the "first event" in life which he remembered was being taken by his nurse to a crag above the Derwent. The experience he describes parallels Wordsworth's account of similar occasions (*Prelude* I, 269–281); and the parallel appears more dramatic through the odd coincidence of particulars such as the same river, and the presence of a nurse. Ruskin writes of "a continual perception of Sanctity in the whole of nature, from the slightest thing to the vastest." He undergoes "an indefinable thrill, such as we sometimes imagine to indicate the presence of a disembodied spirit. I could only feel this perfectly when I was alone; and then it would often make me shiver from head to foot with the joy and fear of it . . . ." He complains, in the Romantic manner, of its inexpressibility: "I cannot in the least *describe* the feeling; but I do not think this is my fault, nor that of the English language, for I am afraid, no feeling *is* describable." There is the familiar Romantic desolation at its loss: "These feelings remained in their full intensity till I was eighteen or twenty, and then . . . faded gradually away, in the manner described by Wordsworth in his *Intimations of Immortality*" (III, Ch. 17).

In a more extensive and detailed way, Ruskin's "La Riccia— Sunlight after Storm" in *Modern Painters* (I, Pt.2, Ch.2) appears to parallel Wordsworth's ascent of Snowdon in *The Prelude*. Ruskin's account begins not in darkness and confinement but in storm, which breaks as he climbs. There are, as in the Wordsworth passage, Miltonic overtones: the storm with its thunder and clouds sweeping in "sulphurous blue" takes on a faintly infernal quality, and the whole scene shares something of the cosmology of *Paradise Lost,* as the Claudian aqueduct lights up "the infinity of its arches like the bridge of Chaos." As Ruskin climbs on and the storm passes, the scene changes to one of transcendent brilliance. The account remains that of a physical scene, but its phrasing consistently suggests the Wordsworthian outlook:

> I cannot call it colour, it was conflagration. Purple, and crimson, and scarlet, like the curtains of God's tabernacle, the rejoicing trees sank into the valley in showers of light, every separate leaf quivering with buoyant and burning life; each, as it turned to reflect or to transmit the sunbeam, first a torch and then an emerald . . . . Every blade of grass burned like the golden floor of heaven, opening in sudden gleams as the foliage broke and closed above it, as sheet-lightning opens in a cloud at sunset.

Ruskin is here using color with the same intensification, beyond the limits of ordinary sensed experience, that Wordsworth had done with sound in the Snowdon passage, and which Coleridge had been apt to do with light. It is the familiar Romantic attempt to suggest transcendence by combining sensed phenomena not usually joined. This is not only color; it is light. It is, moreover, light which involves incandescence in the Coleridge manner: "conflagration," "burning life," "a torch," and which mixes elemental fire with water: "wet verdure," "showers of light," and "crystalline sea." The diction, as in Wordsworth, is religious: "the curtain of God's tabernacle," "the golden floor of heaven." The final glimpse of the Campagna is one of cosmic harmony:

> . . . the sacred clouds that have no darkness, and only exist to illumine, were seen in fathomless intervals between the solemn and orbed repose of the stone pines, passing to lose themselves in the last, white, blinding lustre of the measureless line where the Campagna melted into the blaze of the sea.

My concern here is not with Ruskin's subsequent Carlylean (and better-known) journey from Romantic "poet" to late Victorian social critic, but simply to show how thoroughly his early work was permeated by Romantic attitudes and expression. The sort of parallel I use, moreover, is not simply a literary curiosity, but one example among several similarly consistent. One might equally well put the general attitude and style of any of the well-known nature passages in *Modern Painters* beside Coleridge's letter written to Sotheby on September 27, 1802. They read almost the same: here is Coleridge's hypersensitive observation of nature:

My Dear Sir,

The river is full, and Lodore is full, and silver-fillets come out of clouds and glitter in every ravine of all the mountains; and the hail lies like snow, upon their tops, and the impetuous gusts from Borrowdale snatch the water up high, and continually at the bottom of the lake it is not distinguishable from snow slanting before the wind—and under this seeming snowdrift the sunshine *gleams,* and over all the nether half of the Lake it is *bright* and *dazzles,* a cauldron of melted silver boiling! It is in very truth a sunny, misty, cloudy, dazzling, omniform day. . . .

If we now move towards the end of the century, it is to find that the all-embracing outlook which the Romantics had built on transcendental experience has predictably shrunk back to its starting point in the senses—in Pater's famous phrase "not the fruit of experience, but experience itself." It is true that the philosophic rallying cry of the Aesthetic movement—expressed with a positively symbolic compression in Wilde's *Dorian Gray* Preface—was anti-Romantic (or rather thwarted Romanticism) in its insistence that only sensations of beauty are art, and that it is precisely a *lack* of meaning beyond itself that makes "experience" so precious. Thus experience became transformed from a spiritual to the highly sensual concept it is in Nineties poetry.

Wilde is traditionally taken as leader of this movement, and it is ironic that the Decadent poets and artists he brings to mind provide a hollow biographic echo of the Romantics in their escapes to the Continent, their flaunting of convention, and the brevity of several of their lives. It is an irony doubled by the negativism of their assertion.

But Wilde himself, if his work is read with Romantic poetry in mind, emerges as considerably more than the traditional apostle of Aestheticism. At many points, especially in his later work, there emerges a man who knew exactly what it was he had failed to do; who became utterly self-aware in knowing that the "beauty" he had aimed at creating for much of his career was, even so far as it was achieved, tragically lacking in significance to the human condition. The bulk of his work, of course, belongs to the "Nineties" tradition, and it is, I believe, a mistake to take the plot of *The Picture of Dorian Gray* and infer a "moral" orientation, for the novel itself provides little evidence that its "justice" is much more than an artistic symmetry.[9]

But in the Preface itself is the observation that "The nineteenth century dislike of Romanticism is the rage of Caliban seeing his own face in a glass." And if one is willing to look beyond the theatrical language and take what Wilde says at all seriously, *De Profundis* reveals a pathetic glimpse, from time to time, of a lost Romantic wholeness of belief. Wilde reprimands himself for having "treated art as the supreme reality and life as a mere mode of fiction." He claims in *De Profundis* that the "sun-lit side" of the garden of the world had, however, not been his only preoccupation, that "I had to pass on. The other half of the garden had its secrets for me also. Of course all this is foreshadowed and prefigured in my books." [10] This may, if one wishes, be dismissed as affectation, and here after the fact of his fall.

Perhaps. But Wilde's most telling poems are not simply art for art's sake, or pleasure for pleasure's sake, or mere sensationalism. They carry that same undercurrent of a vision of Romantic integration that never happened; a vision which could have been realized, but now, from the point of view the poems take, lost beyond reach. *The Harlot's House,* which appears the archetype of *Yellow Book* verse, is neither so simple nor so confined, and it is not pointless that through the poem's presentation of an amoral world in the dead mechanistic symbol of the house, there should sound, in wistful rather than bitter paradox, the strains of the "Treues Liebes Herz" of Strauss.

The "slim silhouetted skeletons," the "clock-work puppet," the "phantom lover" and the horrible Marionette which smokes "its" cigarette are grotesques; they are the epitome of action or pleasure without significance, but they imply, like all grotesques, a norm—here commitment or love—from which they have been perverted. The poem emerges as something beyond a Nineties "coup," for it depends on a series of oppositions, one sort nakedly put forward in the poem, the other implied by them. The poem works on something very like a Romantic series of dualities, between the Harlot's House and moral commitment; between lust and love; between mechanism and humanity, the actual and the potential, between death and life. And the poem's ending accords more with the hesitant promise of the positive side of these dichotomies than with the atmosphere of sin:

> The shadows ceased to wheel and whirl,
> And down the long and silent street,
> The dawn with silver-sandalled feet,
> Crept like a frightened girl.

Similarly, behind the standard (and correct though omissive) view of *The Ballad of Reading Gaol* as a moving social plea against capital punishment, stands the substantial shadow of a poem desperately trying to assert a vestige, or a pathetic vision, of a lost Romantic moral order. The poem is in a sense the obverse of Romantic poetry, but it is a poem of regret at the loss of something the hanged man merely symbolizes. If each man kills the thing he loves, if living has indeed become destruction, one cannot read the poem as indictment of this without its provoking a continual, positive sense of what life might otherwise be. At moments, in fact, the implicit Romanticism becomes explicit, if weak: thus the natural round continues to stand for a universal and kindly acceptance which men have grown to lack:

> They think a murderer's heart would taint
> Each simple seed they sow.
> It is not true! God's kindly earth
> Is kindlier than men know,
> And the red rose would but blow more red,
> The white rose whiter blow.

This is scarcely the violently assertive view of the nature-death relationship of *Adonais,* but it is of the same kind. And, again, the poem's final note is not of social, but of moral protest:

> And all men kill the thing they love,
> By all let this be heard . . . .

The poem's social protest is real enough, but it is also only a result of its deeper indictment, which concerns human nature—specifically the gulf between its potential and its actuality.

In Reading Prison in early 1897, looking back upon his literary past, Wilde could at once comment on it, assess himself at that present time, and state the direction of the development he hoped for in future. He saw his past less as achievement than as missed potential, and, in view of his reputation as leader of the nineties' *avant-garde,* there is a final irony in the terms of his declaration, which are far more suited to the first decades of the century than the last:

> Still, I am conscious now that behind all this Beauty, satisfying though it be, there is some Spirit hidden of which the painted forms and shapes are but modes of manifestation, and it is with this Spirit that I desire to become in harmony. I have grown tired of the artic-

ulate utterances of men and things. The Mystical in Art, the Mystical in Life, the mystical in Nature—this is what I am looking for. . . .[11]

2. AFTER THE VICTORIANS ২ঙ The experience of Romantic transcendence is genuine human experience, documented in a variety of epochs and atmospheres. The fervor of the assertion it produced in the late eighteenth and early nineteenth centuries appears unique, but that is a matter of degree, not of kind. And if "The poem . . . is a portion of the world of experience as viewed and valued by a human being," as Cleanth Brooks suggests,[12] it is to be doubted whether Romantic poetry can ever be entirely irrelevant to the literature which succeeds it. The twentieth century spiritual climate, disturbed by more pressing and multifarious but essentially the same disillusioning questions as the last, has arrived at an existential extreme the reverse of Romantic commitment. One can hardly read its literature, however, without being constantly touched by Romantic parallels and echoes.[13] In large part this is because Romantic poetry, with its essence in religious commitment, operates in the same area as the literature of existential non-commitment, though drawing opposite conclusions. The artistic development of Blake prefigures that of Yeats, whom Douglas Bush calls "a poet of religious temperament," going on to explain that "he had been cut off by science from Christianity and felt obliged to construct an imaginary world of symbols in which he could feel at home." [14]

A like sense of Romantic relevance to a time, and a writer, appearing alien to Romanticism is seen in Shaw. One of Shaw's less celebrated critical pronouncements was that to move from Tennyson to Browning was "a *dégringolade*—a fearful come down." [15] It is an opinion superficially surprising if we envisage Shaw the "realist," but Shaw was only the sort of realist created by the thwarting of the Romantic he essentially was. He makes it quite clear in the Preface to *Back to Methuselah* that he turned against Darwinism not because he had, finally, an intellectual case against it, but because he found it emotionally unbearable:

> . . . the Darwinian process may be described as a chapter of accidents. As such, it seems simple because you do not at first realize all that it involves. But when its whole significance dawns on you,

your heart sinks into a heap of sand within you. There is a hideous fatalism about it, a ghastly and damnable reduction of beauty and intelligence, of strength and purpose, of honour and aspiration, to such casually picturesque changes as an avalanche may make in a mountain landscape, or a railway accident in a human figure. To call this Natural Selection is a blasphemy, possible to many for whom Nature is nothing but a casual aggregation of inert and dead matter, but eternally impossible to the spirits and souls of the righteous.

His own attempt to find religious commitment in the modern situation was ultimately to make a god of human intelligence, and to worship it in specifically Romantic terms; they are best put by Lilith in the final words of *Back to Methuselah:*

> . . . [man and woman] press on to the goal of redemption from the flesh, to the vortex freed from matter, to the whirlpool in pure intelligence that, when the world began, was a whirlpool in pure force. And though all that they have done seems but the first hour of the infinite work of creation, yet I will not supersede them until they have forded this last stream that lies between flesh and spirit, and disentangled their life from the matter that has always mocked it.

In this light, Shaw's evaluation of Tennyson and Browning follows inevitably.

There have been, of course, in this century, poems directly and simply Romantic in the experience they present, their effort to echo it, and the sort of commitment they imply. Occasionally they have been arresting—Ralph Hodgson's *Song of Honour,* for instance, though they always remain aberrations.

Modern poems which relate closely to the Romantics and yet do remain vital invariably reflect the irony between the desire for Romantic flowering and the barren modern ground which must be its only soil. The Romantic possibility, for that is what it has become, is *one among others.* In his summary of his work on the poems of Robert Frost, Reuben Brower concludes that "as total expressions, the poems have implied various relations, from momentary experiences of Romantic vision and Wordsworthian co-operation between the perceiving mind and natural things, to ironic withdrawal from vision and highly sophisticated attitudes to language, faith and truth . . ." [16] Professor Brower makes several illuminating comparisons between Frost and Wordsworth in his book; the best example of Frost's handling of the search for Romantic relationship is perhaps his poem *The Most of It:* [17]

> He thought he kept the universe alone;
> For all the voice in answer he could wake
> Was but the mocking echo of his own
> From some tree-hidden cliff across the lake.
> Some morning from the boulder-broken beach
> He would cry out on life, that what it wants
> Is not its own love back in copy speech,
> But counter-love, original response.
> And nothing ever came of what he cried
> Unless it was the embodiment that crashed
> In the cliff's talus on the other side,
> And then in the far distant water splashed,
> But after a time allowed for it to swim,
> Instead of proving human when it neared
> And someone else additional to him,
> As a great buck it powerfully appeared,
> Pushing the crumpled water up ahead,
> And landed pouring like a waterfall,
> And stumbled through the rocks with horny tread,
> And forced the underbrush—and that was all.

The first line, as Brower points out, is ironic in terms of the rest of the poem—there is *something* beyond, and we are right to look for it. The desire of the speaker is for commitment, for some meaningful and responsive attachment to the conditions of existence which nature symbolizes.

> He would cry out on life, that what it wants
> Is not its own love back in copy speech,
> But counter-love, original response.

The response, despite—and because of—the irony of "Nothing ever came of what he cried" is not nothing but something. It is qualified ("unless it was"); it is the essence of brute impersonality ("an embodiment"); and the speaker, true to his time, can only respond to it with the habits of reasonable calculation ("after a time allowed for it to swim"). It seems alien and unconcerned, but it may, for all we know, relate to the human need. The poem is one of Romantic searching, and even of irony at the idea of abandoning that search; what it finds is agnostic and quixotic, yet it keeps alive a sense of the possibility of belief.

Modern attitudes towards this possibility show great variation. To illustrate one, I should like to cite a brief and brilliant poem by Richard Eberhart:[18]

For a Lamb

I saw on the slant hill a putrid lamb,
Propped with daisies. The sleep looked deep,
The face nudged in the green pillow
But the guts were out for crows to eat.

Where's the lamb? whose tender plaint
Said all for the mute breezes.
Say he's in the wind somewhere,
Say, there's a lamb in the daisies.

The poem is about death—death and putrescence seen against all the implications of innocent ideality that the lamb has carried in Blake and elsewhere. It recalls, tangentially and for a brief moment, in "Say it's in the wind somewhere," the voice of Lucy "That whistles in the wind," and all the old assertions of Wordsworth and Shelley about death; but its ending returns us to our time, our world, our situation:

Say, there's a lamb in the daisies.

The comma after this "Say," with its pregnant and appalling pause, is almost the most sharply meaningful thing in the poem. The last line can scarcely be anything but a tonal shrug: it is the voice of our century. But this is not the shrug that dismisses the trivial: one does not shrug in this way unless it is something very substantial, and potentially much cared about even if beyond hope, that is being shrugged off. I do not think the poem really works as it can without a background context of Romantic aspiration on the subject of mortality.

In a parallel way, Romantic assumptions and impulses, scaled down or given a psychological validity, continue as reflections of human experience and aspiration in literature of other concerns overall. In the novel *Doctor Zhivago*, the Doctor tells Anna Ivanovna, at her sickbed, what happens to human consciousness at death. Consciousness is poison, he points out, when it is applied to ourselves (consider psychosomatic illness, insomnia, etc.): it must go outwards. "You in others—this is your soul. . . . You have always been in others and you will remain in others. And what does it matter to you if later on that is called your memory?" [19] It is scarcely the answer of *Adonais* or a Lucy poem, but it relates directly to them.

The Romantic impulse, as is well known, is strong in Joyce's *Dubliners*, and the volume offers a compact and powerful means of experiencing the subtlety and variety of modern Romantic sensibility. In the climax of the work, the story "The Dead," there co-exist, as Romantic dualities in the protagonist Gabriel's consciousness, the world of the Misses Morkans' annual dance, of the Irish question, of "galoshes" against the snow, and of his respectable niche, and beyond all these is the world of the outside, always beyond the windows that Gabriel is continually drawn to: it is the universe of the snow itself, and of the dead boy Michael Furey. When Gabriel, at the end of the story, transcends the first of these levels to the second, his experience, in the way of the Romantic poet, has been provoked by his own developing solitude, his love of his wife, and her account of that remote, past love for her with which Furey had died. It ends in a spiritual journey, the familiar, mounting stages of which move towards a universal consciousness. Gabriel feels that it is better to "pass boldly into that other world, in the full glory of some passion," than to age here. He feels a catalytic gush of love for his wife sweep over him. His soul approaches the region of the dead; he feels his own identity fade, "the solid world . . . dissolving and dwindling." The culmination is the magnificent symbol of the snow which unites all, from his own journey westward to the "dark central plain" of Ireland, from the "treeless hills" to the Bog of Allen and the "dark mutinous Shannon waves":

> It was falling, too, upon every part of the lonely churchyard on the hill where Michael Furey lay buried. It lay thickly drifted on the crooked crosses and headstones, on the spears of the little gate, on the barren thorns. His soul swooned slowly as he heard the snow falling faintly through the universe and faintly falling, like the descent of their last end, upon all the living and the dead.[20]

In his essay *Inside the Whale* George Orwell, explaining the rush of writers to the Communist cause in the thirties, remarked that the Party was "something to believe in." That the search for commitment is universal can be assumed, but in periods when belief seems hopeless or irrelevant whole areas of human awareness, including the experience of literature, become obscured. The very force of Romantic belief becomes an obstacle to a total view of its poetry, yet paradoxically it is that force which generates the transcendence the best Romantic work achieves—and which the modern reader, often enough, receives as "art" only. But Romantic experience, commitment, philosophy and art cannot be separated without loss. It is only as one that they move us as they can. And even their Victorian diminution, intermittently but revealingly and a little pathetically, can create that heightened sense that it may be possible to relate the lonely consciousness to something beyond itself. Without that possibility, we remain inert prisoners of the here and now.

NOTES

[1] See, for instance, Frank Kermode's *Romantic Image* (New York, 1957); J. Hillis Miller's *The Disappearance of God* (1963) and *Poets of Reality* (1965), both published at Cambridge, Mass., by the Belknap Press of the Harvard University Press.

[2] This is not true of Swinburne, whose Romantic affiliations, and his individual development of them, are worth close study, especially in later work like *The Lake of Gaube*.

[3] See Earl R. Wasserman, *The Finer Tone*: *Keats' Major Poems* (Baltimore: Johns Hopkins Press, 1953), pp. 97 ff.

[4] These choices, again, are quite arbitrary: to "cover" the major possibilities would be to repeat this book using a mass of late-Victorian and twentieth-century material. Here, I am simply opting for the precision which examples can offer, with a minimum of distortion to the literature concerned.

[5] *Praeterita*, I, Ch. 6.

[6] In this entire suggestion, I owe much, in both conception and detail, to Mrs. Vivian Woodyard, a postgraduate student at the University of California.

[7] "The Open Sky," *Modern Painters*, I, Pt. 2, Ch. 1.

[8] *Ibid.*

[9] Wilde, when it suited him, was ready to claim for his novel a moral and didactic value (see, for example, his letter on the novel's "terrible moral" written to the *St. James Gazette*, June 26, 1890). In other words he was willing to take the precise opposite of his position in the novel's preface. At other times he was more evasive (see letters of July-August, 1880, to the *Scots Observer*). The relevant letters are in Rupert Hart-Davis' *The Letters of Oscar Wilde* (London, 1962), pp. 258–259, 268–272. One takes one's choice, but on the whole I think claims for the ethical import of *The Picture of Dorian Gray* should be taken with quite a lot of salt.

[10] Hart-Davis, *The Letters of Oscar Wilde*, p. 475.

[11] "De Profundis" letter to Douglas, Hart-Davis, p. 509.

[12] "Implications of an Organic Theory of Poetry," *Literature and Belief* (New York, 1957), p. 69.

[13] Obviously this is true of writers in the "Romantic tradition": D. H. Lawrence, Yeats, Wallace Stevens, Dylan Thomas, Robert Frost and so on. But equally inviting material is to be found, as critics frequently show, in "anti-Romantic" writers such as T. S. Eliot or the Imagist poets, or (as I shall suggest) in Joyce. So few modern writers are untouched by Romanticism that I suspect each critic's list of "Romantically-colored" writers turns out to be significant chiefly as a statement of his own interests and tastes.

[14] "Tradition and Experience," *Literature and Belief*, p. 32.

[15] "Am I an Educated Person?" *Sixteen Self-Sketches* (New York, 1954), p. 113.

[16] *The Poetry of Robert Frost: Constellations of Intention* (New York, 1963), p. 130.

[17] From *Complete Poems of Robert Frost.* Copyright 1942 by Robert Frost. Reprinted by permission of Holt, Rinehart and Winston, Inc.

[18] From *Collected Poems 1930–1960* by Richard Eberhart. © 1960 by Richard Eberhart. Reprinted by permission of Oxford University Press, Inc.

[19] Boris Pasternak, *Doctor Zhivago,* translated by Max Hayward and Manya Harari (New York, 1958), p. 68.

[20] Quoted by permission of The Viking Press, Inc.

TEXTUAL NOTES

In quoting poetry in this book, the following editions have principally been used:

The Complete Writings of William Blake, edited by Geoffrey Keynes. London, New York, and Toronto: Oxford University Press, 1966.

The Poems of Samuel Taylor Coleridge, edited by E. H. Coleridge. London, New York, and Toronto: Oxford University Press, 1912, 1945.

The Poetical Works of Wordsworth, edited by Thomas Hutchinson, revised by Ernest de Selincourt. London, New York, and Toronto: Oxford University Press, 1904, 1946.

The Poetical Works of Lord Byron. London, New York, and Toronto: Oxford University Press, 1904, 1952.

The Complete Poetical Works of Percy Bysshe Shelley, edited by Thomas Hutchinson. London, New York, and Toronto: Oxford University Press, 1933.

The Poetical Works of John Keats, edited by H. Buxton Forman. London, New York, and Toronto: Oxford University Press, 1908, 1940.

The Poetical Works of Matthew Arnold, edited by C. B. Tinker and H. F. Lowry. London, New York, and Toronto: Oxford University Press, 1950.

The Poetical Works of Robert Browning. London, New York, and Toronto: Oxford University Press, 1905, 1964.

Unpublished Early Poems, Alfred Lord Tennyson, edited by Charles Tennyson. New York: The Macmillan Co., 1932.

The Works of Alfred Lord Tennyson. London: Macmillan and Co., 1896.

INDEX

Burton, Robert, 48
Bush, Douglas, 248
Byron, George Gordon, Lord, 32–34, 71, 141; *Childe Harold,* 32–33; *Manfred,* 32, 33

Carlyle, Thomas, 51–58, 61, 64, 73, 84, 89, 100, 127, 137, 138–139, 186, 217, 233; dualistic thought, 55; Romantic vision in, 57, Romantic vision, loss of, 62–63; Romantics, attacks on, 52–53, 58; *Sartor Resartus,* 52–58, 67 n. 35, 68 n. 36, 89, 186; science, view of, 53–54
Clough, Arthur Hugh, 85, 86, 113, 114
Cohen, J. M., 126, 128, 140, 158
Coleridge, Hartley, 11
Coleridge, Samuel Taylor, 6–14, 25–26, 228, 244–245; *Christabel,* 13; *Dejection: An Ode,* 13–14; *Eolian Harp, The,* 6–8, 65 n. 3; Fancy and Imagination, 25–26; *Frost at Midnight,* 11–12; *Kubla Khan,* 72, 82, 147, 171; *On Method,* 25; *Rime of the Ancient Mariner, The,* 12–13, 65 n. 5; *This Lime-Tree Bower My Prison,* 8–10, 150, 179
Coleridge, Sara, 6, 7, 8
Collins, William, 6, 7, 10
Cowper, William: *The Castaway,* 84

Darley, George: *Nepenthe,* 72
Darwin, Charles, 61, 130; *The Origin of Species,* 100, 210
DeVane, William Clyde, 126, 128, 129, 130, 137, 138, 161
Donne, John, 114, 119 n. 14, 151
Dostoevsky, Fyoder, 33

Eberhart, Richard: *For a Lamb,* 251

Eliot, T. S., 194, 220, 221; *Four Quartets,* 233
Emerson, Ralph Waldo, 149

Faust legend, 33
Fitzgerald, Edward, 175, 196; *Rubaiyat,* 100, 145, 206–207
Frost, Robert: *The Most of It,* 249–250
Froude, James Anthony, 52

Godwin, William: *Political Justice,* 31
Goethe, Johann Wolfgang von, 57, 225; *Werther,* 33–34, 57–58, 178, 181
Gray, Thomas, 6, 10

Hallam, Arthur Henry, 220, 221, 222, 223, 224, 226, 227, 230
Hardy, Thomas, 231
Hegel, Georg Wilhelm Friedrich, 149
Herrick, Robert, 169
Hitchener, Elizabeth, 39
Hodgson, Ralph: *Song of Honour,* 249
Hopkins, Gerard Manley, 141, 242
Houghton, Walter, 63–64
Housman, A. E., 231

Johnson, E. D. H., 77, 169–170, 202–203
Joyce, James, 168, 252; *Dubliners,* "The Dead," 252

Keats, John, 30, 32, 42–51, 90, 149; earliest work, 43, 199; *Endymion,* 44–47, 49, 181; *Eve of St. Agnes, The,* 47, 181; *Fall of Hyperion, The,* 42; Greek myth, use of, 44;